Radicalism and Social Change in Jamaica, 1960-1972

Radicalism and Social Change in Jamaica, 1960-1972

Obika Gray

The University
of Tennessee Press

KNOXVILLE

Library of Congress Cataloging in Publication Data

Gray, Obika, 1948-   .
    Radicalism and social change in Jamaica, 1960–1972 / Obika Gray.
        p.   cm.
    Includes bibliographical references.
    ISBN 0-87049-660-3 (cloth: alk. paper)
    ISBN 0-87049-661-1 (pbk. : alk. paper)
    1. Radicalism — Jamaica.   2. Social movements — Jamaica.
3. Jamaica — Politics and government — 1962-   . I. Title.
HN230.Z9R34   1990
303.48'4'097292 — dc20   90-35009   CIP

several prerequisites for a democracy, of which economic modernization is only one. In the view of these analysts, there are also other important political and cultural criteria, not the least of which is the existence of a "democratic political culture." Therefore modernization theorists could claim that, despite its low level of economic development, the Jamaican case actually confirms the validity of their related hypotheses about the social bases of democratic governments, because of an important intermediate variable: the high value placed on pluralism and moderation in politics by both elites and masses in Jamaica. There is indeed some truth in this assertion; a substantial and deeply rooted commitment to political competition and consensual conflict resolution is evident among all classes in Jamaica, particularly among the political leadership and the bourgeoisie. Notwithstanding this fact, however, the assertions in the modernization literature concerning both the determinants of democratic rule and its existence in Jamaica are still problematical.

Difficulties arise when transhistorical prerequisites and inflexible correlation of variables are regarded as universal determinants of democracy. Lacking a firm basis in the contradictory evidence produced by historical research, such explanations ignore significant ambiguities associated with the evolution of capitalist democratic rule in the West. One of these anomalies is that none of the political revolutions in Europe and North America established substantive popular democracy at the time of their occurrence. As Goran Therborn's imaginative comparative investigation shows, the trajectory toward a democracy in Europe was a contingent, indeterminate, and exclusivist phenomenon which was dependent on a complex array of factors.[14] The decisive ones identified by Therborn are: defeat of the working class by a bourgeoisie, which then made concessions to the laboring classes; the waning of revolutionary upheaval in one country, which opened the way for liberalization in neighboring states; competition among bourgeois factions, which led to appeals and concessions to the masses; and, most strikingly, outright imposition of democratic government by victorious states upon defeated rivals and colonial nations. Going beyond the correlational analysis of modernization theory and breaking with its emphasis on prepolitical predispositions of elites, this new attention to conjunctural and political relations among classes is a valuable corrective to the sometimes tautological explanations advanced for the origins of democratic government in the West.

Contributing to the problems generated by the lack of historical accuracy is the tendency of some writers to narrow the definition of democracy and apply it to states which merely allow citizens the free exercise of the franchise in competitive elections.[15] This electoralist approach has allowed certain Third World states, such as Jamaica, to be identified as unambiguously democratic, even though such states may govern in a coercive manner and deprive citizens of substantive justice. Moreover, in addition to the problems raised by the restrictive view, this conception of democratic rule all too easily can conflate the institutional patterns and safeguards of democratic government in the advanced capitalist states with those in Third World countries such as Jamaica. While this conflation of features usefully may call attention to broad similarities in electoral practices and common normative orientations in different countries, it blurs clear distinctions and elides dissimilarities between states with competitive electoral systems. In fact, this emphasis on similarities in electoral forms actually may mask sharp differences in the exercise of power in Third World states and Western democracies. Narrowly identifying democracy with competitive electoral systems ignores important constraints on democracy and participation besides the unhindered exercise of the franchise. Indeed, defining democracy as electoral competition ignores countervailing patterns in the Third World. These include the existence of parallel channels of power and legitimacy which weaken or supplant constitutionally prescribed practices, making them adjuncts to, rather than the effective determinants of, power, democracy, or social justice in these societies. "Demonstration elections" in highly autocratic Central American nations provide an extreme case in point. In some of these nations, where the army rules behind a civilian facade, elections are held and people vote for parties in a demonstration of liberty which often earns these nations the approval they need in the international community; however, this exercise has negligible impact on the effective domains of power and even less on the enjoyment of political liberties. Although the Central American example is an extreme case, a not-too-dissimilar pattern exists in other Third World states where weak restraints on the abuse of state power and proscriptions on independent political activity prevail. This sharp difference between the Euo-American systems and those in the Third World calls into question the practice of seeing a substantive identity between First and Third World democracies by looking at their electoral practices, when in fact there are substantial differences in the politics of the two types of states.

When the issues are framed in these terms, it appears that Carl Stone, the Jamaican political scientist, is correct in arguing that while Jamaica has a durable, competitive electoral system, the exercise of political power in that country does not conform to the well-entrenched democratic pattern established in North America and Europe. Stone has observed that the form of political rule in Jamaica deviates substantially from the liberal democratic model and is not simply another version or variant of democracies in the advanced capitalist states.[16] I share Stone's view prove their condition but repeatedly emphasized the necessity of labor's cooperation with employers.[22] Less than a year before the fateful 1938 rebellion, therefore, Bustamante – a leading personality with close ties to labor, a major player in the newly-created trade union – had adopted an ideological position at odds with the workers' mood.

Notwithstanding its anticolonial impulse, Bustamante's position pressed upon workers the attribute of submissive dependency. In advocating this stance, Bustamante had adopted the ruling-class injunction that the laboring class be well behaved and respectful of their white superiors. But even as Bustamante appealed to the submissive dimension of popular consciousness, he was only one individual in a wider complex of movements and organizations focused on reforming the colonial system. It will be recalled that by 1936 the middle class, in search of a wider unity, had begun creating organizations and developing ideologies. This emergent sentiment bore fruit in Harlem, New York. There, on 1 September 1936, four Jamaican emigres – Rev. Ethelred Brown, Jaime O'Meally, W.A. Domingo, and W. Adolph Roberts – founded the Jamaica Progressive League (JPL), an organization devoted to securing self-government for Jamaica.[23] Of the founders, two – O'Meally and Domingo – already were seasoned political activists, having played significant roles in Marcus Garvey's Universal Negro Improvement Association and in U.S.-based black socialist organizations. In their turn, Ethelred Brown was a prominent Unitarian churchman, while Roberts was a journalist, writer, and cultural nationalist.

Within months of the founding of the JPL in New York, the burgeoning Jamaican middle class's demand for change took organizational form in Jamaica. On 29 February 1937, a coterie of young intellectuals – H.P. Jacobs, Frank Hill, and O.T. Fairclough – put out the first issue of *Public Opinion*, a journal devoted to reform in the colony. Like many members of their class who took up this cause, the journal's founders had not yet developed a coherent nationalist position. However, they did possess organizational skill sufficient to start the journal and a compelling desire to see a more active role for natives in the island's future. Hill brought to the venture his experience as a journalist on several local newspapers, and Fairclough contributed his skills as a former assistant bank manager in Haiti.[24] Together Hill and Fairclough brought on board H.P. Jacobs, a young Englishman and University of Manchester graduate, to complete the trio. Befitting its roles as stimulus to middle-class action and organ of economic and political reform in the colony, *Public Opinion*'s inaugural issue called on those seeking reform to cooperate and to provide effective leadership on issues of concern to Jamaicans.

This middle-class activism continued into 1937, when several important developments took place. These included the creation in March of the National Reform Association (NRA), an organization designed to unify the several forces seeking change, followed in December by the founding of a Jamaican branch of the JPL. The two newly created organizations had overlapping personnel, and close personal ties existed among the reformers. Hence, as Post shows, the NRA had among its founders H.P. Jacobs from *Public Opinion* and Ken Hill, brother of Frank Hill. The third founding member and the president of the NRA was Noel Nethersole, a former Rhodes Scholar and solicitor from a prominent family. At the same time, the local branch of the JPL counted Adolphe Roberts as its founder. Notwithstanding this growth of middle-class organizations in 1937, neither a national organization nor a unifying leader had yet emerged. Evidently aware of this, O.T. Fairclough tried to enlist a prominent young barrister and friend — Norman Washington Manley — as president of the NRA. Manley, however, was reluctant to lead and refused Fairclough's offer.[25]

In turning to this reluctant nationalist, the middle class notables had identified an individual of some distinction. Born in Manchester Parish in 1893, Manley had excelled in his studies and won a scholarship in 1914 to study law at Oxford University. Upon completion of his studies, he returned to Jamaica in 1922 and was called to the bar in the same year. By 1937, Manley not only had distinguished himself as a brilliant barrister but also had shown that he was conscious of the lamentable situation of the Jamaican poor. His response to their plight was to lend his services to the Jamaica Banana Producers' Association (JBPA), a struggling growers' cooperative. Among other things, Manley helped draw up the JBPA's constitution and defended the co-op in disputes with the United Fruit Company. Manley used this contact with laborers to learn about their social and economic condition. Consequently, when the call from Fairclough came, the young barrister's attention and political inclinations seemed directed more toward ameliorating the problems besetting small farmers and peasants than toward assuming leadership of a fledgling nationalist organization. In fact, a few months after turning down the leadership of the NRA, Manley founded his own organization, Jamaica Welfare Limited, to promote rural community development. By the end of 1937, then, several leaders, including Bustamante, were agitating for reforms and forging alliances with labor. By May 1938, however, events had overtaken these developments. Neither Bustamante's pacifying influence nor Manley's useful work with the JBPA were enough to bar a popular revolt. In fact, Bustamante's improbable calls for law-abiding behavior were cast aside, as landless peasants, workers, and the unemployed rebelled, with scarce regard for the etiquette of their behavior.

cal backdoor agitators, political plotters and political conspirators."³⁹ In the face of this unrelenting opposition to the PNP and to the Marxist contingent within it, the PNP finally gave up its efforts at cooperating with the BITU. In the end, Bustamante's announcement in August 1942 that he intended to form his own party as a counterforce to the PNP capped the divisions within the movement. This move to create a political alternative to the PNP received a further boost when London recalled the governor for talks on constitutional change.

This turn of events stimulated party development in the colony. In March 1943, the Jamaica Democratic Party (JDP) was formed to represent local capitalist interests. This was followed in July by the founding of Bustamante's political party, the Jamaica Labour Party (JLP). However, as Eaton notes, the new party "was nothing more than a political label for the Bustamante Industrial Trade Union. The J.L.P. like the B.I.T.U. was Bustamante."⁴⁰ Notwithstanding the split in the nationalist movement and the problems caused by Bustamante's personalist control over both the BITU and the JLP, the 1938 rebellion was a watershed event, as it opened the way for the devolution of power into native hands. In 1944 a new constitution was promulgated, which granted universal adult suffrage. This development opened the way for mass-based electoral politics, albeit under vigilant colonial supervision that would last another eighteen years. The next section reviews developments between 1944 and the achievement of political independence in 1962. Discussion will be limited to three issues: the structuring of the authoritarian state, the demise of a leftwing alternative to the PNP, and the role of foreign capital in the transformation of the economy and the class system.

Authoritarianism and Dependent Development

With the 1944 abolition of restrictions on the franchise, the colonial power took into account some old and new realities after May and June 1938. Among the new developments were an assertive working class and the existence of two ideologically moderate political parties, with their allied trade unions, the BITU and the TUC. The old reality which remained was the continued subordination of the Jamaican poor to the estate system and to the power of the still-existing colonial state apparatus. Consequently, even as the 1944 constitution recognized the change in social relations after 1938, the constitution continued to limit popular representation in the legislature.⁴¹ After all, the rebellion had not overthrown the colonial state apparatus, nor were the colonial military forces in danger of defeat. The colonial state therefore remained intact, and with it British supervision of the colony.[42] Thus, while the extension of the franchise to the masses represented a significant advance for them, the political advantage remained with the British, who adopted a policy of democratic tutelage.

All the same, this development was important, since it began grafting limited forms of democratic rule to the autocratic colonial state structure. In this way, the nondemocratic form of colonial rule was adjusted to accept the longstanding claim for greater native representation in the legislature. What did not change, however, was British supremacy over the political transition and British control of the colonial state. By orchestrating the transition in this way, Britain no doubt hoped to remain in control of the pace of events, while observing the proclivities of the new recruits in the legislature. Indeed, the December 1944 general election, the first to be held under universal suffrage, was won by the JLP, inaugurating a scenario in which colonial supervision coexisted with popular electoral politics for the next eighteen years.

This outcome, which saw the existence of popular suffrage within a colonial state, can be explained by several factors. The balance of forces favored the colonial rulers, the native leaders shared the imperial idea of gradualism, and the popular classes looked to this leadership for political direction. The creation of this form of state therefore was based both on the limitations of the national movement and on the political advantage retained by Britain. Given these relations of power, it may be argued that this pattern of decolonization, with its prolonged transition after 1944, was not a unilateral imposition of the British; on the contrary, Britain's preferred format of "constitutional decolonization" converged easily with labor's demobilization and the native leadership's gradualist inclinations.

This adaptation of the weaknesses of the nationalist movement to the process of constitutional decolonization produced a state of affairs untenable for the popular classes. It led not to the expansion of their independent influence on national politics, but rather to labor's demobilization and incorporation within the dominant union-party cartels. In 1944 and again in 1949, this newly enfranchised electorate gave the JLP consecutive victories in the general elections. On both occasions, Bustamante accused the PNP of communism and characterized PNP calls for self-government within the empire as an untimely renunciation of longstanding colonial ties. However, despite Bustamante's use of charges of anticommunism and disloyalty to empire to discredit the PNP, these attacks failed to bar a PNP victory at the polls in 1955. Thus, despite the parties' ideological differences and disagreements about Jamaica's future, this transfer of power confirmed the political leadership's consensus on constitutionalism and the dominance of the two-party sys-

Table 1. *Electoral Results in Jamaica, 1944-62*

	Votes Cast	Voter Turnout %	JLP		PNP		Other	
			Vote %	Seats	Vote %	Seats	Vote %	Seats
1944	349,127	52.5	41.4	22	23.5	5	35.1	5
1949	467,179	63.8	42.7	17	43.5	13	13.8	2
1955	486,644	63.9	39.0	14	50.5	18	10.5	—
1959	557,794	65.4	44.3	16	54.8	29	.9	—
1962	575,779	72.3	50.0	26	48.6	19	1.4	—

Source: Michael Kaufman, *Jamaica Under Manley,* (Westport, Lawrence Hill, 1985), 51.

tem. This consolidation of two-party politics is evident from the electoral returns reported in table 1.

Still, this victory for the institutionalization of party politics was not without its problems, as the all-too-vigorous competition for political spoils led to party-instigated violence and political intimidation of the electorate. To make matters worse, these early years of electoral activity were notable for the extent to which the anticolonial struggle was displaced by the electoral struggle. Inevitably, the quest for independence suffered, as intense political partisanship diverted the population's attention from self-government to party loyalty. This development further delayed the pace of decolonization, and it was left to London to speed up the transition by issuing a constitution in 1953.[43]

Decline of the Left and New Economic Developments

The PNP's triumph in the 1955 elections was more than a victory over the JLP; the PNP's electoral success consolidated the position of conservative party members and heralded a new direction for both the party and the country.[44] The 1955 victory came on the heels of tension in the party between leftists and the center-right. These conflicts over the party's direction had culminated in the 1952 expulsion of four radicals—Ken and Frank Hill, Arthur Henry, and Richard Hart. This purge and the 1955 elections marked both the reversal of fortunes for the radicals and the ideological ascendancy of the center-right in the PNP. In part, this shift to the right was a defensive reaction to Bustamante's effective attacks on the PNP's socialist ideology and on the presence of leftists in the party. More fundamentally, however, the purge was a response to mounting policy disagreements between center-right party members and the leftists who were a dominant ideological force in the TUC. Indeed, as the party membership grew to include more middle- and upper-class members, and as Cold War sentiment gripped the party and the country, the radicals became more of a liability.[45] Consequently, in addition to expelling the radicals, the PNP disaffiliated itself from the TUC and established a new organization, the National Workers Union (NWU), to reconstitute the party's share of the labor movement.

A further consequence of the new development inside the PNP was the 1955 electoral defeat of the ex-PNP leftists, now opposed to the PNP-NWU and JLP-BITU hegemony. One of these, the Marxist lawyer Richard Hart, tried to continue the political education of labor by forming the People's Educational Organization (PEO) in 1953. In the same year, Hart and Ferdinand Smith, the Jamaican Marxist who was assistant secretary of the World Federation of Trade Unions (WFTU), created the Jamaica Federation of Trade Unions (JFTU). Later that year, the best organized and strongest of the JFTU affiliates, the Sugar and Agricultural Workers' Union (SAWU), called a strike. The goal was to gain better wages and working conditions for sugar workers and to win recognition for the new union. However, because they were inspired by leftwing leaders with links to the WFTU, these initiatives met the determined opposition of the colonial state.

Unable to win recognition for the fledgling union and seemingly blind to the dangers of demoralization among the JFTU workers, Hart and his colleagues took a political gamble. Despite the growing enervation of the leftist movement, they contested the 1955 national elections. The resulting massive defeat of Hart's political party, the People's Freedom Movement (PFM), confirmed both the thoroughness of labor's integration within the dominant party-unions and the political desperation of the leftists. Ever the organizer of forces sympathetic to socialism, Hart had overestimated the strength of the Left and, in the aftermath of the electoral defeat, suffered the bitter disillusionment of the JFTU-PFM cadres. By 1957, in the face of inexorable constitutional developments and the opening of the country to foreign capital, the organizations bearing the imprint of Hart's efforts—the PEO, the JFTU, and PFM—had gone into simultaneous decline.

A third consequence of both the PNP's ascent to power and its expulsion of the leftists was the free hand the party now had to encourage the flow of foreign investment into the economy. By purging its leftwingers, the PNP not only allayed capitalist fears about its ideological direction, but also freed itself of constraint on the creation of an Industrial Development Corporation.[46] Consequently, when the PNP took political office in 1955, it fully supported a policy of industrial growth based on foreign investment, with a smaller role for fractions of domestic capital. The year 1955 therefore brought a significant departure in economic policy, as the PNP pursued a policy of industrialization under the auspices of foreign capital.

From the PNP's perspective, this policy was necessary because of the following difficulties: the low level of capital formation in the island; the clamor for assistance to domestic manufacturing; stagnation in agricultural growth; and high unemployment.[47] To resolve these issues, the party opted for a strategy of dependent economic growth. The perennial challenge of unemployment and the absence of an industrial base were to be tackled using conceptions of underdevelopment long held by the party.[48] As the PNP saw it, the problems confronting the country were not the result of dependence on the capitalist world economy. Rather, the economic difficulties were viewed as having origins which were mainly internal and which also were specific to an autonomous national economy that lacked an industrial sector to absorb the growing number of unemployed workers. In the PNP's view, this sector could be created through sponsorship of external economic intervention. In sum, the policy of dependent development was the result of a diagnosis that the economic backwardness of the island was not due mainly to the historical effects of colonial exploitation, but rather to the internal weaknesses of an independent, backward economy.

The way forward for the newly elected regime was to remedy the colony's lack of resources, particularly its insufficiency of capital. This conception of the problem led to the strategy of relying on foreign capital investment. In dealing with the greater effects of dependent incorporation in the capitalist world economy, then, the PNP responded by deepening this involvement. In 1956 the new regime passed two more Incentive Laws. These were additional components in what had emerged as a model of accumulation organized around state sponsorship of foreign capital.

This externally-impelled model of industrialization has been widely discussed in the literature on economic dependence and amply documented in the Jamaican case. The Jamaican studies, however, have a major deficiency.[49] They failed to discuss the relationship between this phase of capitalist development in the colony and the formation of social classes. This gap has hindered discussion of the pattern of class differentiation which occurred in this final phase of colonialism. While this deficiency cannot be remedied here, it is possible to sketch the general characteristics of foreign-induced economic expansion in Jamaica, and to make certain inferences about its effects both on class formation and on the character of the state by 1962.

The Dominance of Foreign Capital in the Economy

By 1955, substantial inflows of new capital had entered the Jamaican economy, much of it in the form of direct private investment. Initially, the bulk of this investment went into bauxite mining, but portions of it entered such areas as construction, banking, and manufacturing. With the passage in 1956 of both the Export Incentives Encouragement Law and the Import Incentive Law, the PNP pursued the foreign-led model of accumulation. Relying on generous incentives to both foreign and domestic capital, the accumulation strategy sought to raise the level of export production, foster import substitution, and increase foreign direct investment.

The scope and penetration of this investment into the Jamaican economy have been described by several West Indian economists.[50] Their data show the massive infusion of foreign investment in the economy in the 1950s. From the mid-fifties to the early sixties, net foreign investment comprised more than 40 percent of all investments.[51] Of course, while the bulk of this investment was concentrated in the mining sector, foreign loans and investment in the financial sector also made their contribution. Equally significant, from the standpoint of the PNP's attempt to foster the development of a domestic bourgeoisie in manufacturing, is the fact that foreign capital still retained a substantial role even in the manufacturing sector. Thus, throughout the period under consideration, not only did foreign capital attain a dominant role in those enterprises which were capital-intensive and overwhelmingly export-oriented, but also this capital was a significant partner in those sectors which were ostensibly reserved for local capital.[52] By the late fifties, then, this model of development had extended the reach of foreign control into new nonagricultural sectors.

The hegemony of North American capital in the economy brought large inflows of capital investment and created the desired growth in manufacturing. Yet, as developments in the fifties revealed, the model of dependent economic growth was producing uneven economic effects. On the one hand, it certainly propelled the economy toward impressive growth rates and engendered necessary diversification. On the other hand, the impact in reducing the rate of unemployment and the level of imports — the main targets of this model of industrialization — was negligible.[53] Equally important were uneven effects on class formation and social relations. While it is not possible to delineate the multiple effects of this phase of capitalist development on internal class relations, one cannot avoid mentioning certain features of the process.

Dependent Capitalism and Class Formation

Let us take the dominant classes first. The massive infusion of direct external investment substantially reorganized the hegemonic group in the society. Where British capital had played a leading role up to the 1940s, the fifties saw the displacement of British by United States and Canadian capital. Reflecting the eclipse of Britain as a world power, the advent of North American capital in the island, particularly its nonagricultural fraction, marked a new phase in the process of dependent industrialization. Thus, while the British bourgeoisie retained a significant position in such areas as agriculture, banking, insurance, and communications, its members increasingly were relegated to playing a role secondary to North American capital, particularly its American fraction.

However, where private British capital traditionally had avoided productive industrial investment in favor of profits in the agricultural and commercial sectors, the American penetration resulted in a significant shift in the pattern of investment. By advancing into the neglected areas of manufacturing and industrial production, North American capital in effect showed this phase of imperialism to be radically different from earlier periods, characterized as they were by the extraction of raw materials and the dominance of merchant capital in the simple import-export economy. With direct investment as the mechanism of penetration, the effect of this phase of imperialism was to foster the real expansion of productive sectors of the domestic economy while sustaining the overall relationship of economic dependence. This mode of investment and its particular concentration and volume produced both the eclipse of British capital and the rearrangement of the local class structure.

This restructuring was most apparent with the ascendancy of a domestic bourgeoisie in manufacturing and light industry. Buoyed both by state-sponsored incentives and by partnerships with foreign capital, this group came to control the dominant segment of domestic capital. Enjoying a privileged role in the process of dependent industrialization, this segment of capital effectively displaced both the older plantation-based bourgeoisie and those entrepreneurs who remained exclusively in the mercantile sector. Because the Jamaican bourgeoisie's location in landholding, wholesale-retail distribution, real-estate speculation, and import-export trade was multiple and overlapping, it is difficult to make a sharp demarcation between fractions of indigenous capital. However, it is possible to identify the formation of a manufacturing-industrial fraction in the fifties. Typifying this development was the emergence of several family firms engaged in manufacturing. Among them were Caribbean Metal Products, Ltd., started in 1954 by the Mahfood family, and the I.C.D. Group, founded by the Matalons.[54]

The path to the accumulation of capital taken by the Matalon family is instructive, since their businesses occupy prime positions in leading sectors of manufacturing and so illustrate the ascending fortunes of indigenous capital in the new industries. Having started out in haberdashery, the family moved into the distribution trade, with the creation in 1946 of its Commodities Service Company. With the postwar expansion of the economy, the family assumed a leading role among indigenous manufacturers. With Aaron Matalon serving several terms as president of the Jamaica Manufacturers' Association, and with his brother Moses on the board of the Jamaica Industrial Development Corporation, the family's fortune expanded with the boom in construction, real estate, and manufacturing.[55] Relying in part on their ties to the ruling PNP regime, the Matalons were among the main beneficiaries of state-sponsored projects in such areas as construction, most notably in housing for middle-and lower-income families in Kingston.[56] By the first years of the 1960s, the Matalons had built a diversified economic empire under the umbrella of ICD, Ltd. Its subsidiaries were engaged in the construction of houses, port development, food merchandising, and pharmaceuticals.

Playing a complementary role in the economically dominant group were other segments of domestic capital in the commercial, trading, and agricultural sectors. While clearly not the main beneficiaries of the policy of dependent industrialization, the entrepreneurs in commerce and the distribution trade nonetheless benefitted from the overall expansion of the economy. Family firms such as those in the import-export trade owned by the DaCostas and Brandons thrived as a consequence of the growth created by the PNP's economic policies. This strengthening of the classes in the commercial sector could hardly have been avoided for, while the postwar years saw an increased diversification of the economy, the latter retained its basic import-export character. As a result, even as import substitution remained the announced goal of the new regime, the structure of dependence actually produced an inexorable increase in the level of imports. Between 1950 and 1959, for example, imports rose from 49.6 to 187 million Jamaican dollars. As a percentage of GNP, this change amounted to an increase of 12 percent. What these figures suggest is that the commercial bourgeoisie was by no means eclipsed as a force in the dominant group, despite the fact that they were neither directly promoted by the regime nor allowed to capture the greater share of the surplus accruing to the industrial fraction of capital.

As regards the landowning group, it was suggested above that this agricultural bourgeoisie had been displaced from its dominant role within the overall bourgeoisie. The modality of this displacement, however, should be seen as a gradual process, rather than as a sudden shift which occurred in the late fifties. As such, the erosion of the economic dominance of the landed bourgeoisie, while directly related to the increasing stagnation of the agricultural sector, was also linked to the internationalization of capital and its impact on the island in the first half of the twentieth century.

Between 1928 and 1938, for instance, the agricultural bourgeoisie was losing ground to foreign multinationals such as Tate and Lyle in sugar production, and the United Fruit Company in banana cultivation.[57] By the forties, the native rural bourgeoisie was relegated to a secondary role in landholding, as these multinationals shared vast tracts of agricultural lands among themselves. With the onset of dependent industrialization in the fifties and the increased state assistance to small and middle farmers, the big agricultural bourgeoisie's role in the economic expansion of the island was further diminished.

Of course, this slippage in the economic fortunes of the big planters did not substantially alter their traditional relations with the state, weaken their dominance over rural politics, nor expose them to policies which would divest them of their holdings.[58] This lingering power notwithstanding, it remains the case that the internationalization of capital, and particularly its penetration of both the agricultural and the manufacturing-industrial sectors of the Jamaican economy, had produced a reorganization which effectively diminished the role assigned to the landed bourgeoisie. In sum, the process of dependent development produced a reshuffling of the positions in the economically dominant group; the Americans replaced the British as the leading monopoly fraction, and an indigenous manufacturing bourgeoisie rose above other domestic fractions in commerce and agriculture. In light of this transformation in the class structure, the ethnic-minority character of both foreign monopoly capital and the domestic bourgeoisie became politically important. This ethnic-minority status of the capital-owning group was to pose problems for a regime preparing to assume political control in a situation in which the subordinate classes — workers, peasants, and unemployed poor — were predominantly of African descent.

Table 2. Number of Farms by Size Group, 1954–68

Year	All Farms	0–5 Acres	5–25 Acres	25–100 Acres	100–500 Acres	500+ Acres
1954	198,883	139,043	53,024	5,603	881	332
1958	199,489	141,224	53,300	4,012	639	314
1961	158,577	112,626	41,053	3,785	766	347
1968	190,582	149,703	36,881	3,004	699	295

Source: Jamaica. Department of Statistics. Census of Agriculture: 1968–69. Tables 3, 13. (Sept. 1972).

The Subordinate Classes

The process of postwar economic growth was notable not only for the differentiation and restructuring which occurred among the dominant classes, but also for its effects on the subordinate classes. One of these was the deepening of the crisis of the peasantry. The advent of foreign capital in the fifties not only left intact the rural class inequalities, but also accelerated the process of peasant proletarianization by facilitating a spectacular increase in rural-urban migration. The starkness of the rural inequalities is represented, in part, by data on landholding. In 1958, the bulk of all farms — 98 percent — contained twenty-five acres or less (table 2). However, for the same year (table 3), these farms constituted only 45 percent of all land being farmed. Indeed, three years later there was a precipitous drop in the number of farms and in land being cultivated on small- and medium-sized farms. The simultaneous increase, in 1961, of the number of farms of more than 100 acres, at a time when total acreage in farms declined, suggests that large farms were expanding at the expense of small and middle-sized farms.

What, then, was the fate of the thousands of "dispossessed" farmers?[59] One inference is that, where these exfarmers did not join the rural working class or the itinerant poor, they became part of the postwar exodus to the urban areas. Once in the major towns, they could become part of the urban proletariat. It seems more likely, however, that, given their limited skills, they became part of the unemployed phalanx surroundng the urban working class.

Nowhere was this contingent of displaced peasants and other rural strata more evident than in the main urban complex of Kingston and Saint Andrew Parish. There, the influx from the countryside, spurred in part by the rapid urbanization of Kingston, contributed massively to a jump in that city's population, from 203,000 in 1943 to 376,000 in 1961.[60] This spectacular increase in the area's population — an 85

Table 3. Acreage of Land in Farms by Size Group

Year	0–5 Acres	5–25 Acres	25–100 Acres	100–500 Acres	500⁺ Acres	Total Acreage
1954	249,074	502,924	232,178	214,131	716,068	1,914,357
1958	270,781	546,300	176,872	130,994	697,796	1,822,743
1961	198,000	389,441	167,607	185,596	770,786	1,711,430
1968	223,818	333,548	125,104	148,501	676,426	1,507,397

Source: Jamaica. Department of Statistics. Census of Agriculture: 1968–69. Tables 5, 15. (Sept. 1972).

percent increase in seventeen years—not only reflected a significant depopulation of the countryside but also presaged the subsequent political importance of the uprooted peasants now displaced to the urban areas. Despite the state's piecemeal efforts to stem the tide, these smallholders and members of the rural poor almost certainly joined the exodus from the countryside to the capital city. However, whereas many of their counterparts in the 1850s had been forced by colonial edict to quit the land, this exodus to the urban areas in the 1950s was less a matter of colonial policy than of capitalism's tendency to uproot rural populations in a "forced march" to the urban-commercial centers. Having experienced a precipitous drop in landholding in the 1958–61 period, and pulled by the swirl of dependent industrialization with its urban bias (town versus country), it is not surprising that various strata of the displaced peasantry pressed up against the tiny urban working class.

The Urban Working Class

The Jamaican working class historically has been in a precarious position under dependent capitalism. Largely because of the underdevelopment of the colony and the longstanding British policy of restricting the development of industry, the formation of a stable Jamaican working class—one with durable links to the workplace and among its members—was aborted. For example, the 1943 census revealed that, out of a labor force of 505,100, 56 percent or 284,000 were employed (working one week or more). Of this latter total, 89,000 were not working at the time of the census. More significant, however, 70 percent (200,000) of these wage-earners "were only casually employed, some working as little as one week for the year."[61] In sum, with only 30 percent of all wage-earners holding full-time jobs, a serious crisis of unemployment and underemployment existed in the colony.

The typical situation facing a Jamaican worker in the forties and fifties, therefore, was one involving casual employment and the palpable attendant threat of becoming one of the thousands of permanently unemployed. This vulnerability to chronic unemployment was particularly evident in the urban areas. There the process of dependent economic expansion, while broadening the base of the urban working class, simultaneously exposed it to the constant threat of unemployment. Although the development of manufacturing, commerce, construction, and service sectors created new jobs, the low level of employment in these sectors failed to keep pace with natural population increases, the influx of rural migrants, and the rapid growth in the number of persons joining the labor force.[62] In short, neither the scores of manufacturing firms sponsored by incentive legislation nor the investments by foreign capital managed to stem the tide of urban unemployment and underemployment.[63]

Since the city of Kingston experienced the highest rate of unemployment, wage-earners there were caught in the "scissors" of dependent industrialization. On the one hand, the presence of a mass of unemployed and semiemployed workers, teetering above the permanently unemployed lumpenproletariat, cheapened the workers' labor power. In fact, the existence of this reserve labor force provided employers with a ready weapon with which to intimidate workers who were dissatisfied with low pay and unsatisfactory working conditions. On the other hand, for these same workers, employment in the city, even on a casual basis, was far more attractive than permanent unemployment or the prospect of returning to the countryside, with its uncertainties.[64] In short, this strategy of industrialization, far from improving the workers' lot, exposed them to a miserable existence shuttling back and forth between casual work and no work at all.

Commenting on this situation, the economist W. Arthur Lewis aptly described what certainly must have been the circumstances typically facing one of the urban unemployed: "One of the consequences of unemployment is unemployability. One day you work, next day you cadge a meal from your aunt. The day after you steal something small, the day after that you get a half-day's work, then you mind somebody else's car for a shilling, and so on."[65]

Later chapters will examine how the unemployed and others sympathetic to them reacted to the meanness of this urban existence.

and upper classes contributed to increased restiveness among sections of the lower class and inclined them toward Rastafarian leaders who emphasized exodus to Africa as a way out of their desperate situation. Several individuals in Kingston emerged as sponsors of this project for repatriation.[9]

The Reverend Claudius Henry was the most durable and controversial of this group. His activities among the Kingston poor between 1958 and 1960 made him a leading militant among Rastafarians demanding repatriation to Africa. However, Henry's significance went beyond his activism on behalf of a return to the African continent. His personality incorporated many of the contradictions and agonies which gripped the displaced peasantry at the time. It will be recalled that the peasantry had been forced onto the urban labor market, exposed to the impersonal sway of the new capital, and subjected to a changing political situation. In short, the Rastafarians had to confront both the dynamics of decolonization coming from above and the expanding presence of foreign capital. Changing political relations and the widening presence of productive capital triggered an eruption of Rastafarian protest in which Henry played a leading role.

Like many of his countrymen before him, Henry had a sojourn abroad, living for some thirteen years in the United States before returning home in December 1957. Still mindful, perhaps, of the colonial government's hostility toward itinerant preachers, and still smarting from his arrest in 1935 for preaching without a permit, Henry had won his license in 1950 and been formally ordained in the United States three years later. Undoubtedly affected by his stay in America and linking this experience to his longstanding contact with the Jamaican peasantry,[10] he returned to the island deeply convinced of the need for moral reform among the black poor and, moreover, for someone to organize them for a return to Africa.

Taking the title "Repairer of the Breach,"[11] Henry established the African Reformed Church in December 1958, which soon attracted several hundred worshippers. This congregation, overwhelmingly drawn from the urban lower classes, was exposed to the unapologetic, militant anticolonialism in Rastafarian ideology. Whether through pamphleteering, individual proselytizing, or sermons delivered on the church's public address system, Henry summoned his listeners to break with the existing colonial state and its political representatives. Using a discourse which sharply polarized "self-government under British Colonial Rule," and effective independence on the African continent, Henry articulated an alternative nationalism which appealed to the black poor's deepest yearnings for a better life. Between May 1959 and January 1960, tens of thousands of pamphlets were printed carrying the message of this counter-nationalism.[12] One of these, printed in July 1959, expressed a leading idea in Rastafarian discourse:

> Dear Readers, should we at this time sacrifice such a righteous Government, for Jamaica [sic] Self-Government, or any other Self-Government, in the world? . . . shall we sacrifice the continent of Africa for the island of Jamaica? Shall we refuse God's offer for repatriation back home to Africa and a life of everlasting peace and freedom, with Him under our own vine and fig tree, and go back into slavery, under these wicked, unrighteous and oppressive rulers of Jamaica? God forbid.[13]

For those churchgoers who might have had residual loyalties to the political parties and their leaders, Henry warned: "They have nothing to offer us! All their sweet promises and what they hope to obtain out of self-government under British colonial rule can only lead us into destruction and captivity because their leaders are all 'blind', leaders of the 'blind' and they shall all fall into the ditch of God's Judgement, captivity, war and slavery."[14]

We may notice in this Rastafarian discourse, apart from its counter-nationalist theme, characteristics common to ideologies. First, specific "reports" are issued about the world, along with "commands" to change it in accordance with an alternative idea.[15] Second is an organization of idea elements, such that Rastafarian ideology is placed in sharp antagonism to another, competing idea — self-government. Third and most significant in the Jamaican context is the principle that groups *other* than the middle class are regarded as self-determining and capable of acting to change their circumstances in the world. Consequently, a significant feature of Rastafarian ideology was the agency it assigned to the lower classes. They were now seen as capable of independent initiatives, free of dependence on middle-class leadership.

Such agency, however, often was linked to biblical prophecies, which the Rastafarians interpreted literally. Consequently, like other self-appointed prophets before him, Henry set a date for the coming repatriation but then had to turn aways hundreds of believers, since no resources for this exodus existed.[16] Such failed predictions, based on prophesy and on confusion about alleged financial guarantees from political leaders, intensified the Rastafarians' frustration and spurred their enmity toward the native political leadership.

In the wake of this setback, Henry blamed the prime minister, Norman Manley, for thwarting his efforts to repatriate the believers. In a fiery sermon in December 1959, Henry is alleged to have called on his congregation to "get your weapon (sic) ready because we want Mr. Manley's head to play with." In the same sermon, delivered over a public address system, Henry reportedly said that if the congregation did "not get to leave Jamaica back to Africa, they should take off his [Manley's] head and kick it up Rosalie Avenue like [a] football."[17] In the context of this open challenge from the African Reformed Church, and more generally from the increasing number of Rastafarians in West Kingston, the state stepped up its suppression of these militants. In this period, the police conducted several raids against Rastafarian camps in the shanties of West Kingston. Given Henry's inflammatory sermons, it is not surprising that his church was a target of these raids.

One such raid, on 6 April 1960, uncovered an arms cache. Henry and several others subsequently were charged with treason, felony, and breaches of the firearms and dangerous drugs laws.[18] Following these raids, the police crushed an attempted putsch in June, planned by Henry's son Ronald, and several Afro-Americans. Both the failed putsch and a letter addressed to Cuban President Fidel Castro disclosed the willingness of elements in the Rastafarian movement to take up arms against the state.[19] This putschist orientation among some Rastafarians no doubt validated the larger society's fear that these militants constituted a dire threat to national security. But while this attempt at armed insurrection was a palpable threat to the security of the state, it remained an isolated episode in an otherwise nonviolent accommodation of workers and peasants to the status quo. Notwithstanding the growing restiveness among the unemployed and sections of the working class, the resort to arms to overthrow the government was not repeated, nor was it supported by the majority in these two groups.

Despite the fact that this incident was isolated, limited, and easily dealt with, the government saw this threat as a portent of the future. It therefore increased the surveillance of radical groups and stepped up its repression of nonviolent forms of protest. Coming as they did against the background of the Cold War and the recent Cuban Revolution, the Rastafarians' actions spurred increased concern for security on the island. Fears of subversion from both external and internal opponents now gripped the leadership of the transitional state. This heightened sense of vulnerability and fear of destabilization were to lead native leaders to rely on the same prohibitive laws used by the colonial state to maintain security. Consequently, in the months following the attempted putsch in June, exclusion orders were used to keep militant U.S. Garveyites from entering the island.[20] Hence, the waning of colonial rule was not attended by a corresponding easing of the old prohibitive laws. Rather, colonial state security concerns now seeped into political rule under internal self-government.

This resort to restrictive legislation, fed by official fear of subversion, was reinforced by the racial assertiveness of the urban lower class. To the authorities, this development probably appeared as a campaign of racial destabilization. The Back-to-Africa demands, the persistent and expanding consciousness of racial subordination among large sections of the black unemployed poor, and their denunciation of privileges enjoyed by "light-skinned people" all contributed to the tension palpable in this period. In fact, by October 1960, the Chinese again became targets of racial "attacks,"[21] as tensions produced by high unemployment in Kingston and black resentment against Chinese retailers and Chinese overrepresentation in commercial establishments focused on this group.[22] Even so, it may be argued that, rather than representing a campaign of subversion, the racial upsurge really was a protest against existing *class* inequalities. After all, in the changing political and economic context of the late fifties and early sixties, income, material benefits, and educational and job opportunities were unequally distributed among the classes. This unequal distribution of rewards reflected the historical stratification of these classes along racial and color lines. Consequently, notwithstanding the salience of race and nationality in the urban insurgency, it was primarily class conflicts — so intimately intertwined with race and color in this society — that were being played out in racial terms. Stated less ambiguously, the urban poor had resorted to "race" as a means of protesting their class deprivations. This development also contributed its irony, since it was at the very moment when foreign racial rule was on the wane and crumbling, that racial conflicts were erupting between groups of Jamaican nationals.

In explaining why this paradox should have existed, commentators have observed that, despite the attainment of independence and the waning of the strict class-color correlation associated with the old plantation society, the social structure in the postcolonial years still retained residues of the old "racial-class" system. This was particularly true in the early postcolonial period, when the darker-skinned, upwardly-mobile elements of the middle class were in the first stages of their ascent. The social structure was in flux and so inevitably retained features of the old order. Thus, upwardly-mobile blacks readily found places in the bureaucracy and in the professions, as political decolonization "darkened" the racial composition of the group administering institutions in the state and society. Not only did membership in the political directorate demonstrate this racial shift, but also important administrative positions in allied institutions such as the university, the civil service, and the security forces were opened to local blacks.

A parallel though far weaker decolonization occurred within the ranks of the upper class. For the most part, the composition of this class remained racially exclusive, since this stratum consisted primarily of members of the business class — a category in which native blacks had yet to make significant inroads. There was, however, *some* heterogeneity within the upper class, composed as it was of Chinese, Syrian, and Jewish nationals, British and North American managers, and a few blacks.

This incorporation of dark-skinned blacks into the middle and upper sectors of the class system did not imply, however, either the immediate eclipse of all whites in top administrative and professional positions, or the wholesale displacement of the Afro-European segment from their already privileged positions in the society and the economy. As in most decolonizing societies, there were limits *initially* to the rate of incorporation of blacks in middle- and upper-class positions, and to the numbers of advantaged blacks in the pool from which recruits could be drawn. Moreover, cultural dependency among the recruits muted the impact of this growing de-Europeanization of the class structure, as the dark-skinned blacks who joined whites and people of mixed race in the upper echelons of the class structure took as their cultural reference point not the African nationality of the black lower class, but rather the Anglophile orientation of the white and colored population.[23] Thus, despite an incipient transformation of the class structure in the early postcolonial years, the dominant cultural values remained essentially unaltered, and the vast majority of blacks remained outside the intermediate and upper levels of the middle class. It was only in lowest sector of this class, with its clerks, schoolteachers, and salespersons of all varieties, that we would have encountered the dark-skinned population in some numbers above the peasantry, manual workers, and the unemployed. This class structure, with its internal principle of ethnic stratification correlated with gradations of color, reproduced some salient contradictions. The most obvious was the historical one: the continuing polarization of black laborers and the racial-minority business class. As a result, an overlay of ethnic antagonism was added to the tensions in the wage relation between workers and capitalists.

Still another contradiction was spawned by the alliance between native entrepreneurs and party politicians. By 1960, relations between the native bourgeoisie and the two political parties had evolved into cooperation and identity of interest. Indeed, despite the potential for racial conflict inside the state, the bonds of this alliance extended to the recruitment of members of the domestic business class into the state system as partners in the exercise of power. Thus, concurrent with the marginalization of significant sections of the black population, the political leadership was consolidating an intimate and privileged relationship with the local ethnic minority bourgeoisie. In these circumstances, the urban poor easily might have regarded government policy as displaying a form of political favoritism.

Pressed, then, by the Rastafarian challenge to the stability of these intrinsically contradictory arrangements, the leadership of both political parties responded by elaborating a defensive political ideology which I shall call "Jamaican Exceptionalism." In it Jamaica was depicted as possessing an exceptional consensual culture which had earned it an international reputation for political stability and interracial harmony.[24] In this respect, Exceptionalism was a novel ideological invention, designed to address the dilemmas of the incipient independent state. This ideology, it may be argued, had two concurrent purposes: to dampen mounting racial protest against emergent class inequalities, and to create the political and ideological conditions necessary for foreign investment. This latter aim was particularly important, since the success of the strategy of economic development depended on providing the necessary political security for foreign investors. Exceptionalism therefore was both a counter-ideology meant to stem challenges to class inequalities posed by expanding race consciousness, and a means to secure the moral-ideological framework for the country's development strategy. As such, this ideology was both a pragmatic response to unfolding developments and a solution to the ideological deficit incurred in the colonial period.

At this juncture, the ubiquitous Bustamante emerged as a master exponent of the new ideology. Drawing on his talent for fashioning unities out of inherently conflictual social relations, and exhibiting his instincts for ferreting out human propensities for cooperation and reconciliation, Bustamante joined the controversy. Recalling his attitude to race and class conflicts under colonialism, the labor leader noted:

> In the early days of Jamaica's social and economic revolution, there were two principles that were most important to me. The first was that capital and labour should learn to work together — capital had to learn to respect and be fair to labour. Labour had to learn, in spite of any past advantages taken of workers, that destroying capital would destroy one's hopes of development and thereby destroy labour itself. The second principle was, that people of all races must learn to live together, work together and respect one another. To me acceptance of both of these principles was not only fundamental but vital to Jamaica's future, if we were to gain a reputation for stability.[25]

With this identification of the two contradictions and his longstanding orientation toward them, Bustamante went further, linking the ideology of Exceptionalism to political security for capital:

> People in the world have come to point at Jamaica as a leading example — as a small country where reason, law and order are fundamental to the country and our people, and where races work and live in harmony with ever increasing respect for each other, and capital therefore has regarded us as a safe place to come while local capital gained faith to join in doing their part in our development.[26]

The British governor, Sir Kenneth Blackburn, picked up this theme, enunciating an ideological unity on this issue apparent within official circles in Jamaica. He observed that "in a world which is at present sadly disturbed by ideological and racial differences, Jamaica has established a reputation second to none for tolerance, for harmony between peoples of all kinds, and so for happiness and progress."[27]

What these ideological elaborations emanating from the politicians suggested was a determined effort to assert cultural and moral leadership over the subordinate classes. But this effort was not geared toward exercising leadership only over the Rastafarians, or even over the large numbers of unemployed workers. While such workers certainly were "target populations" for the ideology of Exceptionalism, it seems likely that the laboring classes — the employed workers and peasants — were the real targets of that moral leadership. It need only be remembered that just such leadership, using not-too-dissimilar themes, had been exercised over these classes when the 1938 crisis erupted. But what could be the threat from the laboring classes in 1960, a period in which they were effectively demobilized? Why would the appeal from the politically dominant groups be directed more to them than to the restless urban poor?

Part of the answer may lie in the tenuous position of those among the laboring classes who actually *held* jobs, and in the persistence of racial discrimination in the workplace. In this context, Rastafarian ideology could have a special salience for the producing classes; it could bring them under its influence, with destabilizing consequences. In short, since many workers did not have stable ties to the workplace and feared falling into the ranks of the unemployed, the possibility existed that workers might come to recognize themselves in Rastafarian ideology, and perhaps link its themes to labor's discontent in the workplace. The potential for linking the grievances of black laborers with the Rastafarians' global, racially-emphatic critique of the society constituted a real danger. Consequently, in addition to realistic fears about the flight of foreign capital, a related danger for the state, it may be argued, was a potential alliance between labor and the unemployed, based on a recognition of their common deprivations. Hence, although black labor was disarmed by its earlier demobilization, in the context of a persisting racial-class structure, workers remained susceptible to the emancipatory themes in Rastafarian racial ideology.

Still, it should be said that the politicians' ideological appeals did not necessarily fall on deaf ears outside the middle and upper classes.[28] The ideology of Exceptionalism certainly had a positive appeal for members of the subordinate classes, including workers, peasants, the self-employed, and even the respectable poor. The invocation of decency, hard work, racial cooperation, and civic pride affirmed values shared by many Jamaicans. This could hardly have been otherwise in a highly religious country, steeped in the positive aspects of Western civic values as well as in Western rationalizations for unequal rewards to the races. Consequently, there were vast segments of the population which, despite their experience of racial discrimination and opposition to it, found Exceptionalism appealing. Nonetheless, it seems probable that labor had to be immunized further against the contagion of Rastafarian ideology, if only to prevent the worsening of an already deteriorating situation. Under these circumstances, it is understandable that the regime would depict black labor's relationship to capital and to the racial minorities as harmonious, exceptional, and exemplary.

But what of labor's memories of racial oppression? How were these handled by exceptionalism-as-ideology? In part, Exceptionalism ceded some ground by acknowledging past racial conflicts. However, those antagonisms were characterized as a bane of the past. In fact, to innoculate labor against the virulence of black consciousness, the political leadership and other dominant forces now designated racial consciousness as an atavism — a "throwback" to old contradictions now long resolved. This certainly was the view held by Norman Manley. When pressed to speak publicly on the controversy,[29] he reiterated the theme of social harmony threatened by the spectre of black consciousness:

> Ugly forces are rising in our country. All over the land peole have begun to preach race hatred — colour against colour, race against race. Movements are being formed dedicated to the destruction of the very idea of inter-racial harmony. I could understand that sort of thing 20 years ago, but today I say bluntly that it is a dangerous throw back into the past that threatens to undermine and destroy one of the greatest and finest things we have ever tried to achieve.[30]

In our terms, this speech lamented the existence of challenges to the party leaders' power to construct a "subject" labor force which would recognize itself as having an identity of interest with capital. That this still-tenuous consolidation of a cooperative ethic was in jeopardy is apparent from Manely's emphasis on the dire consequences for national survival if this ethic was supplanted by racial confrontations. Addressing the potential loss of investment because of assertions of black nationalism, Manley spoke bluntly of the conditions necessary for capital investment in the island:

> Jamaica's whole future depends upon our reputation for political stability and for sensible government. We live in a competitive world. There is not much capital free to move. Everybody is fighting to get money brought into their country so that you may procure the capital goods which is the founda-

tion of development. Those countries get help that have reputation [*sic*] for stability; for people will come here and spend their money and develop things because they feel secure.[31]

Amazingly, these developments late in 1960 were a near-identical replay of certain aspects of the 1938 scenario. That is, another expression of rebelliousness by a section of the subordinate class once more had produced an intervention by the same leaders, who sought to defuse this militancy by appealing for cooperation with capital. But, despite such similarities, there were profound differences in the two episodes. First, there was a critical difference in the kinds of social forces involved in the two situations. In 1938, the main actors were rural and urban workers; in 1959–60, the urban poor were the main protagonists.

Second, different options were available to handle the protest. In 1938, the timing of the workers' revolt coincided with Bustamante's activism and with the middle-class search for a nationalist organization. The fortuitous convergence of these processes led to the integration of the workers' movement into the organizations created by Bustamante and Norman Manley. Consequently, a significant aspect of the 1938 episode was the political leadership's creation of representative organizations which effectively encapsulated workers' wage demands. Those demands were organizable and eventually were represented in the structures created by the emergent leadership.

This mode of resolving the demands of the urban unemployed was not immediately available in 1960. The growing mass of unemployed workers, and the existence of a layer of permanently unemployed among them, presented formidable problems for integration or demobilization. For example, in 1960 the unemployed workers' demand for jobs could not easily be addressed by the established trade unions. This was so mainly because the demand for employment and the creation of jobs touched on *structural* problems of the Jamaican economy, which could not easily be resolved by wage-bargaining organizations. At the same time, the policy of industrialization under the auspices of foreign capital – a policy designed in part to reduce unemployment – itself was contributing to joblessness and the social crisis.[32] The year 1960 therefore presented a new challenge for the state, as foreign investment was unable to reduce unemployment substantially, and the existing political organizations were unable as yet to integrate the restive urban unemployed into the new pattern of politics. The late colonial period had produced an anomalous situation: the existence of a volatile mass of unemployed workers and allied strata, outside the constraints of the official political structures. The rise of this militant social force, enjoying autonomy outside the ken of official political leadership, also distinguished this period from the 1938 episode. In time, this autonomy would give the urban unemployed unique leverage in national politics, as various political groups vied for their support.

A third important difference between the two crisis episodes was the articulation of 1950s protest in explicitly racial terms. This racial consciousness blocked any alliance between the middle class and the unemployed. Unlike the motives of the 1938 crisis, which articulated some of labor's aspirations and demands with the contradiction within the middle class, the yearnings of the unemployed in the late fifties were not assimilable to the now-amicable relations between the middle class and the colonial power. From the point of view of the middle class, the evolution of constitutional decolonization up to 1960 had resolved its conflicts with the colonial power. In other words, the middle-class leadership was waiting patiently for political power to be transferred to it. From its perspective, therefore, continued opposition to colonialism and the resurrection of issues of racial domination were anachronistic. The *Daily Gleaner* advanced this position best, with its repudiation of a demonstration for Trinidadian independence planned by Eric Williams, the nationalist leader in Trinidad. The Jamaican newspaper noted dryly, "We have said before that Dr. Williams apparently does not recognize that the question of West Indian Independence is not a new battle to be fought out but a battle which has already been won. All that is left is for the West Indies to ask for independence; there is no need for battle or demonstration."[33] Given the pervasiveness of this thinking within influential circles, it was a short step to the conclusion that the resurfacing of racial protest in the island was atavistic, if not "the work of the devil." In short, with the middle class's continuing apprenticeship to state power, the contradictions that once had stimulated its opposition to British rule now had been resolved to its members' satisfaction.

This development fundamentally affected the relationship between the middle class and those classes and groups who persisted in making charges of racial and other forms of discrimination. As is now apparent, these claims were advanced mostly by the Rastafarians, but such criticisms certainly involved non-Rastafarian elements among the urban population as well. These elements included salaried members of the lower middle class, independent artisans, and casual laborers. Despite the postwar boom, the economic situation of these sectors remained uncertain. Whereas, for example, entrepreneurs in import-export trade, manufacturing, and distribution, along with the middle class in the professions, thrived, conditions were shakier for those blacks who were neither ranking members of the middle class nor part of the steadily employed manual working class.

If we look first at the very bottom rungs of the middle class on the eve of independence, among the elements to be found there were clerks, cashiers, bank tellers, telephone operators, secretaries, and receptionists. For blacks aspiring to nonmanual jobs in this sector of the economy, the expanding availability of these positions offered an avenue to respectability and upward mobility. Unfortunately for many other aspirants to these posts, employers sometimes reserved them for light-skinned members of the population. Despite the waning of the tight class-color correlation, residual but significant forms of color discrimination remained in the distribution of rewards. Not surprisingly, those who found themselves blocked by this discrimination felt aggrieved and attributed their experience to color prejudice. For this group, then, black nationalism undoubtedly would have had an appeal.

The situation of the independent artisans — the furniture makers, electricians, masons, mechanics, shoemakers, and billboard artists — was more complex. The overall expansion of the urban economy certainly boosted the fortunes of those who had usable manual skills. For example, the growth in the building trade was a boon to construction and allied workers. They found jobs not only at large-scale construction projects, but also in niches created by homeowners' desires for property improvement. Still, these new opportunities for skilled manual labor were not without their own contradictions. For one thing, there was a limit on the number of workers who could be hired at construction sites, and there were usually more applicants than jobs. Consequently, for many artisans steady employment was unlikely, and this fact undoubtedly forced them into the uncertainties of self-employment.

Second, for construction workers steady work usually meant employment on government projects, which at this time inevitably entangled workers in party and trade-union rivalries. The maturing politics of clientelism, which required workers' political loyalty in exchange for jobs and favors, ensnared some artisans while helping others. Those who felt independent enough to reject this sharp political rivalry and its sometimes accompanying violence had the option of pursuing uncertain self-employment. The demand by this category of skilled laborers for job creation and an end to political discrimination complemented the Rastafarians' racially-focused criticisms of injustice under black rule.

Finally, state policies and political decolonization contributed in their own ways to discriminatory results. The postwar industrialization strategy, for example, benefited primarily the middle and upper classes, through commercialization of the economy, urban construction, and an import policy favoring expensive consumer goods. Similarly, the expansion of the state necessarily involved a demand for administrative and other personnel, and here too the middle class was a beneficiary.

As a result, "personal" discriminatory social practices in the larger society were buttressed by the "impersonal" discrimination of postwar economic policy.

As if this widening protest against discrimination and economic hardship were not enough, the governing PNP regime was challenged on other important issues by the People's Political Party (PPP), an organization flying Garveyite colors. Founded in April 1961 by Millard Johnson, a black lawyer and unreconstructed black nationalist, the PPP organized its opposition around several broad themes. They included the need for cultural ties with Africa, a reduction of foreign capital's dominance in the economy, assistance to small businesses, an end to racial discrimination in employment, and rejection of the West Indies Federation.

From its founding to the national elections a year later, the PPP focused on these issues and succeeded in calling public attention to its views. Although the PPP was a marginal force on the political scene, Johnson's activism gave the PNP cause for concern.[34] At a ministers' conference in June 1961, Vernon Arnett, the finance minister, warned his party in a report that "it is clear that it would be unsafe to treat the Millard Johnson movement lightly. He is succeeding in holding interest and he is known to be a determined and persistent person."[35] Remarking on the PPP's possible appeal for many outside the middle and upper classes, the finance minister's report continued: "But, of course, the real danger is that the unemployed, the underemployed, and the lowest paid labouring and cultivating classes may start turning towards Johnson as offering them something which neither the PNP nor the JLP has offered."[36] Arnett, of course, was referring to the PPP's fusion of a culturally authentic ideology with promises to secure a vastly improved position for black labor in the economy. This synthesis was at the heart of the PPP's program, and—as Vernon Arnett's comments suggest-it gave the PPP a major ideological advantage over the established parties.

Although Johnson sought to extend this leverage to the issue of Jamaica's continuing membership in the West Indies Federation, this broader focus was of little concern to unemployed workers preoccupied with their desperate economic circumstances. Because of its political isolation and inability to advance specific proposals for the economic ills facing the country, the PPP collapsed after a crushing electoral defeat in 1962.[37] As a party of black nationalism, the PPP was unable to offer the population more than cultural revitalization and criticism of existing ills. Nonetheless, this organization's agitation against racial discrimination in the early sixties kept that issue alive and complemented the more socially destabilizing protest of the Rastafarians and allied strata.[38]

As a time of significant economic change and political reorganization, then, the late fifties and early sixties had produced major social tensions. Substantial segments of the black urban population had opposed the official "definition of the situation" as a triumph of black rule and an end to racial oppression. Instead, racial identity and its links to social and economic disadvantages had been projected as national issues. The ensuing ideological struggles and the repeated rebuttals by opponents of black consciousness in 1960 testified to this race and class demarcation of the conflict. In this period, a remarkable ideological unity cemented the defenders of Exceptionalism, as they mounted an offensive against the resurgence of race consciousness. The recurrence of identical themes, especially in the conceptions of the domestic entrepreneurs and the upper and middle ranks of the intermediate class, disclosed a marked concordance of allied class positions on the issue of race.

Touching as it did on the privileges being enjoyed by people of light skin color, Rastafarian ideology apparently had struck a sensitive spot in the politically dominant group. Despite its isolation, the Rastafarian movement had created a small but perceptible fissure in the ramparts of the state. The group's protest against cultural and economic discrimination against black Jamaicans eventually set up a conflict between the regime and the educational apparatus, beginning when a small group of scholars at the University of the West Indies produced a mildly sympathetic study of the Rastafarian movement.[39] Despite the moderate tone of this now-classic study, it generated reactions bordering on panic. Perhaps fearing that legitimacy might accrue to the movement from being an object of academic scrutiny and compassion, various groups condemned the report. Following up on sharp criticisms by the *Daily Gleaner*,[40] the head of the Catholic Church dismissed the study as "unworthy of scholars" and reminded them that the "paramount consideration was the security of the state."[41] At the same time, the conflict forced the PNP into sharply defining the differences between Exceptionalism and black nationalism. At the November 1960 party conference, Norman Manley addressed the membership with some exasperation:

> And then comrades, there is this matter that I so hate to have to talk about. I see people on platforms all over the place preaching colour, trying to build up a spirit of skin against skin and race against race. It is the work of the devil . . . in our country, where all our political institutions are in the hands of our own people and where we are rapidly reaching the day when merit alone counts, . . . who the hell cares that some men are black? Who cares that I am a brown man? Who cares that comrade Arnett is nearly white? Who cares? Any of you care?[42]

This fulmination against racial consciousness was not simply a matter of personal pique, however. More importantly, it was an expression of maturing social conflicts which had erupted between a middle class that had inherited political power, and sections of the urban unemployed who lived on the margins of society. It will be remembered that these new conflicts appeared in the wake of the resolution of conflicts involving obstacles to middle-class mobility. By late 1960, the apprenticeship process had dissolved these latter disputes with the British state over the devolution of power and the entry of natives into hitherto inaccessible positions in the state and economy. In the ensuing months, between the November 1960 PNP conference and the acquisition of political independence in August 1962, this ideological struggle continued unabated. Even where other significant political issues intruded,[43] the obvious unemployment crisis and its ideological effect, in the form of race consciousness, dominated the political scene. As this period drew to a close, the political leadership was baffled by what must have been a vexing turn of events. This denouement of the colonial period in effect had produced a new ideological crisis; the dominant classes apparently were unable to exercise moral leadership over a section of the subordinate population.

This failure of hegemony over the urban unemployed was reflected in a revealing comment by a PNP member of Parliament, Ivan Lloyd. In calling for more state action to quell the urban discontent and to "bring people back to normal" in Kingston, Lloyd remarked:

> I am glad indeed, that our rural population, that the country people have not at all been infected by this virus. They are still living in their own original concepts of right and wrong. They have no conception and any sensitiveness as regards race and colour and things of that sort . . . I am sure Members of both sides of the House would like to see it remain so. In that respect, I hope that our politicians, especially those from the Corporate Area, when they come to our country parts, I am hoping that they [leave] our country people alone.[44]

Despite continued affirmation of the official ideology, the ideological setback in Kingston clearly had produced an aura of uncertainty, a guardedness and inconstancy of mood at the top, as various state policies and individual outbursts disclosed a not-so-sanguine outlook on the future.[45] Indeed, as official fears of subversion, as well as slippage in investor confidence, mounted, the state adopted more restrictive measures.[46] Instead of holding out the prospect of national unity and an expansion of individual freedom, the imminence of self-rule seemed to promise continued conflict and increasingly prohibitive state interventions. In this context of deepening social inequalities, increasing racial protest, and hints of a fortress mentality at the top, assorted attempts were made to develop alternative forms of organization and new modes of opposition to challenge the independent state. The first few of these initiatives are examined in the following chapter.

CHAPTER 4

Militant Laborism
and Popular Protest

The resurfacing of a black nationalism led by Rastafarians in the urban areas produced a major political and ideological crisis for the regime. Coming in the final months of the transition to independence, this resurgence of racial consciousness among the urban unemployed put on the defensive a regime already made apprehensive by the impact of the Cuban Revolution on the region. By the last months of 1961, not only had the politically dominant group responded with the ideology of Exceptionalism, but also it had attempted to install an ideological quarantine around the island. This *cordon sanitaire* was devised to block the spread of socialist ideas and to proscribe Afro-Americans of Black Muslim or militant Garveyite sympathies. In addition to a determined attempt to contain the diffusion of black consciousness internally, efforts were made to cut the island off from radical ideological currents in the United States and the socialist countries.

Such ideological vigilance under the PNP was consistent with the preemptive and restrictive pattern of rule under colonialism, demonstrating the ideological convergence of both political parties in their opposition to communism and black nationalism. With the JLP's return to power in the April 1962 elections, this prohibitive orientation persisted, indicating that these defensive responses were not regime-specific but instead were determined by state security concerns in the new period. In the context of this heightened vigilance, political independence in August 1962 yielded not a model democratic state, but rather a disfigured parliamentary government in which national security concerns tended to override individual rights and civil liberties. Despite constitutional provisions affirming the norms of democratic rule and the protection of fundamental rights, this new independent state found itself torn between past and future. On the one hand, the transfer of the parliamentary model of government created a democratic bridge to the future, as political independence under a liberal-democratic constitution produced an emancipatory advance over colonial absolutism. On the other hand, fears for the state's vulnerability in a turbulent period disposed the JLP to adopt defensive measures rooted in the absolutist colonial past. Political rule in this early postcolonial period therefore had inscribed within it facets of both democratic rule and colonial authoritarianism.

This latter was evident, for example, in the retention of colonial laws after independence. Remarking on this tension between the promulgation of a liberal democratic constitution and the retention of the panoply of colonial legislation, constitutional scholar Lloyd Barnett drew the following conclusions about the contradictory character of Jamaica's postcolonial government:

> There are numerous laws, many of them enacted in the days of strictly colonial government and gubernatorial absolutism, which conflict with the spirit of the constitutional guarantees. Many of these laws, such as the Passport Law, . . . and the Undesirable Publications (Prohibition of Importation) Law have been the instruments of arbitrary ministerial abrogation of the fundamental freedoms. By virtue of the wide discretions which they vest in the Executive they continue to be a threat to the individual.[1]

The conflict between the democratic promise of the constitution and the persistence of highly restrictive colonial legislation suggests that the independent state really was a political hybrid, combining aspects of two political forms: bourgeois parliamentary rule and colonial absolutism. This democracy infused with absolutist tendencies contained weak, underdeveloped elements of both forms of political rule. Authoritarian democracy in Jamaica therefore should be seen as a form of rule in which substantive elements of parliamentary government coexists with restrictive, arbitrary, and nonreviewable state interventions designed to deter populations, movements, and ideologies deemed threatening to the status quo. This system of rule is designated as "weak" in the double sense that both the authoritarian and democratic features of the state are stunted, due to historical factors. For instance, it may be argued that one historical determinant that prevented the emergence of an even more restrictive postcolonial state was the gradual and relatively peaceful transition to independence between 1940 and 1962. These years brought neither heightened tensions between landowners and workers, irreconcilable antagonisms between the colonial state and nationalist leaders, nor a serious bid for power by a revolutionary anticolonial movement. The absence of these developments allowed for a gradual political liberalization from above and afforded a leisurely native apprenticeship and colonial withdrawal. This devolution of power enhanced the fortunes of moderate indigenous leaders, while strengthening acceptance of the British model of parliamentary government.

A scenario opposite to the one described — such as the crushing of an anti-imperialist movement, or its attainment of a revolutionary victory—would have produced sharply different outcomes, neither of which would have been auspicious for the emergence of *bourgeois* democracy in Jamaica. In sum, the absence of an even more authoritarian form of rule in the early postcolonial years was related partly to such vital outcomes as the lack of a serious threat to British rule from below, and the unambiguous acceptance of liberal-democratic procedures by nationalist leaders. The route to bourgeois democracy in Jamaica, then, was at least related to both an ideological consensus among native leaders and the moderation of conflicts in the late colonial period.

Having alluded to two factors which helped forestall the emergence of an even more restrictive form of postcolonial rule, we need to note that this independent state was not a model democracy. For while such factors as constitutional provisions, the ideological inclinations of the political leadership, and a long mass apprenticeship in party politics allowed for the unfolding of substantive democratic practices, other influences imposed limits on the scope and content of this democracy. Aside from such weighty constraints as the structural continuities between the colonial and postcolonial states, the burdens of an underdeveloped economy with its poor differentiation of classes, and sharp social and economic divisions, other factors throttled the full flowering of a democratic state and diminished official respect for civil liberties.

First, despite the political liberalization afforded by the transfer of the Westminster model of parliamentary government, the prior nondemocratic colonial order provided few opportunities for natives' full enjoyment of fundamental rights or civil liberties. Consequently, precedents in law or society that might have developed around these two ideas were generally sacrificed to the exigencies of law and order and the principle of imperial control. Whatever libertarian practices arose with political independence had to do so against a weak colonial tradition of respect for civil and political liberties. Given the almost nonexistent tradition of upholding natives' civil liberties, it is not surprising that, despite a democratic apparatus, postcolonial rule began by encroaching on these liberties.

That these breaches occurred is not without its irony, however. Indeed, they suggest a related influence which weakened the democratic content of the independent state. Implicated here is the paradox that, although Jamaican anticolonialism had implicit within it a defense of civil liberties, strenuous agitation for implementation of these principles appears to have been subordinated to the global demands for native participation in the economy, greater political inclusion in the colonial bureaucracy, and eventually direct rule by nationals. Compared with the emphasis on majority rule, civil liberties, as an idea

worth defending in universal terms (particularly as it affected the protection of all dissident opinions), apparently elicited less sympathy
from the native political leadership which fought for self-rule and drew
up the independence constitution.

This slighting of civil liberties during the late colonial period — due
to limits imposed by the politics of the nationalist leaders and their
probable belief that abuses would be a moot question in a democratic,
self-governing country — evidently produced a disregard for the protection of dissenting political opinions and movements in the early postcolonial years. In sum, despite the patent abuses of colonial rule, civil
liberties and their protection in the early postcolonial period found few
champions among the indigenous leadership.[2]

Finally, the conjunction at independence of several factors inimical
to the easy assertion of the new state's political authority also created pressures for heightened state vigilance, which in turn further encroached on political liberties. Like its Third World counterparts at this
stage of evolution, the Jamaican state was faced with the challenge of
asserting its political authority over a postcolonial society marked by
social inequalities and economic divisions. It has been noted that this
political authority was suspect and was established only shakily amid
concurrent ideological challenges from domestic and international
movements. These challenges — the eruption of black nationalism at
home and abroad, the shattering impact of the Cuban Revolution as
an exemplar of an alternative model of development — inevitably generated defensive state responses.

In this context of local dissidence and officially perceived vulnerability to the contaminative influence of foreign ideologies and movements, the structural tendency of the postcolonial state to assert its
power over the new society gained additional impetus. Thus state security and law-and-order — already associated with the creation of stability
and the guarantee of political security for capital — were further justified by fear of communist and black nationalist subversion. Preemptive
measures to proscribe these threats consequently expanded the authoritarian character of the state, even as the fragile, newly-established democratic norms sought roots in the new society. Under these various
circumstances, Jamaican democracy emerged flawed and disfigured.
Where the carefully supervised transition to independence seems, on
the one hand, partly to have favored the emergence of a democratic
postcolonial regime, both the formative history of Jamaican society
and the challenges of the postcolonial order, on the other hand, inclined the fledgling independent state in an illiberal direction.

This drift toward state security, censorship, and other abuses did not
deter political activists however. In fact, the 1962 JLP victory was

matched by a tentative renewal of socialist activism in the country, as well as an expansion of independent forms of popular urban protest. For example, socialist activism reemerged in 1962, after a period of dormancy and isolation in the wake of the ignominious defeat in the fifties. Despite being cut off from labor and crippled by the legacy to their arduous passage, socialist formations — heirs to the beleaguered Marxist tradition — sprouted afresh in the year of political independence.

Testifying to the vitality of that tradition and bringing to fruition Richard Hart's efforts to develop a Marxist political culture among workers, two new groups emerged.[3] One, the Young Socialist League, was created inside the PNP; the other, the Unemployed Workers' Council (UWC), surfaced among the shanty dwellers of West Kingston. The former renewed attempts to put the PNP back on the socialist path, while the latter conducted a grassroots struggle on behalf of the urban poor. This chapter explores the UWC's activism among the Kingston poor and discusses how the latter developed a politics which was informed by the erosion of deference, the assertion of race consciousness, and open disregard for the etiquette of the respectable classes.

The Origins of the Unemployed Workers' Council

As we have seen, by 1957 dissension within the JFTU had disorganized the leftwing forces. After the suppression of the JFTU in the sugar strike, several militants had opposed Hart's creation of the PFM on the grounds that it was premature and detracted from building the already beleaguered leftist trade union movement. The subsequent electoral defeat of the PFM and the steadfast refusal of the colonial government to recognize the JFTU led to the disintegration of the ex-PNP Left that remained committed to a Marxist politics.

Among those sharply critical of Hart's leadership was Ben Monroe, a willful, self-assured cabinetmaker from the depressed working-class community of Southwest Saint Andrew. Schooled as a militant inside the PEO and active in the 1954 JFTU strike movement, Monroe led the opposition to the PFM's leadership. Evidently with the same unbridled outspoken bravado and assertiveness of character for which the West Kingston poor were to gain notoriety, Monroe criticized Hart's leadership. His charges included a lack of internal democracy within the PFM, political opportunism, absence of reflection on the 1952 split, and exhaustion of the material and human resources of the JFTU in the abortive election and strikes.[4] What distressed Monroe most was his belief that Hart had been hasty in creating the PFM. In Monroe's view, "Enough work was not really done in analyzing the experiences which were gained from the development of the PNP and what had resulted from the split. We felt that the leadership of the PFM assumed that because the people had moved to support the PNP's socialism, [then] they would have automatically followed the PFM."[5] The PFM leadership apparently did not respond effectively to these allegations, and this failure also helped seal the fate of the Left opposition.[6]

With the collapse of the leftist organizations in the late fifties, Monroe turned to his Southwest Saint Andrew community and formed the Congress of Progressive Youths (COPY)—his version of the PEO. Inside COPY, the group around Monroe studied the Communist classics, including Engels' *Anti-Dühring* and *Dialectics of Nature*. However, it was Lenin's political writings that most absorbed the group as it searched for theoretical and organizational principles with which to understand the local political scene. Indeed, of the several ideological influences which were to animate the UWC, Leninism—particularly its critique of imperialism and its antipathy toward refomist parties of the Left— was the most enduring.

This abiding Leninist influence was leavened by a close analysis of the local scene and by the tenets of such international organizations as the United Nations. The UN's Charter on Human Rights, and particularly Article 23 on the "Right to Work," occupied a central place in the UWC's activism. As a consequence of the UWC's ceaseless championing of the UN doctrine, the principle of "natural" economic, political, and social rights—which had yet to find legitimacy in the island— became a radical force for political mobilization and growth of awareness among the urban unemployed. The UWC leadership was so committed to the UN's defense of the right to employment as an inalienable human right, that the UWC saluted Article 23 by naming the UWC journal of political agitation "The Right to Work." Similarly, the Cuban Revolution in 1959 emboldened activists in COPY. Like many radicals in the region, they paid close attention to this revolutionary development on a nearby island. In time, these activists were able to read literature in English directly from the source, as the Cuban consulate in Jamaica breached the ideological quarantine by disseminating, in bulk, various works on the revolution.[7]

As a result of study and reflection based on these varied ideological influences, in March 1962, Monroe and a few ex-PFM cadres[8] launched an urban poor peoples' organization, the Unemployed Workers' Council. Under Monroe's leadership, the council adopted several positions. These included: a commitment to socialism, affirmation of the right to work, criticism of the drift toward suppression of liberties, opposition to external control of the local economy, and resistance to the two-party practice of clientelism and victimization in employment. In addition, the council showed a willingness to take direct action on behalf of the unorganized urban poor. In taking up these positions, the UWC distanced itself from the political practice of the JFTU-PFM, which the council felt had succumbed to a leftwing version of the political unionism practiced by the dominant parties and unions. Since the council was resolutely opposed to all varieties of political unionism, it condemned what it saw as the emergence of this practice within leftwing organizations.

To better appreciate the UWC's sharp critique of the PFM's tactics, recall the dominant parties' abuse of workers in the forties and fifties. At that time, both political parties not only engaged in electoral rivalries, but also competed to bring workers into their affiliated unions. This competition for working-class support spawned an intense and often violent politics of bargaining rights. Each union fought the other with everything at its command — including strikes, hired thugs, and demonstrations — in order to share in the right to represent workers. As a consequence, the expiration of labor contracts and the launching of new construction projects inevitably led to bitter conflicts and pitched battles between the unions at construction sites. The council opposed this well-entrenched party-linked union rivalry, and this stand distinguished it as an early advocate of worker self-management and independence from political unionism.[9] In fact, where political exigencies subsequently led other radicals to focus their opposition mainly against the JLP-BITU structure and so to spare the PNP and NWU, the council was unflagging in its antagonism to *both* cartels.

If the UWC's opposition to all forms of political unionism tended to give it a maverick coloration among leftwing forces, its activism among the unemployed and its defense of destitute slum dwellers loaned it a specificity unmatched in the history of Jamaican postwar social movements.[10] That is, the council constituted a pioneering attempt to organize a social force of increasing importance in the island's political life. Underdeveloped capitalism had spawned a large unemployed labor force which roamed the rural towns and villages and comprised a considerable mass in the urban areas.[11] The destitution of this sector gave it a volatility easily excited by any provocation. The 1938 labor revolt, for instance, found some urban slum dwellers at the workers' side battling the police, while others took to sacking Chinese shops and "demand[ing] money with menaces from anyone who looked 'respectable.'"[12] Having already remarked on the general militancy of the unemployed in the late fifties around the issues of race and nationalism, next we shall differentiate groups within this mass. This exploration will allow us to glimpse their ways of life and to observe the political tendencies which drew UWC activists to the urban unemployed.

The Specificity of the Urban Unemployed: The City of Kingston

It is possible to identify three main layers among the Kingston poor in the early sixties: a segment of self-employed tradesmen, a variegated mass of petty vendors, and a stratum of destitute hard-core unemployed. Surrounding all three layers were allied semiemployed casual laborers of all types. The topmost layer among the poor was composed of artisans and skilled craftsmen who worked mainly on their "own account," although in some instances they hired themselves out for an odd job here and there. This category included self-taught tradesmen such as carpenters, sign artists, tailors, furniture makers, shoemakers, and automobile repairmen. Although some in this group, such as the carpenters and dressmakers, looked to the construction trade or garment factories for employment, the majority earned a livelihood by making or repairing various objects for use by members of the working class. As members of this group practiced their trade in the dismal working-class districts in Kingston, they earned a reputation in these communities for the skill and quality of their work. Predominantly black in color, this segment exhibited contradictory political tendencies. In fact, many in this group were part of the respectable poor—a group particularly susceptible to Bustamante's appeals for forbearance in the face of provocation and deprivation.

While taking no satisfaction from their meagre economic circumstances, the tradesmen were stoutly committed to lawfulness, decency, and reputation for good character as sources of dignity. For instance, the independent artisans derived a guild pride from their work and their self-reliance and were apt to share in the ideology of the upper and middle classes, who emphasized to the poor the enobling value of work and the possibility of upward mobility through sacrifice. Understandably, these tradesmen—many of whom were shielded from harsh everyday contact with the classes above them—were less inclined than some to adopt the militant postures of the Rastafarians and other militant unemployed elements. Nonetheless, their lowly social origins, dark skin color, and proximity to the more destitute poor placed these craftsmen in a relation of active sympathy with the more militant unemployed. Class affinity therefore put the tradesmen in a position of latent opposition to the politically dominant group.

At the same time, the moderate outlook of this fraction of the urban poor was balanced by the presence among them of some Rastafarians. The latter, equally proud of their status as independent artisans, provided a bold contrast to the ideological moderation of their peers in this community. Despite their militancy, of course, the Rastafarians' unyielding desire to live under their "own vine and fig tree" — an allusion to their aspiration for economic self-sufficiency — bespoke a petty entrepreneurial mentality not too dissimilar to that of the respectable poor. Ironically, this outlook gave the Rastafarians an ideological affinity with their more conformist peers.

Lower in the hierarchy was yet another "own-account" category. Compared to the artisanal layer above it, this contingent was younger, unskilled, less cohesive, and more inclined to reckless, rebellious displays. Here a rich assortment of social types subsisted through petty entrepreneurship. Unable to find employment and lacking the skills to take up an independent trade, this stratum resorted to desperately hawking petty commodities. Offering such items as novelties, clothing, confectionary, and animals, members of this layer eked out an existence on the street corners and marketplaces in Kingston. Whether they plied their trade from fixed stalls or moved about the steaming streets of the city, the vendors came into direct contact with their social betters and with groups of the unemployed. The character and the simultaneity of these social relations produced in the vendors an antipathy toward the middle class.

For example, in conducting its business in the commercial districts, the middle class came into contact with street vendors. The nature of this social contact engendered mutual contempt between these two segments of the Kingston population. As we have observed, the Jamaican middle class possessed an exalted sense of its cultural affinity with the upper class and therefore dealt imperiously with the darker, poorer classes below it. This stance was evident in the contemptuous and paternalistic relationship members of the urban middle class maintained with the maids and "gardener boys" who worked in middle-class homes. Workers there often were subjected to abuse and humiliation that ranged from sniping remarks about their lifestyles to outright physical abuse. Given this background of class contempt, it is not surprising that members of the urban middle class demanded submissive compliance from the street vendors. In the marketplace, for instance, the middle class could adopt a supercilious posture, enforce class distance, and even attempt to impose its own price on the vendors. When the cumulative effects of these behaviors inflamed the vendors, the middle-class individual would quickly resort to a wheedling paternalism to calm them. The everyday occurrence of these practices, reflecting the contemptuous middle-class view of the vendors as the "riff-raff" of society, at the individual level reproduced the antagonistic class and race relations characteristic of the larger society.

If the street vendors' relations with the middle class sharpened the antagonism of these petty entrepreneurs, then their association with allied unemployed strata such as the lumpenproletariat gave an extra fillip to the vendors' antipathies toward the dominant classes. The ties between the "lumpen" and the street vendors reflected a shared alienation and mutual experience of cultural injury, which congealed into tense hostility toward the middle class, ethnic-minority capitalists, and Chinese shopkeepers. In the context of Jamaica's poorly differentiated class structure, it is difficult to make a sharp demarcation between petty street entrepreneurs and members of the urban lumpenproletariat. It is probable that there was movement back and forth between the two categories. Some vendors almost certainly gave up the wearisome hawking in the blistering heat for the uncertain occupation of the lumpenproletariat, while members of the latter may have tried their hands at petty entrepreneurship. Whatever the direction of this movement, the lumpenproletariat's way of life — its bravado, nihilism, and guerrilla-like forays into the commercial districts to intimidate those who appeared respectable and well-to-do — met with wonderment on the part of people from allied unemployed strata, many of whom assumed these postures.

For their part, many among the lumpenproletariat lived by their wits, engaging in artifice, crime, and predatory acts. Here were to be found the practitioners of ghetto wiliness: the various con-men, small-scale marijuana dealers, and nimble-fingered pickpockets who targeted the Chinese, the visiting tourists, and the well-dressed and made them victims of crime. More dangerous were the bandits and holdup men, whose forays against banks and commercial establishments and whose unsparing disregard for innocent lives could hardly be regarded as politically defensible. But there was more to the protest of the urban poor than simple criminality. Of significance was the class-antagonistic morality that infused these predatory acts. For example, the militant hard-core unemployed, who existed outside the confines of all the "normalizing" institutions of the society, developed a subculture of alienation. This outlook was at once anomic and ideologically antagonistic in its assault on the standards of civic virtue and the modes of bourgeois respectability being deployed by the political leadership and the upper class. To the latter's status superiority, paternalism, and insistence on deference, the lumpenproletariat responded with an antagonistic nihilism. They defied political authority, rejected the dominant cultural sensibility, and affirmed ghetto culture and ideology as legitimate rivals to the dominant Anglophile tendency. This celebration of ghetto morality exalted a combative refusal to be submissive, a spontaneous militant affirmation of blackness, a disposition to adopt menacing postures toward those perceived as "oppressors," and a readiness to challenge those found guilty of vaunting their class position and "high" skin color.

For their part, the middle and upper classes invariably interpreted these tendencies as a lack of "breeding" associated with lower-class behavior. It may be argued, however, that what the anomic practice of the unemployed and allied strata actually disclosed was an attempt to counter class arrogance by adopting forms of behavior that ridiculed and caricatured the middle- and upper-class ways of life. This antagonistic morality, expressing a growing defiance and an erosion of deference, radiated throughout the lower ranks of the unemployed, marking them with a sensibility which called into question the adhesion of the urban poor to the official consensualist ideology.

The Phenomenon of the Rebellious Urban Youths

Nowhere was this open disregard for the etiquette of the respectable classes more apparent in the early sixties than among the unemployed male youths of Kingston. Beginning about 1961 and blossoming fully three years later, a rebellious youth movement erupted as a distinct force among the unemployed.[13] Self-consciously identifying themselves as "rude boys" or "rudies," this contingent of young males adopted exhibitionistic forms of behavior which made them the bane of those charged with summoning the subordinate classes to the dominant ideology.[14] In inventing what might be called a culture of resistance, the youths selected those aspects of the moral codes most cherished by the middle and upper classes and inverted them. In matters of speech, dress, comportment, forms of salutation, and even the etiquette of courtship, the rebellious youths reversed the official codes. They deliberately went without socks; shirts were not tucked in; wash rags were substituted for handkerchiefs and left to hang out of their back pockets. Caps were worn askew atop an uncombed head, and other ways were found to assume an alternative costume. To the speech affectations of the middle class, the youths responded with a variation of working-class speech. Indeed, not unlike the Rastafarians, they developed a form of speech which probably gave better expression to their cultural experience by allowing for unorthodox linkages among emotion, language, and sound.[15]

As a stratum of the urban unemployed, the rebellious youths developed rituals and ideas associated with, but still distinct from, those of the Rastafarians. As the antecedent movement that had engaged the dominant classes in ideological battle, the Rastafarians had assumed a moral leadership among the urban poor. Their militant black nationalism, with its Garveyite remembrances, struck a responsive chord among the unemployed. An attractive ideological summons for the latter, the appeal pulled many in its train. The Rastafarians allowed adherents to "live" their opposition to the dominant groups through black nationalism, and to do so in explicitly Rastafarian terms. Indeed, under the prevailing conditions of censorship, it could be argued that the Rastafarians broke through the official strictures on social discourse and breached the state ideological quarantine. This they did by constructing an alternative site for free political communication, which many among the unemployed quickly occupied. By exploiting the vehicle of talk, based on the interpretation of the Bible – a medium readily at hand in the homes of the poor – the Rastafarians allowed many among the unemployed to attain dissidence. In this way the Rastafarians strengthened their moral dominance among sections of the urban poor, widening and deepening their separation from the normalized classes in the society. The significance of the Rastafarians in the early sixties was that, under conditions of cultural ridicule and police suppression of the urban unemployed, they held open a political space for dissidence among the poor. The Rastafarians created an indispensable holding action against the pressures of the regime and built an ideological safehouse for the unemployed and urban ghetto youths.

But the Rastafarians also called upon these allied social forces to *temper* their militancy with discipline and asceticism. For Rastafarians, oppression in Jamaica called for a studied retreat and disengagement. Furthermore, unfolding events demanded constant study and analysis, and this entailed meditation, discussion, and reading the Bible, seeking for answers. All this activity implied a special competence on the part of recruits to the Rastafarian point of view. Moreover, to belong to this culture of resistance, enlistees had to meet the rigorous intellectual demands of the Rastafarian community and remain faithful to the idea of repatriation. It is at this point that the differences between Rastafarians and the rebellious youths become obvious. Although the youths were influenced by Rastafarian notions of black emancipation, they were less inclined to show fidelity to the idea of repatriation and the web of related metaphysics and rituals. The militant youths stopped short of a thoroughgoing embrace of Rastafarian ideology. Instead, they drew haphazardly on Rastafarian ideology, borrowing those notions they found useful in indicting their antagonists or in affirming the legitimacy of ghetto culture. Thus, early militant slogans such as "Is fi wi time now," and "Black man time come," which were raised initially by Rastafarians, found their way into the lexicon of militant youths. Similarly, the Rastafarian antipathy toward work which paid "slave wages" was transmitted to the rude boys. While many among the urban poor certainly availed themselves of the unpredictable "day's work" which came their way, the rebellious youths stoutly rejected the low pay and abuse which sometimes accompanied casual employment.

But where Rastafarians linked these anathemas to a militancy informed by an ideology and a vision of black empowerment, the "rudies" possessed no such coherence of outlook. Theirs was a spontaneous affirmation of moralities rooted in the everyday life of the ghetto. These moralities encompassed such traits as political cynicism, aspirations for a better life, the celebration of instinctual needs, and in-group camaraderie, as well as the cultivation of a fearsome, violent personality. Under these circumstances, the rebellious youths remained vulnerable to the vices of ghetto life and susceptible to the thrills of youthful exuberance. Despite evidence of an antagonistic morality among urban youth, these bits and pieces of their cultural makeup did not constitute either a coherent political ideology or a clear vision of an alternative society. This anomic, inchoate consciousness made the rebellious youths even more frightening to the rest of society than the sometimes stoic Rastafarians.

The ideological disorganization among the rebellious youths was tied to the commingling of Rastafarianism and the Americanization of Jamaican culture. On the one side, the imbibing of nationalist ideas from the Rastafarians inclined the young people toward an uncertain political awareness which found expression in a ready pride in blackness and a rejection of the cultural status quo. On the other side, the Americanization of the local culture brought the youths under the negative influence of one of the U.S. cultural exports — cowboy movies. The torrent of "westerns" imported in this early period and shown almost exclusively in working-class communities stimulated the formation of gangs among working-class youths and marked them with a fateful recklessness.

Consciously modeling themselves on the marauding outlaw gangs in these films, the youths turned fiction into fact. By mid-1963, this imitation had culminated int the inevitable horizontal violence and struggle for turf among juvenile gangs. The emerging pattern of gang warfare, combined with a marked hedonism and materialist ethic, set the youths off sharply from the Rastafarians. Protest among urban ghetto youths assumed a distinctive form, as their antagonism reflected the double cultural impact of Rastafarianism and American outlaw dramaturgy. Western forms of outlaw culture, materialist values, racial assertiveness, and susceptibility to the perils of ghetto culture all were fused in the rebellious youths' identity. The uneasy coexistence of these disparate cultural influences in the rude boys' identity gave them a distinctive outlook and defined the boundaries between them and the Rastafarians. Their unstable ideological composition gave ghetto youth militancy an ambiguous flavor, as claims for social justice competed with expressions of instinctual needs. Youth consciousness therefore exhibited a clouded recognition of social inequalities and an anomic, antisocial temper.

This spontaneous militancy and instinctive apprehension of social injustice attracted radical organizations like the UWC and the Young Socialist League. While neither organization stated its position on the antisocial temper in popular protest, it is arguable that socialists in both the UWC and the YSL probably were repelled by the youths' nihilism but saw in these young people possibilities for political mobilization and education. The unlikely interest of leftist organizations in the most destitute sections of the society was almost certainly due to two other factors. One was the unavailability of the working class for radical political mobilization, since it had come under the leadership of the dominant party-unions. Furthermore, despite the growth of the urban working class in the postwar period, its social weight was being diminished by the growth of the unemployed. The sheer numbers of the latter and their capacity for antisystemic opposition certainly recommended them to radical activists.

The other determinant which assigned importance to the ghetto youths was the politically disastrous absence of a well-developed section of the Jamaican middle class willing to articulate alternative perspectives on the problems of culture and freedom in the new society. Given this lack, opinion formation on such matters was left largely to others in the middle class — state officials, politicians, and conservative writers at the *Daily Gleaner* — who worked within the existing consensus. As circumstances therefore would have it, a break with these opinions came from the urban poor and from a minority of intellectuals. Absent a "ruptural" middle-class critique of the status quo, that assignment fell by default to militants among the urban poor, with all the dangers attendant thereupon.

UWC Activism among Unemployed Workers

For the activist in the UWC, insurgency and bold display of cultural opposition among sections of the urban poor marked the latter as a strategic, though not necessarily decisive, social force. The council recognized that of all the subordinate classes and groups in the society, none appeared as willing as the urban unemployed to take an openly oppositional role against the authoritarian state. Mindful of this militance, the UWC attached itself to this group, in order to get them jobs and raise their level of political awareness. Despite this interest in the urban unemployed, the council had no illusion about which class was fundamental to the transformation of the society. Consistent with its allegiance to a Marxist-Leninist politics, the UWC was even more committed to the idea of the decisive political role of the working class. In addition, the council was not unmindful of the contradictory political tendencies of the unemployed. While appreciating their defiant character, UWC activists were equally aware of the susceptibility of unemployed labor to various inducements from employers and the trade unions. This vulnerability placed the unemployed in opposition to the workers' movement. Workers' strikes often were broken by the use of scabs recruited from the ranks of the unemployed.[16] Similarly, in the struggle for bargaining rights, the dominant trade unions also drew on the unemployed force for the political henchmen who fought to maintain the established unions' share of the workforce and blocked the organizing efforts of leftists unions.[17] The problem for the council, therefore, was how to reconcile a commitment to the working class — now demobilized and reduced to militant economism — with the recognition that the urban poor had assumed the role of a militant but ideologically unstable vanguard.

The council's resolution of this anomaly disclosed a historical torsion in the ideology of the Jamaican Left, and revealed an incongruity long implicit in its political practice. This was the coexistence of a resolute commitment to militant laborism, with an unyielding exclusion of popular anti–status quo ideologies from socialist discourse.[18] The consequences of this demarcation were significant: recurrent ambiguity in the Left's response to racial and religious representations in popular protests, and continuing tactical and conceptual blind spots. These blind spots included a tendency to reduce all social struggles to the class struggle; a bias in treating ideological struggle as a means to defend "class" but not "race," and a practice which implied that labor activism was sufficient to challenge the *moral* sway of the dominant classes.

In adapting its socialist politics to the anti–status quo dramaturgy of the rebellious youths and the black nationalism of the Rastafarians, the council glossed over the specificity of these forms of protests and simply attempted to win these groups to an alliance with workers. While this position accorded with the principle of unity of labor and captured the vulnerability of workers to victimization and unemployment, it elided the problem of an important difference between the two populations. For example, despite the uncertainties for many employed workers, their participation in a stable wage nexus set them apart from jobless workers excluded from it. In the early sixties, to be an employed unionized manual worker meant having ties to a structure of power with which an accommodation had to be reached. Workers therefore adapted themselves to the terms of the labor-capitalist and the trade union–worker relations. Although unionized workers could lash out against abuses of either unions or employers, their militancy was domesticated within the conflict-management mechanism, which reserved a place for the continued economic participation of these workers. No rejection of society was therefore involved in these workers' conflicts with either unions or employers. The same could not be said of militant jobless workers. Their orientation was rejectionist, antisystemic, and, in the case of the Rastafarians, even secessionist. In short, while there were obvious exceptions, the core of the UWC's jobless constituency, having few ties with the rest of society, wanted little to do with it; and the structure of the economy saw to it that this group remained excluded.

As this exclusionary orientation toward the unemployed persisted, their employed, unionized counterparts were being domesticated and were adapting to their involvement in the economy. Under these circumstances, the UWC docrine of the unity of labor could have only rhetorical significance, because of the substantive differences in the politics and circumstances of the two populations. As for the racial and religious themes in the ideology of the unemployed, the UWC failed to accord them any significance within its politics, except to subsume them under "class struggle." In this respect, Monroe's position on the Rastafarians' protest is instructive for the chasm it revealed between socialist politics and nativist movements and ideologies. In a retrospective assessment, Monroe noted:

> The racial question had really developed around repatriation . . . We did not share the views of the Rastafarians and we did not want to go in opposition [to them] on the question of religion. We recognized that the movement had two basic sections; a highly religious section and a revolutionary section. But on the question of God, we did not think it important to struggle, to contend with the Rastafarian's religion at the time. . . . We only tried to bring them forward to a position of political struggle to defend important economic and political gains. Our position was liberation in Jamaica, and we believed we could make a contribution to the international black liberation struggle in that way.[19]

Expressed here in pristine form is the dilemma identified above: how to respond to a social force which exhibited a renowned militancy yet insisted on couching this protest in religious language. The UWC's solution was to avoid opposition to the Rastafarians and their religious thinking, while limiting the absorption of their ideology into the council's politics. At the same time, the Rastafarians' lack of employment and their capacity for opposition was used to bring them into the workers' movement. Since the council basically viewed all sections of the urban poor as "unemployed workers," it was a short step to an instrumentalist and reductionist approach to the racial struggles of these strata. That is, the UWC's practice became instrumentalist by seeing the Rastafarian protest as a means to advance labor's struggle, without attending to the political significance of the Rastafarians' emphasis on nationality.

The UWC's politics were reductionist because the council collapsed the specificity of the cultural opposition of the unemployed into the economic conflicts of the working class. Fidelity to a militant laborism prevented the UWC from appreciating the unique character of the urban poor's opposition and the destabilizing impact of black consciousness on political power. Operating with these limiting conceptions, the council worked to build an alliance between workers and the unemployed.

The opportunity for direct action came in March 1962, with the dredging for a refinery along the West Kingston waterfront by the Esso Oil Company, a subsidiary of the U.S.-based Standard Oil Company. The construction of this refinery, part of a development project to build a modern port facility on the Kingston waterfront, brought a large-scale capital construction project into the heart of one of the worst slums in the country. This siting of the refinery in the ghetto inevitably attracted scores of jobseekers who disrupted the dredging operations.[20] Under the UWC's leadership, community residents demanded preference in employment, especially since the project would displace many who depended for a livelihood on fishing in the area. However, the presence of riot police and the apparent willingness of the PNP to discuss the employment of community residents led to a temporary solution.[21] Having won this concession, the UWC sought to have the principle of employment priority for community residents accepted by the JLP, which had come to power in the interim. This demand was rejected, and, as construction continued into 1963, the UWC found itself embroiled in a bargaining-rights dispute between the two party-affiliated unions. Apparently the contractor for the project earlier had concluded an agreement with the PNP-affiliated NWU, which would have given it sole bargaining rights at the site.[22] But with the JLP's return to political power in 1962, this agreement was challenged as the BITU pressed its own claims for representation. The result was restiveness at the site, culminating in a strike by the NWU on Thursday, 3 January.[23] At the same time, the council rallied its supporters for a major demonstration the following Monday, aimed at getting the JLP to accept a demand that the unemployed from the community be recruited on a nonpartisan basis. At this point, a curious alliance emerged between the UWC and the NWU, led by Michael Manley, son of former prime minister Norman Manley. Stymied by the BITU's claim for representation, Michael Manley threw his support to the council's upcoming demonstration, which was timed to coincide with the NWU's strike. The struggle between the two dominant political unions now took a new turn, as the UWC, which opposed them both, found an ally in the NWU.[24]

In response to this upcoming joint demonstration against the BITU, Bustamante, now prime minister, issued the following statement:

> It has been brought to my attention that certain elements, including what is called[the] "Unemployed Workers' Council" are arranging a demonstration to take place at the Oil Refinery site on Monday, 7th, instant, and a mischievous pamphlet has been circulated to this effect, a copy of which is in the Government's possession. In order that there be no misunderstanding, I wish to state that it is Government's policy that workers be recruited through the Government Employment Bureau for engagement on this and other projects and the Government is satisfied that this system is fair and reasonable. I wish to also make it absolutely clear that law and order will be maintained at all times.[25]

With this blunt threat of force, Bustamante reaffirmed the practice of partisan recruitment of labor for government projects through the State Employment Bureau. True to its word, on the day of the demonstration, the JLP sent some two hundred riot police to the construction site, and they tear-gassed several hundred demonstrators, routing NWU strikers and UWC protesters alike. However, instead of sundering the practice of political unionism by creating a closer alliance between the council and the NWU, the assault on the demonstrators led to a closing of ranks between the NWU and the BITU. In an about-face, Manley suddenly called off the strike and concluded a separate agreement with the BITU to submit the issue to arbitration pending a representation poll.[26] In short, the NWU broke its pact with the council and abandoned the hundreds of demonstrators it had mobilized. Thus, the sanctity of job recruitment and of unionization of the work force on the basis of political loyalty was not to be jeopardized by desperate nonpartisan jobseekers.[27]

Despite this NWU betrayal, the council continued its agitation among the West Kingston poor. In March 1963, it held a major demonstration at the public square adjoining the Coronation Market, a main hub for the Kingston poor. There the council demanded public-works programs for jobless workers and called for an end to the exploitation of the country's wealth by "foreign monopolies."[28] Five months later, the UWC continued its lonely struggle to defend the hapless squatters of West Kingston against a state-ordered eviction. In this instance, the regime had served the squatters of Kingston Pen with a notice to quit the site in two months, because the land was needed for the construction of a government housing project.[29] Despite the presence of several hundred squatters at the site, the JLP apparently had made no arrangements for them to be resettled.[30] Instead, the shanty dwellers were asked to fill out a "letter of intent" indicating their desire to be considered for accommodation in the new project. At this point, the UWC called on the squatters to ignore the notice and to resist the impending demolition of their shacks.[31] As the deadline expired, bulldozers, protected by riot police, moved onto the site to begin razing the shanties. They were met, however, by a fusillade of rocks, as chanting demonstrators and desperate mothers with babies in hand blocked the bulldozers' path. Undeterred by this show of defiance, the police fired tear gas into the motley crowd, dispersing it.[32] This display of power elicited from official quarters murmurs of protest at the callousness of the regime for not giving the demonstrators more time to find accommodations.[33] Obviously under pressure to make a humane gesture, Bustamante relented and offered a week's extension. Thus a temporary setback was dealt to the JLP's use of slum clearance as a device for breaking up this shanty town and eventually repopulating the area with political wards of the party who would live in modern facilities.

When this new deadline expired and the settlers still remained on site, the JLP adopted a new strategy. It took to depicting the squatters as wage earners who were slum dwellers by choice. As the minister of housing argued:

> Some of the people living in Kingston Pen are known to be steadily employed and others obtain temporary employment from time to time, and are in no worse position than many others of our citizens, but they have chosen to live in this slum for various reasons which are best known to them. In these circumstances, Government can see no justification for providing alternative accommodation which would be costly and would divert funds which are desperately needed to provide additional housing.[24]

In the wake of this appalling rationalization of the mid-October evictions, the regime backed away from its plan for immediate eviction of the squatters. Instead, it agreed to a three-stage eviction plan with a further deadline of 15 January 1964.[35] With this concession, the UWC's activism on behalf of the unemployed achieved another small advance. In discussing this limited victory, the council proclaimed that "the first battle has undoubtedly been won by the settlers. Government has . . . been forced into recognizing the settlers, and its aim of victimization has been struck the first blow."[36] The council also planned to demand, among other things, that the squatters be given priority in employment

when construction for the new housing development began. It remains
unclear whether these demands were met, since the council's activities
over the next nine months are obscure. It seems likely, though, that the
autocratic character of the JLP regime did not make the outlook hope-
ful. In fact, the regime imposed a month-long ban on the council's activities in the West Kingston area, thus blunting its effectiveness.[37] When
the council "resurfaced" in August 1964, it was no longer defending urban slum dwellers. Rather, it had been drawn ineluctably into the now-
rekindled PNP inner-party struggle. That development brought the UWC
promptly to the side of the Young Socialist League, where the council
played an insurgent role as ally in a concerted effort to win the PNP
back to socialism.[38] Before turning to that engagement, however, let
us examine the regime's widening crisis of legitimation in relation to
certain ideological absences in the UWC's activism.

Exceptionalism and the Politics of Ethnic Chauvinism

It will be recalled that the explicitly racial focus of popular urban protest triggered a defensive state ideological response that I have termed
Jamaican Exceptionalism. This ideology sought to purge the antagonistic
elements from the ideology of the urban unemployed by hailing the
subordinate classes as *exemplary racial neuters* in a world torn by ethnic
disorder and strife. The appeal to the overwhelming black population
was that they were a special people in the world, who lived harmoniously
with other domestic ethnic groups. Consequently, talk of racial discrimination in the postcolonial period was regarded by those in power
as nonsense sowed by provocateurs. This tactic of saluting the population on the basis of superior performance on a scale of comparative
ethnic stability made Exceptionalism far more than a convenient myth.
For many, Exceptionalism was compelling precisely because it alluded to
incontrovertible global comparisons in terms of national demographics.
After all, neither was Jamaican society composed of myriad ethnic or
religious groups, as other Third World societies were, nor was it wracked
by disorders occasioned by such cleavages. The conflicts in the island
certainly paled by comparison with the communalism of, say, the Indian subcontinent. In these terms, Jamaica indeed was different and,
it should also be said, fortunate. In this sense, exceptionalism-as-ideology
spoke truth to history.

Yet, as we have maintained, this legitimating ideology was not innocent. Like all ideologies based on appeal to "facts" in the real world,
Exceptionalism highlighted certain interpretations and left others in the
shadow. In an attempt to rally the subordinate sectors to their inter-

pretation of the national past, exponents of the official view emphasized to blacks their legacy of conformism and their identity as racial neuters without specific racial or class membership. But neither the one-sided idea of conformism nor the myth of an unambiguous cooperation between the races accorded with Jamaican social history. That history, of course, had been punctuated by militancy and racial conflict, as well as by episodes of conformism and quiescence.[39] Those who employ legitimating ideologies, however, are not in the business of "letting the facts speak for themselves." Their bias explains their summoning blacks to find an identity in a mythical history expressed in the national motto, "Out of Many, One People."

Notwithstanding the ostensibly benign flavor of historical comparisons on communal tensions, Jamaica's official ideology remained perverse. Certainly it blurred the experience of racial discrimination and ferreted out residues from the slave past associated with blacks' submissiveness and obeisance toward their social betters. Jamaican Exceptionalism, therefore, seemed to be the antithesis of a "healthy" black nationalism — one which remembered the past and, out of its complexity, recovered for the black majority their best and most socially potent selves. Faced with a challenge to their moral and political power from the "great unwashed" in the urban slums, however, the political leaders and others met the challenge of black consciousness with a vigorous intolerance, albeit in the guise of promoting racial coexistence.

This underlying attitude was quite apparent in 1963, as critics sought to discredit the idea of black nationalism. The *Daily Gleaner* and the Chinese middle class led the attack on black consciousness. Alluding to the national debate on who among the several anticolonial fighters should be considered national heroes, the *Gleaner* in early March doubted there were any besides Bustamante and Norman Manley.[40] In fact, the paper's political reporter dismissed all talk of creating national heroes. For him, Jamaica had no need of heroes, and he rejected such talk as "silly," since "our circumstances have never produced one."[41] However, it was the convergence of the urban poor's black nationalism with a quickened sense of racial discrimination among lower-middle-class blacks which prompted an antiblack reaction.

The occasion for this backlash came when a section of the black lower-middle class — those who had acquired the education, comportment, and know-how to aspire to positions as clerks, secretaries, bank tellers, salespersons, and front-office staffers — became embroiled in a now-familiar conflict: opposition to an alleged Chinese monopoly of coveted positions. In this case, opposition was directed not at Chinese retailers but against an alleged overrepresentation of Chinese nationals in positions requiring the handling of tasks and personnel in banking, tourism, and sales. Reminiscent of the small-capitalist xenophobia with regard to Chinese retailers in the twenties and thirties, this aggrieved sector of the middle class excoriated the Chinese for blocking its members' path to prestigious nonmanual jobs. Once more the Chinese became the target of discontent felt by dark-skinned Jamaicans on the lower rungs of the class structure. Much like their predecessors in the twenties and thirties, this group cried out in the early sixties against the structure of inequality and the continuing color discrimination. Inevitably, they again made the Chinese the target of this anger. Not surprisingly, the Chinese and their defenders responded in kind. After all, the growth of black consciousness at the bottom and intermediate levels of the class structure placed Chinese nationals in the line of xenophobic fire.

Regrettably, some Chinese retaliated by engaging in a racialist elaboration of the official ideology. A case in point was the following letter to the editor by a Chinese writer who, after explaining the success of the Chinese in business by a theory of comparative *ethnic* advantage,[42] noted ominously:

> All I can now say is, be careful all of you who are teaching race-hatred, lest the present situation in Alabama does not develop here in years to come but with the Chinese and white Jamaicans being victimized. . . . This whole concept now held by many Afro-Jamaicans that Jamaica is a Black Man's Country and Black Man Must Rule no matter what, even if the country is probably ruined in the process, is all wrong and makes a complete mockery of our motto.[43]

Similarly, William Strong, a leading columnist for the *Gleaner*, devoted two editorials to this issue in October. They are worth quoting in full. Writing on 8 October, he depicted the ethnic minorities as victims of a "misguided nationalism."

> The aggressiveness of our Negro population—even some of the educated ones—in demonstrating their Jamaicanism is making the other racial groups in the island uncomfortable. It is driving sensitive groups back into the social shells out of which they ventured in pre-Independence years in response to a desire, an urge, a conviction to integrate. This aggressiveness, this misguided nationalism, is seriously affecting relationships with other racial groups whose adoption of Jamaica as home is comparatively recent—but many of whom are better citizens than the Negroes who jostle, heckle and insult them wherever they go.[44]

Strong was, of course, referring to the lack of deference and militant postures adopted by the Rastafarians, rebellious youths, and allied strata. To be sure, the menacing actions Strong described did occur. Indeed, black aspirants to positions in the colonial economy and society historically had resorted to the most rabid of chauvinistic attacks on Chinese

Jamaicans. Every crude stereotype, ranging from their dishonesty as entrepreneurs to their accented use of English, was hurled at this group, which lamentably was caught in a vise between big capital and the mass of black Jamaicans jockying for position in the changing economy and society.[45] So indeed there was operating here a mutual chauvinism, one with deep historical roots now reflected in this exchange of abuse.

Still, the responses of the urban poor, while unflattering and clearly socially unacceptable, must be understood in relation to the humiliation, cultural injury, and economic hardship they suffered daily. Moreover, in the absence of a single figure of renown and social credibility who could speak out for the legitimacy of black nationalism without insulting other races, the burden of defending black consciousness fell to the urban poor, with the attendant danger that their spontaneous ideological reactions would collapse into unabashed chauvinism.

It was to this danger that Strong directed his second editorial, observing:

> Jamaicanism is not a colour . . . or a fiercely aggressive attitude towards people who are not black. Jamaicanism is a state of mind, based on a sense of civic responsibility, on good manners, on respect for all others who inhabit our island . . . Jamaicanism is not "black man time." Jamaicanism is raceless . . . Jamaicanism is realization and acceptance of the fact that Jamaica is neither a black nor a white nor a pink country, but a country in which all men may dwell together in unity and good fellowship.[46]

Paradoxically, in the face of this sharp ideological contest, the UWC remained strangely silent, preferring instead to criticize the "dictatorial powers" of the independence constitution and the suppression of the "democratic organizations of the working class."[47]

Despite being rooted in the very forces which were engaged in this "debate," the council managed to remain aloof from the conflict between black nationalism and Jamaican Exceptionalism. Thus, at a time when the politically dominant forces were struggling to consolidate their hegemony by delimiting the influence of black nationalism, the council held to its position of pristine laborism. In so doing, it failed to link the economic class struggle with other nonclass conflicts, such as racial tensions. This failing had the effect of limiting the council to a politics which implied that the militant defense of economic rights was a sufficient basis on which to organize political opposition. Agents of the Jamaican state, however, were deeply concerned about the reproduction of their moral and cultural sway, now threatened by the urban upsurge. Therefore, they waged an unremitting struggle against the spread of race-consciousness among the workers and peasants.

Gripped by the unfortunate economism of its outlook, the UWC in effect abandoned the terrain of identity and culture to the urban poor and the dominant social classes. Militant laborism thus became a fetter preventing the UWC from waging an effective ideological struggle against the dominant social classes, because the UWC failed to advance positions encapsulating both economic and cultural issues. Consequently, despite its abiding attention to the important issues of unemployment (which highlighted the structural crisis and called into question the strategy of economic development) and political unionism (which identified a basic problem of the political structure), the UWC's exaggerated fidelity to these issues led it to neglect the surrounding cultural conflicts, further narrowing the scope of its already limited appeal.

CHAPTER 5

The Politics of the
Young Socialist League

In the preceding chapter, we have seen how the social struggles of the urban poor and unemployed youths precipitated an ideological crisis for the state, which it attempted to surmount with the ideology of Exceptionalism. Even as insurgency among the unemployed created sharp uneasiness among the upper class, it also attracted the attention of a small contingent of former PNP leftists. Through the UWC, these militants sought to mobilize the urban poor around bread-and-butter issues and tried to link their needs to those of the working class. By late 1963, the struggles of the urban unemployed commanded the attention of those who wished to challenge the system and those who wanted to keep it intact. Given the central role that the urban poor had come to play in the calculations of the state and its opponents, it is not surprising that the PNP also was subject to the effects of this autonomous insurgent mass movement.

Having long abandoned its socialism, the PNP was in the throes of trying to redefine itself in the wake of its defeat in the 1962 elections. Faced with the prospect of being out of office for several years, and confronting a marked decline in its popular appeal, the party sought a way out of its dilemma. At its conference after the elections, the PNP created a Policy Advisory Committee (PAC) to assist it in developing options as the problems of unemployment, social inequality, and cultural malaise deepened. Assisting in this reassessment was a small, politically committed group of junior party members.[1] Disillusioned by the party's repudiation of socialism and troubled by its lack of direction in the face of the social malaise and the illiberal policies of the JLP, this group formed a Provisional Committee to invigorate the seemingly moribund PNP. This initiative led in September 1962 to the creation of a group within the PNP called the Young Socialist League (YSL). In its draft constitution, the league committed itself to advancing the cause of democratic socialism and to encouraging greater participation of youth in the country's affairs. Consequently, within six months of the creation of the UWC in March 1962, another contingent of leftists, committed to a socialist Jamaica, had emerged on the political scene.

As with the UWC before it, much of the stimulus for the creation of the league stemmed from the restiveness among urban youths. The league therefore tried to harness this energy by directing its organizing efforts to the young people. In justifying this course, the YSL maintained that "only the youth have the audacity to challenge the present economic and social structure, the vitality to effect the necessary change, and the vision of a new social order."[2] The timing of this bold initiative immediately won the support of the PNP leadership. Both Norman Manley, the party leader, and Aaron Matalon, the industrialist, endorsed the new organization by addressing the YSL's inaugural meeting.[3] Indeed, Matalon identified himself with the league's goals by calling for drastic reforms in the structure of agriculture. Thinking perhaps that this fulsome endorsement was a signal that the PNP was prepared to consider allowing the Young Socialists membership on its policy-making body, the YSL requested that the league be allowed to become an affiliate of the party. In its reply, the PNP asserted that YSL representation on its decision-making bodies was out of the question. Affiliation might be possible, however, if the YSL promised to adhere to party policy. Responding to this rebuff, the league noted in its first annual report that it could not accept these terms and reported that "our efforts in this direction have therefore been abandoned."[4]

Despite this setback, the Young Socialists remained in the party while organizing the league outside the PNP. In 1962-63, the YSL sponsored a series of public forums on a variety of topics. These included "The European Common Market and Its Possible Effects on Jamaica" and "The Road to Socialism in Independent Jamaica." At this early stage, however, the league remained organizationally weak and was plagued with a lack of discipline within its ranks.[5] Despite these problems, the league adopted an internationalist outlook by establishing contacts and working relations with socialist youth organizations in the United States and Britain. For example, the league cooperated with the Young Socialists of Britain and collaborated with the Young People's Socialist League of New York on a statement to the United Nations on disarmament. As the YSL set about developing the organizational means to mobilize Jamaican youths, the PNP also was taking steps to strengthen its ties with workers, the unemployed, and the peasantry. In 1963, the PNP party conference established an advisory committee on employment and land reform. Its mandate was to develop recommendations on these issues for the 1964 party conference.

With the PNP apparently positioning itself for an important policy statement, several members of the league who were not party members moved quickly to enter its ranks. As one of them noted several years later:

> We were of course aware of the party's checkered history in regard to social-
> ism, but it was generally felt that, as socialists in the YSL, we could ill afford
> to ignore this apparent attempt by the PNP to correct the errors of its past.
> It was obvious to us then, as it is now, that the party would need a new
> image and an influx of young and new blood if it hoped to convince the
> country of its sincerity in reverting to the socialist position which it had
> abandoned after the expulsion of its leftwing in 1952[6]

The presupposition of some of the Young Socialists was that, if the impending policy reforms were to be really meaningful, they would have to enter the party to struggle for the adoption of a radical program. In this respect, they were exhibiting a sensitivity not only to the earlier capitulation of the party to foreign capital, but also to the continued presence of prominent capitalists in it and to the dominance of the party's right wing in policy matters. Despite this apparently distrustful and adversarial posture toward the party, league members nonetheless shared a basic ideological affinity with the PNP. At this early stage, this affinity was reflected in their adoption of the PNP's 1940s conception of socialism. At that time, socialism for the PNP, meant not the antithesis of capitalism but its domestication: nationalization of key industries, assistance to small farmers, establishment of rural cooperatives, and economic security for the working class.

Twenty-two years later, this ideology of democratic socialism was reproduced in the league. In 1962, for example, the YSL identified as one of its main goals making sure that "the sources of wealth and means of production [were] brought under the direct control of government."[7] Similarly, in a pamphlet apparently designed as a study aid, the league, after posing socialism as the alternative to capitalism, proceeded to identify the former with agricultural assistance to small farmers, work for the unemployed, and public ownership of "major industries."[8] Indeed, the extent of this ideological association was so deep that the very motto of the young radicals — "fixity of purpose and continuity of effort" — was lifted directly from the PNP's own motto. This shaping of early league positions by PNP reformist ideology strengthened the YSL's optimism concerning the possibility of achieving socialism in Jamaica despite authoritarian trends. As the league noted, as long as there was no further erosion of civil liberties, then the YSL had "every reason to use methods of peaceful persuasion" to achieve socialism in Jamaica. This was so, the league held, because some countries in Africa were already "setting out along this road." Without elaborating, the league surmised that both "the force of reason and the circumstances of our people favor a socialist victory."[9]

If the magnet of the PNP's democratic socialism pulled it toward reformism and idealism, then the league's identification with the party's radical past drew it to Marxism. It will be remembered that the league was one progeny of the abortive socialist movement within the PNP. The YSL leadership, whether inside or outside the PNP, formed a part of that mass of Jamaicans who remained ideologically close to the PNP in spite of the party's repudiation of socialisn in 1952. In addition, Bustamante's personalism, crude anticommunism, and procapitalist outlook contributed to keeping YSL members politically tied to the PNP, even as they objected to the latter's postwar economic policies. The political education carried out by the old Marxist Left—whether directly or at a distance—left its imprint on the Young Socialists, forcing them toward the PNP, if only to make it fulfill its radical heritage.

These varied ideological moorings meant that the YSL was shaped not only by reformism but also by a tradition of political radicalism and anti-imperialism. The duality of this ideological formation produced considerable tension and numerous contradictions throughout the league's existence. Moreover, prior to March 1964, when formal links were established with radical academics at the University of the West Indies, few in the league had a thorough grounding in socialist literature or a close knowledge of the history of the world communist movement.[10] The discontinuous path of the Marxist movement in the country, the official hostility toward communism, and the JLP's violations of civil liberties all contributed to this uneven development. By 1963 this experience had produced a diffuse anticapitalist radicalism which was, in effect, a struggle to move beyond the PNP positions of the 1940s. Indeed, even by 1964, when the *Monthly Review* school of Marxism[11] had become ascendant within the league, this ideological unevenness remained, as the YSL continued to combine the liberal ethos of democratic socialism's critique of capitalism with trenchant *Monthly Review* positions on imperialism.

Organization and Educational Work

By late 1963, the YSL had taken the first tentative steps in its expansion. By September of that year, it had already established some international ties and had forged a few rural links. However, organizational coherence was still lacking, as the league groped for a strategy of urban organization. For much of 1963, it had attempted a "blanket" approach to the Corporate Area, but this was abandoned at year's end in favor of a more manageable course. By January 1964, after a reshuffling of responsibilities, the league opted for the more practical "area council" strategy of organization. The Corporate Area—the name for the constituencies of Kingston and Saint Andrew — was divided into ten areas: three in Kingston and seven in Saint Andrew, with the University of the West Indies (UWI) and the lower-middle-class Harbour View housing project forming separate areas. By March 1964, area councils had been established in East and West Kingston, West-Central Saint Andrew, and the UWI.[12] By May, a YSL outpost had been established in the United Kingdom among students studying there.

The UWI Area Council played an important role in this phase of the league's development. Formally created in March 1964, this branch provided theoretical guidance, did research, and prepared agitational literature. Major policy statements were drafted by members of the UWI Council, who also served on various committees associated with political education or policy formulation. Some students and faculty at the university helped with the work of the league. Trevor Munroe, a student of political science and subsequently a Rhodes Scholar, was a member of this group. Theoretically gifted and politically active, Munroe was beginning a long career uniting scholarship and activism. During his apprenticeship in the YSL, he not only helped prepare its agitational literature,[13] but also later, in August 1964, attempted to moderate a factional struggle which erupted at the league's Second Congress. Faculty members also assisted in the work of the league. Among them were PNP advisor and economist Leroy Taylor and Bertell Ollman, an American expatriate and student of Marx who was teaching at the university.[14] Ollman brought to the league a grounding in Marxist literature and a knowledge of socialist history which shaped the YSL's major policy statements and internal educational work. Although the agricultural economist George Beckford was not a member of the UWI Council, he too was called on to help draft a policy on agrarian reform "because of his expertise in this area."[15]

Although the emergence of the UWI Area Council signaled an important development in the growth of the league, the YSL nonetheless remained a political organization without broad mass support and without large numbers of political cadres. Despite a tenfold increase in members, from about one hundred in 1962 to about a thousand in 1963, this growth did not signal a corresponding expansion of the YSL's political influence. Indeed, in its 1964 annual report, the executive group observed that the league was having little effect nationally and lamented that in 1963 it still remained "a largely unknown organization."[16]

Acutely aware of this shortcoming, the leadership in the first months of 1964 became increasingly preoccupied with issues of cadre formation, agitational techniques, and leadership development among youths. In early May, these issues were debated by the YSL's executive body, which resolved to locate individuals with potential leadership abilities and recruit them.[17] The league, however, was very much aware of the nihilism among the young urban unemployed population and its isolation from organized political leadership. As a result, the league repeatedly stressed the theme of "self-discipline" and the need for a "sense of responsibility" as qualities necessary for YSL membership. In approaching the task of training league members in political strategy and tactics, an internal document noted that the "aims of instruction [are] to turn out people who can explain and defend Y.S.L. policy, expose political trickery, popularize socialist ideas in their own sphere, [and] become known as activists and militants in any organization which they join."[18]

With such considerations in mind, the leadership called for increased production of literature to train these cadres. Attention was directed to issues in Jamaican, socialist, and "imperialist" history. Pamphlets were suggested with the following titles: "Youth, How to Win a Glorious Future"; "Jamaica in Ten Years — How It Could Be," and "Socialism and Freedom." Finally, speakers for the organization were told to note "regional facts" and, in the country, to mention the name of the "biggest landowner, [the] profits of the largest companies, [and] the greatest social evils [in the country]."[19] Despite an apparent grasp of these aspects of agitation, the leadership was unsuccessful in developing the organizational means to carry them out. Even as it was cogently outlining the league's various political tasks, the leadership faltered in practical organizing and in follow-through.

Paradoxically, part of the difficulty stemmed from lack of discipline at the top. From its very beginning, the league was plagued with unreliability in members of the executive body. Tasks which were assigned were not carried out, leading to delays and organizational readjustments. Absenteeism was a major problem. In one instance, eight members of the executive failed to show up for a meeting.[20] Despite the removal of a few members, the problem persisted. Its seriousness prompted a major internal report in 1964 detailing numerous "failures" of the executive group and their effects on the organization.[21] For the most part, these concerned the lack of "follow-up" in training of cadres, missed opportunities for establishing rural councils, and inability to identify rural youths who could carry out shortterm organizing. In a trenchant criticism of the executive Committee, the 1964 report observed:

> The unreliability of executive members is appalling and there is a distinct lack of interest by many members in the general activities of the League which manifests itself in a refusal to attend any meetings or other activities apart from executive meetings. Even those who occasionally attend meetings are reluctant to undertake any organizing tasks and when they do, discharge them inefficiently.[22]

The problems of discipline and inability to carry out practical tasks apparently spread to the strongest rural council in Savanna-la-Mar. There, a YSL cadre apparently had attempted, on his own, to create an alliance between the league and another organization. It required two trips from Kingston by the president and general secretary, and the expulsion of the cadre, to set things right.[23] But where the internal problems wracking the league prevented it from anchoring itself among youths, the leadership was unable to offset that by turning unfolding developments to its advantage. Surprisingly, the important workers' strike at the Jamaica Broadcasting Company in 1964 found the YSL executive body declaring that the strike "tended to detract [the] league from regular work."[24]

Notwithstanding these deficiencies, others labored to make the league an effective organization. The UWI Area Council, for example, produced many useful and pithy agitational materials. These included "Fact Sheets" on the society and the economy, a document on public ownership, and a long pamphlet on "Freedom and Socialism." The latter was remarkable for its clarity and absence of dogmatism in responding to local fears concerning communism. Indeed, by the start of the league's Second Congress in August 1964, not only had the organization extended its international links to Europe and the immediate English-speaking Caribbean, but it also was represented at the July 26 celebrations in Santiago, Cuba.[25]

The Struggle at the YSL's Second Congress

Despite its internal woes and difficulty in becoming truly a mass organization, members of the league rallied on the occasion of the Second Annual Congress. Held in Kingston at Vauxhall Senior School on 23 August 1964, the congress represented a notable instance of successful organizing, as was evident from the detailed program, with its major reports and resolutions, and from the attendance of delegates from far-flung rural areas.[26] The congress also attracted local observers and visiting representatives and won extensive coverage in the *Daily Gleaner.*

In a major statement drafted for the congress, the league took a nationalist and anti-imperialist position on the existing economic, political, and cultural situation in the country.[27] On political matters, it was sharply critical of the continuing ideological influence of the party-union cartels over the working class. The statement noted the absence of trade-union democracy and denounced the practice of "business unionism," in which "the workers regard their union representatives merely as paid negotiators in the capitalist jungle."[28] Asserting that business-unionism had hampered the growth of a socialist consciousness among the workers, the league maintained that its effect was to leave the "way . . . open for anti-socialist, reactionary 'advisors' from America to confuse honest union workers under the guise of 'educational programmes.'"[29] On the issue of the colonial legacy, the statement criticized the practice of having the English monarch as head of state and the British Privy Council as the final court of appeal. On other matters, the league criticized the cultural models then in vogue. It bemoaned the affectations in speech on the radio – probably a reference to the adoption of British accents by some Jamaican announcers. The YSL also remarked on the unsuitability of formal dress by parliamentarians and noted the official neglect of such black patriots as Marcus Garvey.

It was for the economic area, however, that the league reserved its sharpest critique. It criticized politicians who "merely stress the political side of the nation's freedom" to the neglect of foreign domination of the economy. The league identified significant areas of the national economy controlled by foreign capital: city transportation, sugar factories, communications, mining, refining, construction, and commerce. The league blamed the politicians for this extensive foreign ownership of the economy and for serving as "willing agents of these foreign interests." On the question of agriculture, the "unjust" system of land ownership and the rural unemployment it entailed were also assailed and documented with research.

In offering its own proposals to deal with the island's economic and cultural subordination, the league was remarkably prescient in its suggestions. Indeed, the YSL anticipated by several years many of the demands and programs of the radical Left in the late 1960s, as well as those taken up by the PNP in the 1970s. Among the major proposals the league advanced were the following: a nonaligned foreign policy, an end to foreign ownership of the domestic economy, equitable foreign trade and diversification of trading partners, worker participation in industry, agricultural and consumer cooperatives, and state control of exports and of the wholesale import trade. Besides endorsing the existing practice of state support for marketing, credits, and equipment to small farmers, the league made one other suggestion of some consequence. In advancing a proposal for public ownership, the league betrayed its underlying idealism at the very moment that it was taking up anti-imperialist positions. Thus, in its proposal for the creation of a socialist economy, the YSL argued for the establishment of "public corporations administered by a governing board composed of representatives of managers, technicians and workers but subject to general political direction from above and a strong element of democratic workers' control from below."[30] Apparently reverting to its identification of socialism with "public ownership," the league was now advancing a form of worker-management cooperation and ignoring much of the earlier analysis it had made of the antagonistic social relations in the country. The league offered no analysis of how this cooperation would take place, nor did it suggest the conditions under which such an arrangement would work in Jamaica. In short, the league retreated to a consensual view of class relations with its proposal – a violation of both its avowed commitment to a radical analysis of Jamaica and its recognition of the lack of industrial democracy. Thus, despite an emphasis on class conflict and antagonistic relations between workers and capitalists, the YSL lapsed into a posture which found it defending the PNP, a capitalist party, as an agent of socialism. This outlook led to a major conflict at the congress, as factions clashed over the propriety of having YSL leaders continue as members of the PNP.

This criticism of the league's association with the PNP went to the heart of the YSL's definition of itself. After all, a close and open collaboration between the PNP and the league had been forged at the time of the league's formation. Not only were the original founders of the league members of the PNP, but also the PNP leadership actually supported their political work, no doubt hoping that whatever gains the league made would redound to the benefit of the party. This official indulgence extended to opening the pages of the party's newspaper, *Public Opinion*, to occasional articles and letters by the Young Socialists.[31] More than that, the PNP executive board even protected the league from its detractors inside the party. For example, on one occasion early in 1964, the party's executive structure intervened to protect the Savanna-la-Mar Area Council from a hostile PNP member of Parliament who had threatened to destroy it.[32] Additional support came from the progressive element in the party, including Vernon Arnett and John Maxwell, both of whom were now leading supporters of reform in the country.[33]

But this tolerance of radicalism was not shared by the entire PNP hierarchy. The Right, for instance, remained watchful and suspicious of the league[34] but had to defer to Norman Manley, the party leader. Up to this point, Manley had adopted a centrist position and had taken a protective attitude toward the young radicals. By the middle of 1964, a symbiotic relationship, now some two years old, had been consolidated between the two organizations, with top YSL leaders belonging to both. It was this relationship which was boldly questioned at the congress by Robert Hill, a leading member of the league. In an open letter to the congress,[35] Hill forcefully raised the issue of the propriety of YSL leaders retaining their membership in the PNP. Hill reminded the league of the disastrous consequences of the expulsions of 1952 and pointed out how the current party leadership was temporizing in the face of the prevailing social and economic crisis.

In a scathing polemic against both political parties, Hill wrote, "They are not prepared to use our Political Freedom to put an end to economic exploitation, to wage an implacable struggle . . . against the local and foreign exploiters."[36] Warning the congress not to be misled by the apparent change of heart in the party, he vigorously maintained that the change was an opportunist maneuver and a "gigantic trap to enlist us as a base for their selfish electoral designs, the very base and cadres Manley and his cronies expelled in 1952, the base and workers they no longer have, the base they are planning to turn the Young Socialist League into. To this our reply and our only reply must be: Today the nemesis of your hypocrisy and repeated sell-outs have caught up with you. Now reap where you have sown!"[37]

In his letter, Hill anticipated objections apparently held by a section of the league and its sympathizers. The argument went that the league was not strong enough to break ties with the PNP and that such a tactic would be fruitless, given the authoritarian political environment. Remaining in the PNP, this faction claimed, would provide a "shelter" from the JLP's anticommunism. Hill rejected these arguments as evasive. Responding tartly to the claim that the PNP would protect YSL members against the JLP, Hill asked, "When since have Socialists become in need of shelter from traitors and sycophants to exploitation?"[38]

In refuting the objections, Hill argued that only political engagement could strengthen the league. It was only through political struggle against the "apologizers for imperialism" and by heightening existing contradictions that the YSL could become truly a mass movement, Hill claimed. With manifest impatience, he observed that a lot of energy was being devoted to the training and organization of cadres for the "eventual socialist takeover," but, he remarked, this was really a "do-nothing" policy.

It was on the question of "split loyalties" that Hill was most adamant. He asked how the league, having made such a radical critique of the leadership in the country, could countenance the retention of PNP membership by YSL executives. Hill observed that the masses were waiting for the league to back up its "fearless analysis" by breaking with the PNP — "the action necessary for that analysis to become a reality."[39] He therefore demanded the immediate resignation of YSL executives from the PNP. Their failure to resign, he argued, would be a fatal compromise in the struggle against imperialism: "What we simply cannot afford is to have Comrades who are directing the work of the League to be at one and the same time engaged in directing the work of any other organization. This can only compromise our leaders, confuse our members and would-be supporters, and place a fetter on the thrust of the League."[40] Although Hill made many other proposals, several of which were adopted,[41] it was his demand for the immediate resignation of YSL executives from the PNP which created a stir at the congress. With several officers and militants in the league also active in the PNP and the NWU, Hill's resolution triggered an emotional debate.

Just how much support for his position Hill was able to muster remains unclear. However, it is probable that Hill found an ally in the UWC, given the latter's opposition to collaboration with the PNP and its demonstrated hostility toward the party's endorsement of the league in 1962. Indeed, after the congress, the UWC, despite its alliance with the YSL, resolutely opposed the latter's continued association with the PNP and the NWU.[42] What is not in doubt is the YSL executives' and UWI Area Council's opposition to Hill's proposal. Here Trevor Munroe played a key role in opposing Hill. We have already commented on Munroe's role in assisting the league with research and preparation of agitational literature. Now the *Gleaner* reported his success in getting Hill's proposal killed. He argued that the resolution implied a mass resignation of YSL members from the NWU and the BITU. As the newspaper showed, "This would mean the resignation of Mr. [Hugh] Small from his post as legal advisor to the NWU."[43] In other words, Munroe and the YSL executives took the position that, if adopted, Hill's resolution would isolate the league from organized labor.

This debate suggests a distinct change in league tactics. Although it continued to make overtures to youths, the YSL now was focusing more directly on the working class. In fact, the policy statement delivered to the congress gave clear indications of this turn, with its direct reference to the workers and its claim that "the time is long past when any radical protest could begin among the most depressed sections of the population."[44] Indeed, Hill's polemic assumed as much, arguing as he did that the YSL had a "duty to the workers of Jamaica whose destiny to be the owners of what they produce is the only logic of the League's existence."[45] The Second Congress therefore found the YSL talking less about youths and more about supporting workers, but disagreeing about how this latter should be done. Apparently, after some two years of less than successfully enlisting youths in the cadres, the league had moved openly to concern itself with the working class. It was this agreement on support for workers among all sections of the league that evidently allowed Munroe to beat back Hill's proposal. By formulating the issues not so much in terms of membership in the PNP, but rather in terms of links to labor (and specifically YSL links to the NWU), the alliance against Hill was able to turn his argument concerning the defense of workers' interest against him.

The strategy endorsed by Hill's detractors nonetheless failed to address his major concerns. If the Young Socialists expected to remain in the party or the union, they would have to moderate their criticism of the PNP. If, as they maintained, membership in the PNP was the most effective means of gaining access to organized labor, then some circumspection was implied, lest that access be jeopardized. Not to be circumspect — to attack the PNP, for example, — would be to fly in the face of the league's claim that access to organized labor should not be jeopardized. In other words, rejecting Hill's position seemed to entail moderating criticism of the PNP in favor of forging league links to organized labor. Yet no such tactic was adopted by the YSL. Rather, its *ad hoc* approach to tactics soon put the YSL in the position of undermining its claim that membership in the PNP provided strategic access to labor. Within a month of the congress, the YSL began waging an implacable battle against the PNP's right-wingers on the issue of land reform. The character and resolution of this inner party struggle once more revealed the serious weaknesses in the theory and practice of organizations committed to socialism in this period.[46]

With debates over tactics marking the conclusion of the YSL congress, the focus of events shifted rapidly to the PNP. There, a long-awaited declaration of the party's ideological direction and its proposals on land reform had taken shape. By mid-September 1964, the Policy Advisory Committee, charged with having these proposals ready for the November party conference, had issued its interim report.[47] Reflecting the concerns of the Young Socialists and bearing the imprint of progressive elements in the party who shared the YSL's vision, the PAC put forward a number of recommendations. These included restrictions on land which could be held idle; limits on landholding by foreigners; a five-hundred acre limit on the total acreage which could be held "by any single person, whether individual or company"; and an increased role for the state in agriculture.

Evidently satisfied with the recommendations of the PAC and seeking to allay the right wing's anxieties about the Young Socialists' influence, Norman Manley, true to his centrist predisposition, used the occasion of the party's annual dinner to defend the young Turks. Noting that "there are always young people who wish to make a revolution," Manley added, "We welcome such young people. We need a revolution."[48] While the party leader was, of course, referring to the YSL's contribution to the party's ideological renovation, even this proved to be too much for their detractors inside the party. Speaking to the same gathering, Wills O. Isaacs, a major figure inside the party and a critic of the Left, acknowledged the importance of the Young Socialists to a revitalized PNP. At the same time, he obliquely aired the conservative faction's distrust of the league by questioning their commitment to the party: "We seek to know what sacrifices they are prepared to make for the party. Let them demonstrate that they are prepared to sacrifice personal gain and to go to the country carrying the party program to the people."[49]

Evident here is the sharp rift which had emerged between the Young Socialists and the party's right wing. Although the Young Socialists held no positions on the PAC, they evidently had been successful in influencing its recommendations, and this success presented a setback to the Right.[50] Shielded by Norman Manley and working through sympathetic personalities on the PAC, "entrism," or the tactic of boring from within, seemed to be working. The party would accept for debate at the November 1964 conference, proposals which would put some limit on the landowning class. In addition, the PAC was in the process of drafting a comprehensive statement on the party's ideology and its program for economic development. It was at this juncture that the Unemployed Workers' Council intervened.

Formally allied with the league after the YSL's Second Congress but opposed to the YSL's tactic of entrism, the UWC went on the ideological offensive. In the 23 October issue of its journal, *The Right to Work*, the UWC bitterly reviewed the PNP's capitulation to foreign capital after 1952. The UWC noted that the party now was trying "to regain its lost power and prestige" among the masses by turning once again to socialism, and called for the "defeat of this new PNP conspiracy."[51] While acknowledging that the PNP's land policy was the result of the Young Socialists' "pressure . . . on the party's leadership," the council denounced the league for aligning itself with "the pseudo-socialist wing of the PNP." Reflecting the position taken by Robert Hill at the YSL congress, the council told its supporters that "this New Left orientation inside the PNP . . . is not a genuine orientation of the Party towards the Left. But rather, the expression of a reformist group inside the Party, whose aim is to capture political power, and to serve Imperialism under new disguises."[52] Consistent with its unyielding opposition to any collaboration with the PNP, the council called for the development of an independent movement and the formation of a "genuine socialist-oriented anti-imperialist party." As Ben Monroe viewed it, the way to accomplish this was not to join the PNP—that only implied a futile attempt to control a bourgeois party dominated by able rightwing politicians. Rather, he argued, forces seeking genuine national independence needed to hasten the decomposition of the PNP and deepen the isolation out of which it was trying to emerge, while building alternative forms of organization.

Reflecting on the period, Monroe observed that although the YSL and the UWC lacked popular support and were themselves weak, it was nonetheless important to remain independent of the PNP: "We felt that an independent position could serve the struggle better, because the PNP was fresh in the minds of the people as betraying socialism and every day there was further evidence of the developing crisis of this 'development by exploitation' policy."[53]

Consistent with this tactic of further revealing to the masses the bankruptcy of the dominant organizations, the UWC in its journal, disclosed allegations of fraud against members of the NWU executive board. Until now such allegations had remained an internal union matter. Without directly naming its source, but alluding to "an enquiry into the union's finances by new forces drawn into the NWU executive," the council publicly alleged that fifty thousand pounds in union dues were unaccounted for, and commented on other malfeasance in the union.[54] This disclosure, made without consultation with the YSL and without concern for Hugh Small's position as a legal officer of the NWU, was to play a role in Small's expulsion from the union. It also contributed to strains in the YSL-UWC alliance. Before turning to that episode, however, it is necessary to situate it in the context of the PNP's formal announcement of its policy of democratic socialism, and the dramatic events surrounding the November party conference.

Democratic Socialism and the Abortive November 1964 PNP Conference

Complementing the earlier publication of its land-reform proposals, the PNP, in early November 1964, announced a policy of democratic socialism. The document, which bore the unmistakable stamp of the Young Socialists and their allies in the party, sharply criticized the PNP's postwar policies.[56] Even as it noted that PNP policies between 1955 and 1962 had been substantially adopted by the JLP, the PNP document now repudiated these programs and observed that "with every passing day, it is clear that what Jamaica needs is a new direction and a new road."[57]

Unabashedly presenting the new policy as an attempt to revitalize the PNP as a "revolutionary party," its proponents gave full vent to their radicalism. They denounced the existing inequalities between "the few" and "the many" as a "sham and a fraud."[58] They decried the lack of popular participation in public affairs, lamented private control of "the commanding heights of the economy," and provided a trenchant analysis of the role of postwar foreign capital in the economic underdevelopment of the island.

As a corrective, the document proposed adherence to the "philosophy of Democratic Socialism." Only this ideology, it claimed, "can create that dynamic inspiration and confidence that Jamaica needs."[59] While firmly rejecting the JLP's position of "equality of opportunity" under capitalism, the document observed that while socialism also was about equality, this equality "does not mean a military dictatorship or a 'dictatorship of the proletariat' in which some are more equal than others."[60] Distancing the party from communism with this statement, the document reiterated the proposals on land reform. To these it added an important proposal for the nationalization of the foreign-owned utility, the Jamaica Public Service Company, "as a start in a programme of transferring the ownership of vital sectors of the economy from private to public ownership."[61]

This appeared to be as far as the PNP was prepared to go with its radicalism. Indeed, between the publication of its land-reform proposals in September 1964 and its announcement of socialism in November, the party had already dealt the Young Socialists a rebuff. In fact, despite the Young Socialists' obvious influence on the party's latest proposals, relations between them and the PNP were worsening. As we have seen, the YSL's position in the party was defined by conflict and cooperation. Conservative party members often took YSL members to task for their positions, and the Young Socialists in turn retained their places in the party by avoiding direct attacks on it or making only oblique criticisms of it. Always strained, yet attended by the benevolence of the party leader, this tortured relationship continued through the middle of September 1964. After that, support quickly eroded when the YSL expressed serious reservations about the party's proposals on land reform.

An indication of growing disfavor came when the YSL submitted a rebuttal to the proposal for reforms. In it the writers warned the PNP against adopting a specious policy which would "merely . . . modify the extremes in wealth and poverty without touching the social and economic relationships within the society."[62] Noting that "this type of land reform [was] fraught with danger and is nowhere very distinguished for its success in achieving its own limited objectives," they called on the party to adopt a more meaningful policy. This was only possible, they maintained, by recognizing that "land reform is not so much an administrative process but in reality, a political process with specific social goals and that vested interest groups must be stripped of their power."[63]

While commending the party on its recognition of the need for agrarian reform, the socialists noted that the party had glossed over the plight of tens of thousands of small farmers with holdings of less than five acres. They observed that, although the party spoke of assistance to small farmers, it remained vague on specific proposals to help them. The Young Socialists therefore pressed the PNP to revise its policy statement to include "a 'vital minimum' acreage of land to which all farmers will be entitled" and to establish some form of state-run marketing service which would provide "guaranteed markets at guaranteed prices" as well as subsidies for particular crops.[64]

The YSL observed further that the party had remained silent on its policy towards the dominant social classes, who were likely to oppose these proposals. How, the YSL asked, did the party expect to deal with the landowning class, when that very class not only was represented in the PNP but also provided it with financial support? In perhaps their most direct criticism of the PNP thus far, the young party members observed:

> It is well known that several big landowners are party supporters and contribute to its funds. It is also known that one of the party's leaders is in close contact with perhaps the biggest land-owning family in the country. Will the P.N.P and its leaders be prepared to suffer the inevitable withdrawal of financial support from these quarters? The policy statement lacks the uncompromising ring of conviction which will convince the country that this is so.[65]

This penetrating interrogation evoked a written reply from their mentor, who now abandoned his posture of benign support. Skipping over their criticisms of the policy statement, Norman Manely charged them with making a "gratuitous attack" on the party leadership and with having "some ulterior motive [and] secret purpose of their own."[66] Recalling his earlier support for the league, despite "criticism of their activities," Manley made it clear that this latest action was the last straw and called on the party to take action against them. Closing ranks with the Right-opposition, Manley observed, "We must decide now what to do. We need total unity among ourselves if we are to carry a dynamic new programme throughout Jamaica. We cannot afford to have disruptions alongside of us—better to deal with it now once and for all."[67] With this, he suggested that the party executive board deal with the YSL document "as it thinks fit."

With this turn of events, the November conference took on added significance. Several weeks of publicity and debate had created high expectations among the party faithful that the PNP would be striking out on a new path. Certainly such expectations must have been strongest among those who saw themselves as heirs to the party's radical tradition. Not least among them were both the reformist elements of the urbanized petty bourgeoisie and those sections of the urban working class who were still faithful to the party's radical legacy. If we add those sections of the unemployed workers and the young people, among whom the UWC and the YSL had done political work, then it is probable that a significant number of those attending the conference were in favor of ratification of the land-reform program.

At this stage, any move by the party leadership to repudiate the principles outlined would be likely to antagonize many delegates and open the possibility that the conference might collapse in disarray. Such an outcome appeared all the more likely now, given the open break between the party leader and the Young Socialists. This falling out gave members of the Right the signal to attack the platform directly, something that they had been prevented from doing up to now, because of Manley's benevolent attitude toward the Young Socialists.

On the opening day of the conference, the Right-opposition, benefiting now from the party leader's disgust with the Young Socialists, maneuvered to distance the party from its platform. In his remarks to the conference, Manley set the tone by assailing the Left's criticism of the proposals on land reform. Clearly attempting to allay the fears of the bourgeoisie, he noted that, as the PNP understood it, public ownership meant neither a rejection of foreign capital nor a "Castro-type revolution." Taking issue with the Left's attack on the rural bourgeoisie, Manley repudiated the young Turks for attempting to do too much too quickly. He then drove the point home by linking the call for curbs on the agrarian bourgeoisie with "totalitarianism": "You cannot reorganize a system of landholding within a short time without creating chaos, except in a totalitarian regime. That is the only thing every totalitarian regime has created for itself. You cannot rush it."[68]

Following this retort from the party leader, Vivian Blake, a top party member and a determined foe of the proposals, now offered a preemptive resolution. Remarking on possible fears the reforms might provoke, Blake moved to have the proposals resubmitted to the PAC and called on the conference to declare its support only for the general principle of democratic socialism.[69] This obvious maneuver to adjourn the conference prematurely incensed the Left and its supporters in the hall. Vernon Arnett, member of the PAC and ally of the Young Socialists, rose to denounce Blake and his allies on the PNP executive board. Arnett's actions triggered pandemonium in the hall, as both he and Blake came under vocal abuse from their detractors on the floor. Now supporters of the socialist program, already made restive in the wake of Blake's resolution, responded by rushing to the podium to denounce Blake as a "capitalist," "land baron," and "race-horse owner." The ensuing uproar, which found Wills Isaacs drawing his pistol[70] on supporters of the Left, brought the conference to an abrupt end.

Writing in the wake of this maneuver to beat back the forces calling for a stiffer program on land reform, the *Gleaner's* political reporter was able to discern the motives of those in the party who opposed the reforms:

> It would mean the immediate loss of much support for the party, particularly among influential capitalists and among a large section of the middle class, and this must mean that the party would have a great struggle before it to get itself and its programme accepted by the Jamaican electorate at large. . . . It is this same reckoning which has frightened some sections of the party. They see before them a long dreary stretch in opposition, and they think it foolhardy for the party to risk its chances at the . . . forthcoming [1967] elections in order to state so fundamentally drastic a programme.[71]

Thus, rather than face the prospect of a debate on a policy which was criticized for not going far enough, key party members preempted discussion of it and chose political expediency instead. Having dealt the Young Socialists and their supporters a decisive setback at the conference, members of the Right-opposition moved quickly to consolidate their position. Shortly after the conference, they stepped up their campaign to have the Young Socialists removed from the party. Senior party members Wills O. Isaacs and Florizel Glasspole reportly demanded their ouster.[72] This campaign was to continue into the new year.

For its part, the NWU was less charitable to Hugh Small, who was president of the YSL and legal officer of the union. He was summarily fired after the conference for raising questions about the undemocratic nature of the NWU structure in his talks with workers.[73] In addition, Small's association with the UWC, coupled with the council's earlier disclosure of the misuse of union funds, made it appear that the YSL president had been the source of that information. The explosiveness of the UWC's allegation gave Thossy Kelly, president of the NWU, additional reason to fire Small.

At this juncture, an important aspect of the YSL–UWC alliance came to the fore. Although the two organizations maintained an alliance, it was a tenuous one punctuated by ideological and tactical disputes. It will be recalled that the UWC was implacably opposed to the Young Socialists' affiliation with the PNP. In this context, the UWC's public disclosure of conflicts in the NWU suggested that the council was prepared to jeopardize Small's position in the union. In fact, it is not unlikely that the disclosure could have been made with an eye to torpedoing the YSL's links to the NWU.[74] At any rate, the disclosure led Small's detractors in the union to conclude that he was abusing his position as its legal officer and provided his critics with a pretext for firing him.

The pamphleteering by the council thus strained the alliance and led the league to take steps to dissociate itself from its ally. In fact, the UWC's exaggerations, misstatement of fact, automatic opposition to league positions, and sudden reversals after joint positions had been worked out all took their toll on the partnership. Eventually this failure of discipline, while not precipitating a formal split, did force the league into publicly renouncing its still-continuing relationship with the council. So great was this apprehension of being associated with the activities of the council that many leading figures in the league refused to be publicly identified with the UWC, because they viewed it largely as a creature of the egotism and whims of its leader, Ben Monroe.[75]

Given Monroe's personality and operational style, that judgment certainly has merit. Yet it is of some significance that the UWC's insurgency had focused public attention on the inner workings of the NWU. Moreover, the council's tactics had disrupted the NWU's organizational routine. The UWC's disclosure apparently forced a three-month postponement of the NWU's annual conference and produced several indignant public disclaimers and attacks on the council. The major figures in the party and union — Michael Manley, Thossy Kelly, and Florizel Glasspole — tried to discredit the UWC, variously depicting its members as communist agents, parts of the "lunatic fringe," and anarchists seeking to undermine confidence in the NWU.[76] These retorts, however, could not gloss over apparent problems inside the union. In fact, the UWC's disclosure was given credence by a *Gleaner* columnist known to be hostile to the YSL. Writing on 8 December under the pseudonym "Thomas Wright," the journalist and landowner Morris Cargill observed that "Mr. Michael Manley, along with other high officers, have borrowed money from the Union, and [also like other officers] at present owes the union money — in Mr. Manley's case a matter of a few hundred pounds."[77] This misuse of workers' dues by leading NWU officials gives a clue to the abuses occurring in the union at this time. Undoubtedly, Small's opposition to these practices contributed to his expulsion from the union.

The Young Socialists Respond

In responding to these events, the Young Socialists appeared unsure of their tactics. Their initial reaction was sharply critical of the party's role in supporting Kelly's action against Small. In a letter[78] to the party, the Young Socialists drew the correct conclusion that both the active blocking of parts of the socialist policy in November and the firing of Small had been carried out with the approval of Norman Manley, the party leader. Noting that efforts were afoot in the PNP to proscribe the league, the letter also warned that the league would "take retaliatory measures . . . to put the matter of Hugh Small's dismissal into its proper perspective, [by] accusing those persons who have been most prominent in the attacks upon the League and its president."[79]

Implementing this threat, the league published a pamphlet entitled "The Desperate Men!"[80] It put the recent developments in the context of the inner party struggle which had occurred in 1952, and recalled the collaboration among Isaacs, Glasspole, and Kelly in engineering the ouster of the Left in that year. The pamphlet concluded that this same coterie now was engaged in a smiliar intrigue against the YSL. In this respect, the Young Socialists correctly grasped the traditionally obstructionist role played by this durable trio. In the pamphlet, however, the Young Socialists went beyond simply highlighting the recurrent role of the Right-opposition in thwarting the Left. They also disclosed the extent to which the Young Socialists felt themselves outmaneuvered and cut off from the rank and file during the current inner party struggle.

In an apparent attempt to end this isolation and win supporters to their position, the Young Socialists reversed their previously hostile position on the entire party leadership. They now advanced the view—untenable on its face—that Isaacs and Glasspole were renegades whose hatred of the Left was not shared by the other top leaders in both the union and the party.[81] This unlikely line was improved on further with the claim that both Manleys were in imminent danger of a coup from the Right. Thus, in the case of the NWU, the Young Socialists maintained that what was happening there involved a bid "to undermine Michael Manley, frame Small and clear the way for a complete takeover by Wills Isaacs and his friends."[82] Similarly, the Young Socialists altered their position on Norman Manley. While they had previously maintained that he had thrown his lot in with the Right-opposition, the Young Socialists now revised this view to depict him as a supporter of YSL policies and as an ally who stood in danger of suffering a coup. Thus, in an apparent last-ditch effort to foil the Right, the Young Socialists took to attributing erroneous views to Norman Manley and dubious motives to their opponents in the party. This maneuver to isolate the Right failed. Instead, the latter's opposition to the original policy hardened, with both Glasspole and Isaacs putting additional pressure on the leadership to change the platform.

The rightist militancy and threats paid off.[83] The party leaders drafted, and the National Executive Committee approved, a revised program to be sent to the party conference which was due to reconvene in February 1965. Most striking about the new document was its drastically changed tenor. Whereas the earlier document on democratic socialism, developed under the influence of the Left, had been sharp and trenchant in its analysis of social inequalities, the new statement was tepid and ideologically innocuous.[84] The revised document was purged of references to class exploitation, the role of foreign capital, and the existence of what the Left had called a "small highly privileged minority of local capitalists and land-barons."[85] The revised program scarcely used the term "socialism," preferring to speak of a "mixed economy" and "common ownership." While reserving a role in the economy for both private capital and the state, the new statement backed away from the issue of nationalization.[86] At the same time, a key proposal opposed by the Left — private ownership of land up to a limit of five hundred acres — was reaffirmed, as was the proposal to acquire lands on farms over one hundred acres for distribution to farmers. Other proposals objectionable to the Right, such as a tax on luxury homes and on incomes over five thousand pounds per year were struck down.

Having regained control over both the platform and the ideological direction of the party, the Right-opposition also adopted portions of the Left's original proposals. Suggested reforms in social legislation,[87] trade, and industrial relations were accepted in the revised program. Thus, the new platform was unanimously approved, and in March 1965, the victory of the Right was capped by Glasspole's and Isaac's election to key party posts.[88] After waging a determined ideological struggle against leftwing tendencies in the party, the Right-opposition had achieved a major victory. Not only was the more radical thrust of the Left deflected, but the Right also emerged as the standard-bearer of a reconstituted "socialist" platform. Looked at another way, it may be said that a conservative leadership, intensely opposed to overturning the existing class structure, would be presiding over a platform which largely protected the position of the dominant classes while securing some of the interests of the lower classes. The PNP could, therefore, claim to be committed to social change, while it sidestepped the issue of class domination.

This adept response to the crisis in the party, and its attendant ironies, were not lost on the Young Socialists. Indeed, the suppleness of the PNP response had the effect of refocusing attention on the broader theoretical and strategic issues behind the politics of the league. It will be recalled that, from its inception, the league had been beset by a dispute over strategy. The leadership had to fend off critics who were uncomfortable with the fact that some members of the YSL executive board retained membership in the PNP. We have already seen how, at the Second Congress of the league, a conflict developed between those who favored collaboration with the PNP (Trevor Munroe, Hugh Small, and others on the YSL executive body) and those who opposed it. (Robert Hill, the Unemployed Workers' Council, and others). The latter group had called attention to the dangers inherent in the strategy of collaboration. Not least of these dangers was the risk of divided loyalties, which such a strategy would entail. The group also reminded the league of the PNP's past opportunism and abuse of the Left. Only by building an independent working-class organization, they argued, could the YSL end the

PNP-JLP monopoly over the nation's political life. For all the sharpness with which those concerns brought to the fore the central theoretical and strategic questions confronting the league, their proponents did not prevail. Instead, those who held that affiliation with the PNP afforded links to organized labor won the day. So, after August 1964, the league had embarked on the strategy of collaboration.

Now, six months later, in the wake of both the setback at the PNP conference and the Right's appropriation and containment of the goals of the original socialist platform, the league felt impelled to reassess its approach. Apparently the Young Socialists had learned little from their encounters inside the party, for they persisted in the view that their strategy was appropriate. Indeed, they were adamant in their claim that a militant minority, by boring from within, still could move the PNP to adopt a more radical policy. In what appears to have been an attempt to silence critics who had reminded them of the failure of similar tactics by the Left in 1952, the league gave a blunt reply: "There is no reason why, despite the disillusionment since 1952, the same thing cannot be done on a much larger scale and with more success by a militant and active Left who are not prepared to compromise with the Middle and the Right."[89]

The Young Socialists went beyond this paean to voluntarism by giving the recent events in the party a peculiar twist. In their view, the party's acceptance of the truncated socialist platform had not been a setback for the Left; rather, they claimed, it had helped to move the PNP "further toward socialism."[90] However, this perspective repudiated many of the principles the league earlier had held with respect to the PNP's land-reform plan. In contrast to its prior stand, which expressed a general vigilance against PNP accommodation and a defininte antagonism toward the revised policy, the league now adopted a startlingly indulgent attitude toward the very same policy. It now maintained the surprising position that "the question of whether the PNP can carry out its stated objectives is, after all, of secondary importance to the increased opportunity which the policy provides for enlarging and solidifying the socialist forces now widely dispersed inside and outside the PNP and even the JLP."[91]

In an apparent about-face, the league now deemed it unimportant "whether [the PNP would] take over this or that industry *or even limit the size of large landholdings.*"[92] What was really consequential, the league now maintained, was "how the policy is interpreted."[93] Thus, whereas they once had demanded clear commitments and specific policies from the PNP, the Young Socialists by February 1965 had abandoned those positions in favor of relying on the good "intentions" of the party leadership, should the PNP win the upcoming general elections.[94] Whether this abrupt shift in the politics of the league was yet another attempt to dissemble is unclear.[95] What is not in doubt is that the strategy of boring from within long since had faltered, its fate finally sealed by the victory of the Right in the March 1965 party elections. That accomplishment within the PNP, however, was less an expression of the Right's omnipotence and more a reflection of the political immaturity of the YSL. The relative ease with which the PNP fended off the Young Socialists revealed the latter's low level of political development — a condition that afflicted the Jamaican Left at the time.

Debility was expressed in a limited grasp of the theory and practice of socialism — the politics to which the league aspired. This deficiency resulted in an inchoate, confused, and improvised politics. Given this absence of a firm grounding in socialist politics, it is not surprising that the Young Socialists succumbed to a series of mistakes, not the least of which were the following: (1) an instrumentalist conception of the PNP, which saw it simply as a shell to be taken over by insurgents and made to serve the interests of workers, peasants, and the unemployed; (2) an inability to analyze the emergent balance of forces within the party and the nation, and to adjust YSL tactics accordingly; (3) an idealist conception which presupposed that the national crisis could be addressed within the confines of the two-party system; and (4) a decided inclination to avoid the daunting tasks of political education and organization building in favor of capturing the PNP for the Left.

Whether the Young Socialists made an analysis of these mistakes in the wake of the failure of their strategy is unclear. However, a fortuitous development involving striking sugar workers suggests that, although the Young Socialists finally dropped their illusions about the PNP, they nonetheless remained in the grip of the political opportunism which in part had triggered their involvement with that party.

The Debacle in the Sugar Fields

So far, we have seen how the Young Socialists accommodated themselves to the PNP and compromised themselves in an abortive attempt to reform the party from within. In the wake of these developments came an upsurge of militant strike action by sugar workers at the Frome and Monymusk sugar estates. In April 1965, hundreds of sugar workers at both estates went out on strike to protest the failure of the West Indies Sugar Company (WISCO) to pay them their customary bonus. Compounding the workers' predicament was the reluctance of either the NWU or the BITU — the trade unions representing the workers — to endorse the strike. Convinced at last of the futility of their efforts inside the

PNP, and spurred by an urgent appeal for solidarity from the Frome workers, the Young Socialists plunged into the dispute on the side of the strikers.[96]

The high level of consciousness displayed by the Frome workers was particularly evident in this conflict. Whereas their comrades at the Monymusk estate had given in to appeals from the BITU and NWU that they return to work, the Frome workers rejected these appeals. Instead, they continued their action for more than two weeks, after which they took the bold step of contacting YSL personnel in Savanna-la-Mar for assistance in forming a union.[97] This self-direction by the Frome workers created an unfortunate scenario. It thrust the Young Socialists into the role of organizing a workers' movement against the established unions, at the very moment when the socialists were least prepared to exercise that responsibility.[98] Nonetheless, after an initial meeting at Ricketts River, attended by an estimated four thousand estate workers from both unions, the Young Socialists set about trying to organize the Workers' Liberation Union (WLU).[99]

Hugh Small played a major role in the rapidly unfolding events. Because of his prior experience in union activities and his record of activism on behalf of workers' autonomy, Small was perhaps the one member of the league with a close knowledge of the striking workers' plight. No doubt aware of this commitment, the workers asked Small to help them found the new union. Small responded by traveling through the Westmoreland sugar belt to address the striking workers during the first weeks of May. On 5 May he addressed a late-evening gathering at the Frome estate, where he accused both unions of collaborating with the WISCO management, failing to support the strike, mismanaging union funds, and generally neglecting the workers' interests.[100] Small was particularly critical of the unions for acquiescing in WISCO's attempt to pass off as a wage increase for 1965, that part of the workers' bonus which had been withheld in 1964.[101] In addition, he recalled that the workers had been without a contract for over a year, and that for the past five years they had been receiving bonuses rather than a "basic wage increase."

Small leveled his harshest attack against the structure of political unionism. Evidently aware of the intense divisions this structure had wrought among the working class, he emphasized to the strikers that their unity as a class was more important than their party affiliation. Clearly attempting to invoke the priority of class identity over party allegiance, Small skillfully touched on the workers' current predicament:

> When election time comes that is your business. When I look in front of me all I see is oppressed black people, working class people, exploited by

the will of WISCO so that I don't business what party you want to belong to. What I say is that the worker is all the trade union must be concerned with. Politicans will come and politicians will go but the working class goes on forever.[102]

Similiarly, Small reiterated one of his longstanding criticisms of the dominant unions: their inability, despite the collection of dues, to set aside a strike fund.[103] He explained to the workers how this deficiency strengthened management's hand in labor conflicts, and he accused the union leaders of reinforcing that strength by reassuring WISCO that the workers would not go out on strike.[104] Obviously alert to the historic role the Frome workers had played in the 1938 upheaval, Small urged them to remain faithful to that tradition in dealing with both the WISCO management and the "two cousin unions."[105] In response to the deep frustration which had led hundreds of estate workers to consider defecting from the established unions and to seek out the league, Small posed the alternative:

> Jamaica needs a union that will stand by workers when workers decide to take militant action and go out on strike. Jamaica needs a union that will give workers strike pay when they decide to strike. Jamaica needs a union that is not tied to management and can speak on behalf of the workers. Jamaica needs a union that is not tied to political parties, but can speak on behalf of one united working class movement in Jamaica.[106]

Four days later, Small spoke to another group of workers at Grange Hill.[107] There he repeated the themes of his address at Frome, with an especially vigorous attack on "family political . . . unionism" and union collusion with "sugar barons." Once more decrying the signing of secret agreements behind the workers' backs, Small now linked their discontent to exploitation of black labor by Tate and Lyle, the English multinational coporation:

> fellow workers, make no mistake about it, . . . the sugar barons represent the forces of colonialism and destruction in this country. The West Indies Sugar Company has nothing to do with the West Indies apart from the fact that it is situated in the West Indies and the workers who work in it are West Indians. It is owned by an English Company called Tate & Lyle, and every now and again . . . Peter Runge comes down to Jamaica, and he struts up and down the 60,000 acres, and he looks at the workers sweating in the factory . . . and he goes back to England and tells them that the blacks out there are doing well.[108]

After this critique of foreign capital, Small sought further to isolate the workers from the leadership of the established unions: "[They] betray us by failing to support us in our struggle against the foreign enemy, the unions are not only proving themselves dishonest and unworthy to be called Jamaican, but they were subverting and destroying our independence."[109] In a manner not unlike the Bustamante approach in the 1938 strikes, Small now was making his debut as the people's tribune. At that time, estate workers, rebelling against colonialism, drew to their side members of the reformist middle strata, who then championed labor's cause and spoke to its deepest yearnings.

Despite these similarities, the 1965 conflict occurred in a context vastly different from that of 1938. The twenty-seven-year period since the rebellion had seen the emergence of a postcolonial state structure in which political unionism and two-party competition had become firmly entrenched. Moreover, a native governing class had newly acquired political power, and, despite some signs of restiveness among the urban poor, the political leadership had retained its cohesion based on anticommunism and the ideology of Exceptionalism. These developments had cemented an intense political partisanship among the broad masses of Jamaicans — a condition the league was attempting to reverse in the sugar fields. The decidedly autocratic character of the postcolonial state, with its encroachments on civil liberties and harassment of dissidents, intimidated all but the most resolute activists, making the league's task doubly difficult. That the league was not successful in drawing more workers to its alternative was largely due to the resilence of this structure of allegiance and the character of the state.[110] At the same time, it must be said that the league's inability to create a stable organization, and its extended isolation from the laboring class, did not help its cause.

Despite the difficulties posed by the new turn of events and the league's own obvious limitations, the defection of workers from the established unions and the prospect of a renegade union in the sugar belt threatened the dominance of the BITU and NWU. Even though both unions had been engaged in bitter rivalries for unionization of the estate workers, the threat from the league forged an alliance between the established unions, designed to head off the dissidents. Thugs were brought into the fields to intimidate the league and the dissident workers. These hired hands stoned the fledgling union's open-air meetings at Frome and roughed up league organizers. Hugh Small's speeches were secretly taped by a PNP informer to be used against him later; and when he became involved in a melee with the police, assault charges were brought against him.[111]

This use of violence to harass the Young Socialists was supplemented by state actions to prevent the WLU from becoming a reality. Thus, when the league submitted the constitution for the new union to the government, the registrar of unions blocked its ratification by returning it repeatedly for corrections.[112] Confronted by this militancy among sugar workers, the JLP appointed a Commission of Inquiry to look into the dispute. Coming at the height of the league's activities, this intervention by the state effectively broke the YSL's momentum and shifted the initiative to the established unions.

The commission, whose hearings dragged on for several months,[113] took evidence from the BITU and NWU leaders, the WISCO management, and representatives of the incipient WLU. The latter apparently fared badly before the commission, since the PNP used the hearings to discredit the league and Hugh Small in particular.[114] In cross-examination by the NWU, Small was subjected to a withering attack on his politics, and his association with the Unemployed Workers' Council was used to discredit him. At the same time, the regime acted to curb league members' freedom to travel abroad. In what would be a long campaign of curbs against dissidents, the JLP seized the passport of a YSL member in July 1965 and cancelled that of another for having attended anniversary celebrations of the Cuban Revolution.[115] In September, the police, in an attempt to tie YSL members to riots in the West Kingston area, searched their homes for weapons and prohibited literature.[116]

Small, evidently disheartened by the determination of his opponents, concerned about the neglect of his law practice, and smarting from the grilling he was subjected to before the commission, turned back entreaties within the league to continue his activism among the dissident workers.[117] Indeed, by the time the commission issued its report,[118] the initiative to organize the WLU had collapsed. Other YSL activists were left with the unenviable task of demobilizing the dissident Frome workers. Within a few months of the defeat inside the party, the Young Socialists had suffered an even crueler blow to their hopes by being foiled at the very moment the trade unions showed signs of weakening.

On the heels of this rout in the sugar fields, the PNP executive group took steps to rid the party of the Young Socialists. The party appointed a disciplinary committee to investigate charges against Dennis Daley, one of the founders of the YSL.[119] The committee issued its revealing report in November 1965.[120] In it the practice of political unionism was confirmed and endorsed.[121] Brushing aside Vernon Arnett's defense of Daley, the committee found that both Daley and Small had tried to undermine the party-union cartel. In recommending Daley's expulsion, the committee reminded its critics that "it is part of the policy of the PNP to maintain and preserve the affiliation with the NWU" and that "we do feel strongly that, in the present Jamaican context, no member of the PNP should be allowed to attack the NWU in the way in which Comrade Daley did at the meeting at Rickett's River."[122] Once again a party tribunal had confirmed the class orientation of the PNP and exposed the limits of radical efforts to capture it for socialism.

Although the new year found the Young Socialists still politically engaged, these activities were the twitchings of a dying movement.[123] Nearly four full years of defensive struggle — much of it conducted in isolation from the broad Jamaican masses, and all of it carried out in an inimical political environment — finally took its toll. What had begun as a movement to politicize youths, reform the PNP, and challenge the policies of the postcolonial state disappeared from the political scene in mid-1966.[124] By this time, however, the deepening social crisis had spawned a variegated democratic movement within which the urban unemployed had gained hegemony.

The Deepening Crisis of the Regime: Social Disorder and the Advent of a Nationalist Intelligentsia

In our analysis of the early years of the postcolonial period, we called attention to a major consequence of the prolonged process of uneven development in Jamaica: the uprooting and displacement of the pro-letarianized rural population into the urban centers. We saw that out of this mass of urbanized peasants in Kingston sprang a rebellious anti–status quo movement, whose lack of deference to the Europeanist mold of upper-class behavior and whose bold assertion of a black racial consciousness challenged the political and moral leadership of the dominant classes. It will be recalled that these latter classes evolved the ideology of Exceptionalism, with which they hoped to build national unity. This ideology suppressed antagonistic differences between the departing colonial rulers and the laboring classes, and glossed over con-tradictions between the latter and the politically dominant group.

The result was the development of an ideological ensemble which repulsed a racially-based nationalism among the people, vaunted cul-tural affinities with the British, affirmed the unity of all races within the island, appealed for exemplary conduct by the population, and threatened law-and-order reprisals against "subversives." The conno-tation produced by this ensemble was decidedly authoritarian and hostile to the restive urban poor, indicating some continuity between the outlook of the colonialists and that of the now-dominant native groups.

The reproduction of this outlook was particularly evident among the intermediate and upper ranks of the middle class. Buoyed up by the same process of postwar urbanization and economic diversification that had propelled the native bourgeoisie within the economy, this branch of the middle class had assumed the positions in the state and society that had been opened up by this expansion. As top civil servants and self-employed professionals, members of this class prided themselves on the respectability conferred by their nonmanual occupations. While some of their numbers still inveighed against residual obstacles to their advancement, on the whole their sense of class prerogatives and the thoroughness of their assimilation of colonial ideology made them contemptuous of the laboring classes.

This class arrogance produced, on the one hand, an indigenous reproduction of colonial ruling-class ideology and practices. These placed great weight on decorum, proper manners, and law and order.[1] On the other hand, there was a parallel revulsion against lower-class culture and wariness toward the politically uncooperative poor in the West Kingston slums. It has already been pointed out that this part of Kingston was an incubator for the most diverse forms of anti-*status quo* behavior. By the mid-sixties, the ecology of the West Kingston ghetto had spawned an autonomous resistance culture. Unimpeded by conformity to upper-class values and socialized outside the society's normalizing institutions, the inhabitants of these communities were free to develop their own rules of social interaction. This sovereignty generated limited forms of community, social obligation, and fraternity. It also permitted the flowering of spontaneous ideologies and linguistic innovations out of the conditions of everyday life in the ghettos. In time, these developments found creative outlets in the rise of the popular musician and vocal artist, who, by representing the social history of the ghetto in songs, quickly came into vogue in these communities. As we have observed, however, this relative independence from official society had its costs. Isolation not only allowed for creativity, but also gave many among the Kingston poor an apprenticeship in antisocial behavior. The ecology of the ghetto spawned its share of criminality and indiscipline. In fact, the same conditions of poverty which led to a struggle for survival and generated creative responses in music, art, and language also produced antisocial tendencies among the urban poor.

For example, in 1964, a hitherto-unprecedented upsurge in youth-gang violence and rowdyism attracted the attention of the whole society. Unemployed youths engaged in social banditry and internecine gang violence, menacing store owners and individuals. By the end of the year, the predatory acts, communal violence, and general lawlessness spilled over into some middle-class areas. In fact, it was not unknown for these youths to converge in small groups on theatres outside working-class neighborhoods to watch an American movie. During the showing they would hoot, whistle, and cheer their protagonists with bawdy language, while cowing into silence patrons who dared reproach them. It is probable that not a few films had to be halted because of this rowdyism.

This antisocial behavior in the early sixties evoked varying responses from the officials. The JLP decried the rise of "hooliganism," threatened repression, and implored school and church officials to help in disciplining the unemployed youths.[2] Others averred the possibility of equal opportunity for all, despite sharp social and economic divisions in the society. Thus, Russell Graham, Custos of Saint Andrew, after an obligatory nod to the colonial past that blocked his ascent to his present post, used the attainments of his class to instruct young people that "there is no barrier to the Jamaican today, there is no barrier to anyone regardless from which strata . . . he comes. All he needs is dedication and hard work . . . with no disrespect to the past, . . . 30 years ago one like myself could not be a Custos, things have changed and there are no barriers today."[3]

But where Graham's understanding of the prospects facing youths was clouded by class ideology, one church leader was prescient in recognizing the autonomous and self-ruling character of the broad mass of the urban Jamaican poor. Without drawing out the political implications, the Anglican bishop noted late in 1964 that "the real problem in Jamaica so far as hooliganism is concerned, is not just a question of a few hundreds of youngsters here and there who disturb the public weal and are a nuisance to the community, but it is that people of all ages, particularly between the ages of 15 and 22 . . . come under no influence whatever either of Church or state."[4] In other words, the bishop implicitly was calling attention to the difficulty faced by the dominant classes in exercising moral and political leadership over the unemployed, where the latter were self-governing and largely outside the institutional control of the state. However, this sovereignty was contradictory in its effects. For while it facilitated a dissidence and forms of creativity, it also bequeathed an ever-present malevolence.

Unfortunately, the menacing postures and the recklessness of the militant Kingston poor were not regarded by them and their admirers as distinct from political activism and opposition. Rather, their outlaw behavior was regarded as the ultimate symbol of their self-identification and opposition to the status quo. The paradox inherent in much of the ghetto-based opposition at this stage was that no distinction was made between illegal, outlaw activities and political opposition to the state. For the militant poor, social protest and outlawry were inseparable. Aggressive and intimidating postures, looting businesses, and menacing ethnic-minority merchants and shopkeepers became poor people's way of protesting "injustice" and their own status as outcasts in the society. As such, social-banditry-as-politics defined the ethics of the militant poor.

With embryonic socialist formations already attempting to link socialist opposition to the aspirations of this militant stratum, and in the face of the latter's ability to act with impunity, it is not surprising that the government intervened to influence this trend. For example, between 1963 and 1965, the police were given free rein to contain the unrest stemming from youth gang violence, and several suppressive edicts and curbs were introduced as a result.[5] But while these steps contributed to the state's autocratic cast, they were unavailing. Indeed, a confluence of events in 1965 and 1966 deepened the social crisis.

The first of these occurred in early August 1965, with the shocking news that England once more had sharply reduced immigration from the Commonwealth. Where the previous annual quota had been 28,800, it now was cut drastically, to 8,500 from all the former British colonies.[6] This latest effort to reduce nonwhite immigration was received by the government in Jamaica with dismay and a sense of betrayal, since the reductions dealt a serious blow to its plan for coping with unemployment. In his response, the acting prime minister, Donald Sangster, was quite blunt in informing the Jamaican Parliament of the importance of the export of labor to ease unemployment: "The [unemployment] situation in Jamaica is almost unique and there is no denying that the restrictions may have an adverse effect on the development program, since, as the House is aware, a certain amount of emigration for an initial period was taken into account in the development planning . . . the cutting off of the temporary assistance provided by emigration will certainly have an adverse effect on our economy in general and on our relationship with the United Kingdom."[7] Within weeks of this setback, the West Kingston area was rocked by serious attacks on Chinese nationals and their businesses by infuriated area residents. The latter part of August found these residents stoning and setting ablaze Chinese-owned stores to protest the alleged beating of a female salesclerk by her Chinese employer.[8]

The spark for this outburst came amid tensions generated by the shopkeepers' extension of credit to the black poor. Given the potential for misunderstanding, abuse, and distrust in this nexus, it is not surprising that a dispute ensued, as the shopkeeper attempted to deduct payments for a radio from the employee's check. The sacking of Chinese businesses by the militant urban poor, in defence of an aggrieved worker, not only disclosed sources of continuing tension between retail merchants and the Kingston unemployed, but also affirmed the fusion of banditry and political protest in the actions of the unemployed.[9]

Unable to do much about the crisis of unemployment and the tenuous basis of its ideological leadership, the JLP persisted with its illiberal policies in 1966. The regime struck at the Kingston poor with a slum-clearance policy, fashioned captive populations by constructing new housing for the poor in one of its political strongholds, hired gang leaders as political thugs, imposed security controls at the university, and eventually declared a state of emergency in Kingston.

The opening of these developments in early 1966 was triggered by another attempt to remove hundreds of squatters whose makeshift shacks sprawled over some ten acres of government land now designated for industrial expansion. As we have seen, back in 1963, the government, as part of its industrial development program, had uprooted thousands of squatters in the Kingston Pen area to make way for the Newport West complex and the Esso Oil refinery. At that time, the JLP also had cleared a section of the largest shanty area, then known as "Back-O-Wall," and erected the low-income Tivoli housing project. Now, in an extension of that development project, the JLP hoped to add another port facility, create an industrial complex for small manufacturers, and expand the Tivoli housing project.[10] This planned clearance of the area did not include arrangements for alternative accommodations for the destitute slum dwellers. Their shacks, put together from cardboard boxes, zinc, and bits of scavenged wood, simply were to be demolished so that construction could begin.

In order to appreciate this disdain for the settlers' plight, it should be recalled that the JLP regarded the squatters as a serious threat to stability in Kingston. Not only did their lawlessness imply a repudiation of the image being cultivated by the regime, but their ideologies and political tendencies marked them as opponents of the regime. After all, it was from among these slum dwellers that the Rastafarian and rebellious youths sprang, and it was also among this mass that militant organizations such as the UWC agitated.[11] The anti–status quo attitudes of the West Kingston poor, their combustibility as a social force, and their demonstrations challenging the assignment of work on the basis of party loyalty all help to explain the determination with which the regime sought their eviction.

Indeed, the policy of slum clearance in the West Kingston area, which had become a JLP electoral stronghold, revealed one of the power strategies of Jamaica's authoritarian democracy. In undertaking slum clearance, the JLP accomplished three things. First, it struck back at its political nemesis, the militant urban poor; second, with the expansion of the Tivoli housing project, the JLP continued to break up the shanty towns and reconstitute the area's population as "captive populations" living in modern facilities and obligated to the JLP;[12] and third, the slum clearance allowed the government to proceed with an industrialization strategy which promoted the fortunes of foreign and local capital. In sum, policies which were justified as part of the continuing modernization of Kingston were linked intimately to urgent *political* concerns and to the JLP's accumulation of power.[13]

Beginning in mid-February and culminating in summer 1966, the JLP sent in bulldozers and a one-hundred-man riot squad to remove the squatters. In initial sweeps on 17 and 24 February, more than five hundred slum dwellers and their children were routed from the Payne Avenue and Majesty Pen sites. As scores of children on Payne Avenue watched their "homes" turned to rubble, they found a solitary member of Parliament, Vernon Arnett, joining their mothers in a vain attempt to block the path of the bulldozers.[14] As this initial removal effort progressed, clashes between rival gangs and the police escalated. At the same time, party rivalry seeped into the conflict, as the PNP tried, in the face of JLP resistance, to enter the area to mobilize the residents. This PNP challenge to JLP control of West Kingston in effect signaled the beginning of the 1967 general election campaign.

Retaliating against this PNP "invasion," the JLP on 29 March banned all public meetings in the Corporate Area for sixty days. By June, the status of the youth gangs as pariahs had been altered, as both parties pressed some of them into political service. Increasingly, their clashes assumed a party coloration which reflected the emergence of a new social type on the political scene: the party gunman recruited to protect or invade urban electoral districts. Indeed, the reliance on gunmen to encroach on or to consolidate electoral gains introduced a new dimension in the competition between the two parties. While competitive political violence had formed a part of Jamaican politics since the forties, the violence surrounding the shanty removal program in the mid-sixties was different, in that the official parties began to legitimize the role of the gunman as an *enforcer* in their rivalry, thereby investing an anomic figure with a decisive role in national politics.

As an enforcer, the politicized gunmen now would ward off challenges from the opposing party, enforcing the principle of captive constituencies. At stake for the JLP in the West Kingston area was the protection of its "investment" in the population around the Tivoli project, whose political loyalty was being ensured by various inducements. As for the PNP, its intervention was designed to prevent the JLP from expanding its control over this constituency. After all, the JLP's industrial program, with its focus on West Kingston, could only alarm the PNP. The impending expansion of the Tivoli housing project and the additional plans for modernization of the area, with its benefits to the low-income community, implied a JLP largesse which would pay dividends at the polls.

Out of this PNP attempt to forestall the consolidation of a JLP fiefdom emerged the twin phenomena of *political* gang warfare and the legitimation of the party-recruited gunman. Consequently, violent groups such as the Phoenix and Viking gangs now were absorbed into the party machinery as enforcers for the JLP and PNP, respectively. Paradoxically, what had begun as an attempt by the state to curb crime and communal violence by juvenile gangs now was converted, by the exigencies of party competition, into a domestication of this violence for political purposes.

It was against this backdrop of political violence and gang warfare, that the most extensive eviction of squatters in the postwar history of the country began. On 12 July, some 1,500 of these hapless poor, some with their makeshift shacks in hand, scurried from the Foreshore Road and Industrial Terrace areas, as bulldozers and riot police moved in to begin the final phase of demolition.[15] Those who fled to nearby squatter sites at Riverton and Moonlight cities promptly were turned back by some of the three hundred police on hand. The settlers, apparently intimidated by this show of force and wearied by the entire experience, did not repeat the defiance which had characterized the 1963 eviction. In the aftermath of this blow, only a forlorn band of settlers was left to wander the streets of West Kingston in search of shelter.[16] This counterstrike against the squatters, however, brought only a brief lull in the prolonged conflict between the state and the Kingston poor. In mid-August, the quiet was shattered by a resurgence of political gang warfare. Propelled by the stakes in the approaching elections, enforcers from each party roamed West Kingston, intimidating residents. Remarking on this development, the *Gleaner* reported that "adherents of both . . . political parties stopped people in the streets and openly questioned them about their political affiliation." The report observed that "a beating depended on the answers."[17]

Despite the entry of riot police into working-class neighborhoods such as Denham Town and Trench Town, the party violence continued unabated. The ban on political assembly, introduced in March, was renewed a third time on 28 September, but open clashes between the political gangs kept the area in turmoil. By late September, it was evident that gang warfare had strained the capacity of the police and threatened to reduce West Kingston to a war zone; on 2 October, a truce was imposed by the JLP, in the form of a declaration of a state of emergency.[18]

Even though this action was unique in the postcolonial period, the invocation of the Emergency Powers Act was not particularly remarkable in the context of prior state policy. The state, as we have seen, was authoritarian, preemptive, and monopolistic. By 1966, it already had infringed seriously on the civil liberties of Jamaicans by targeting the Left, the Kingston poor, and other critics. To prevent ideological contamination from outside, the JLP had proscribed "subversive" literature, seized the passports of activists, harassed and intimidated anti-status quo groupings and movements, and barred various activists from entering the island. Although the censorship of ideas and curbs on travel hampered critical discussion of public policy and soured the character of public discourse, what happened to the intelligentsia and other middle-class critics was relatively mild compared to the woeful experience of the urban poor. Having been severely disadvantaged by the character of postcolonial economic and social policy, the urban poor bore the brunt of legislation designed to create law and order. For example, the 1963 law requiring mandatory sentencing, flogging, and hard labor for serious crimes snared many among the poor.[19] Similarly, the 1964 revision of the "ganja law," mandating long prison terms for the possession and use of marijuana, also exacted its toll from the tens of thousands of poor Jamaicans who were involved with this drug.[20] Lastly, the poor suffered the additional indignity of whippings, as the 1965 Flogging Regulation Law improved on colonial punishment by approving the use of "cat-o-nine-tails" and the tamarind switch in the prisons.[21] If incidents of police brutality are included, it would not be an exaggeration to say that draconian laws fell heavily on the poor, and that JLP's policies toward them were harsh.[22]

Well in advance of the state of emergency, then, a general pattern of prohibitive state policies and punitive laws already existed. Against this background, the new emergency edicts did not represent an extraordinary departure. However, prohibitive actions by the state were taking place in the context of an ever-widening two-party clientelism which sought to enlist politically relevant strata of the population on the basis of rewards, favors, and material inducements. This clientelistic process had spawned widespread political victimization and abuse, as both parties rewarded their supporters and victimized their opponents. In light of this link between clientelism and authoritarian rule, it may be argued that the significance of the emergency was not that it created a sharp break in the politics of the state. Rather, its importance was that it exposed the difficulties both parties were experiencing in attempting to encapsulate a deviant force — the juvenile gangs — which up to now had existed outside the grasping network of clientelism and party politics. Thus, the emergency should be seen not simply as an attempt to curb lawlessness *per se*, but rather as a means to define boundaries for the political enforcers, who, in their murderous partnership with the parties, had overreached themselves and were threatening to take the initiative from their sponsors.

While this massive show of force in West Kingston apparently pacified the armed political gangs,[23] it scarcely relieved the crisis besetting the regime. In fact, even as the JLP grappled with the Kingston poor, it simultaneously found itself in the grip of an intense wave of worker unrest and an increased agitation at the university. In activities beginning early in 1966 and cresting in the following year, workers in major sectors of the economy engaged in strikes, walkouts, and other forms of work stoppage. In part, this restiveness reflected an effort by the PNP-affiliated NWU to pressure the regime by endorsing workers' demands in the public sector of the economy. But the upsurge in worker unrest went beyond the NWU's manipulation of labor discontent.[24] The unrest also disclosed a generalized consciousness of economic hardship, reflected in labor's overwhelming dissatisfaction with wages and discontent with political unionism.[25]

This simmering dissatisfaction with the subordination of workers' interests to the imperatives of party politics resulted in the advent of an independent union movement in Kingston. While small independent unions had long existed alongside the dominant unions, this latest sprouting was marked by leaders' affirmation of workers' self-management and rejection of the prevailing mode of unionization, with its bureaucratic, personalistic, and wage bargaining features. But even as this movement highlighted the depth of workers' dissatisfaction with the existing unions, and even though it brought to the fore authentic leaders from the working class, the independent union movement remained limited in its national impact and confined to a small sector of the urban workforce. Only after 1968, when they united under a coordinating body, did the independent unions assume a political role of some consequence.

The University as a Site of Conflict: The Politics of the Intelligentsia, 1960–67

In our analysis so far, we have emphasized the multiform character of the anti-JLP opposition and the nature of the state's response to these challenges. We observed that even as the juridical basis of the state rested on liberal democratic principles, the events of the early to mid-sixties left little doubt about the state's authoritarian exercise of power. In analyzing this disjunction between the official form of the state and the regime's illiberal policies, we maintained that this disjunction was due to several interrelated factors. The persistence of the colonial state structure at independence, and the role assumed in it by Europeanist native classes who had achieved a settlement with the colonial rulers, had unleashed a process which compromised the democratic credentials of the postcolonial state. Opposed to the militant poor by class ideology and exposed to domestic and international challenges at the very moment of consolidating their political power and industrialization policy, the dominant classes and their political representatives resorted to authoritarian methods to sustain their rule. The decreasing reliability of the university intelligentsia in reproducing the dominant ideology aggravated this situation.

For the most part, responsibility for elaborating the official ideology traditionally had fallen on officials of the state and on those occupying positions in institutions such as the church, the schools, and the media. The University of the West Indies (UWI), at Mona, constituted a notable exception to this ready conformity. We have already observed that tensions had existed as early as 1960, when academics commissioned by the government had asserted relative independence from prevailing values by producing a report sympathetic to the Rastafarian movement. By the mid-sixties, events in the region had quickened activism among the intelligentsia, who took governments in the region to task on a range of issues. At Mona, the main campus of the university, this critique was particularly insistent, as a small but significant branch of the intelligentsia adopted positions which brought it into conflict with the JLP. To account for this breach between the ideology of the regime and the orientation of the intelligentsia, we must go beyond psychologistic theories emphasizing the intellectuals' alienation to examine both the origins of the University of the West Indies, and the specific juncture at which members of the native postcolonial university intelligentsia made their appearance as strategic actors on the political scene.

The Origins of the University of the West Indies: Caribbean Upheaval and Imperial Fait Accompli

For all but a few years of its prolonged domination of the West Indies, Britain ignored the need for advanced education among the West Indian peoples. Although a theological college was established as early as 1710 in Barbados, followed in 1921 by an agricultural college in Trinidad, neither institution was created along the lines of the modern unitary university. Nor were they intended as centers of higher learning for the Caribbean peoples.[26] This suggests that, well into the twentieth century, options for higher education in the West Indies were extremely limited. For the lower middle class in Jamaica, attendance at a teacher-training college might have been a possibility. For the capitalists and wealthier sectors of the population, there was the option of sending their progeny to universities abroad or, less likely, of allowing them to stay in Jamaica to take the external degree of the University of London.[27]

For the British, whose control over the colonies was secure, providing advanced education to its West Indian subjects at the apogee of empire was out of the question. In a perverse way, the establishment of an institution of higher learning in the West Indies colonies had to await circumstances which would impel Britain to begin thinking about its departure, as well as the creation of a native class in whose hands the British could securely deposit political power. The necessary impulse for these developments in the Caribbean came with the labor rebellions of the 1930s and their aftermath. In Jamaica, the coming devolution of power was signaled by the 1944 Constitution and the extension of an unrestricted franchise in that year. Indeed, only a year earlier, with the appointment of the Asquith Commission, the British had turned to the matter of examining higher education in the empire.[28] Under a mandate from this commission, a West Indies Committee, chaired by Sir James Irvine, was appointed in January 1944. This committee had as its responsibility the creation of an institution of higher learning, from which the future leaders of the region would be drawn.

The Irvine Committee, which included representatives drawn from territorial legislatures, made a three-month tour of the region and paid visits to McGill and Howard universities to examine the situation of West Indians there.[29] This fact-finding group was not without its anomalies. One had to do with its composition. Of the seven members, two — including the chairman — were vice-chancellors at British universities. In the context of a wider colonial policy in which metropolitan institutional practices were taken as models for administrative rule in the colonies, it seemed unlikely that the European committee members, faced with the challenge of putting in place an educational institution to train future leaders of the region, could ignore the British university model. At the very least, then, the Irvine Committee arrived in the region with an implicit model for the new institution, against which dissenters would have to contend.

Second, although the committee included native representatives, they were drawn from a narrow section of the indigenous population: members of the middle class serving in the colonial legislature or in other official positions. As we have already noted, members of this group had an interest in seeing the liquidation of colonialism but were disinclined to cut institutional ties with the empire. Native members of the Irvine Committee, such as Hugh Springer and J.A. Lukkoo, therefore were least likely to advance models or conceptions of higher education divergent from those held by the Europeans on the committee. Indeed, when a report was issued, there was no dissent by its Caribbean members.[30]

Third, even though the committee was making a visit to address a major deficit of British colonial policy and an issue of supreme importance to the Caribbean peoples, it chose to shield its deliberations from broad public scrutiny and participation. As the committee observed in issuing its report, "All evidence and interviews were regarded as confidential and neither the press nor the public were admitted to the hearings."[31] The committee, by insulating its deliberations from the widest possible debate and participation, thus sharply reduced the Caribbean peoples' influence on a major issue of concern to them.

The reason for this lack of wider consultation can be discerned in the intersection of two processes: the unfolding of contentious nationalist movements in the territories, and British efforts to protect its initiative from local interference. From the British standpoint, since nationalist politics were cresting in the territories, inviting public discussion not only would have produced divergent proposals and territorial rivalries, but also might have permitted the undermining of an operative principle in the committee's deliberations: the creation of a unitary regional institution. In sum, the committee's nonconsultative approach on higher education was a tactic which produced a *fait accompli* for independent Caribbean governments. As a member of the Irvine Committee later observed, the university had to be put, even after its creation, beyond the reach of interfering nationalists:

> The College was protected during its earliest years from the harsh winds and tides of local politics and nationalism. Because many governments were involved and there was as yet no federal government, the constitution of the College was enshrined in a Royal Charter, a fact which gave an additional measure of protection in that it removed the temptation of casual or hasty amendment.[32]

The committee was prescient in anticipating disagreements from the territories. In fact, important disputes did emerge on siting, finances, and even fears that the colonies might become "intellectually impoverished" if the pattern of education abroad were diminished. In fact, the pan-Caribbean regional university eventually recommended by Irvine might not have survived the cut and thrust of these sectional interests, had they been allowed to participate. After all, the subsequent failure of the West Indies Federation and Caribbean governments' fundamental responsibility for its demise offered a compelling case for avoiding the obstacles which might have attended Caribbean leaders' involvement in the creation of an independent institution of higher education. In this respect, ironically, by taking the decisions out of the hands of the territories, Irvine and his committee were responsible for inaugurating the first genuinely pan-Caribbean institution.[33]

At the same time, it must be said that this *fait accompli* produced an institution more attuned to imperial values than to the needs of the Caribbean peoples. It is not surprising that, when the committee's report eventually was released in June 1945, it recommended the founding of a unitary college based on the British model, stipulated that it should be "entirely residential," and proposed a period of tutelage and affiliation with a "university of repute" — in this case, the University of London.[34] This decision effectively ensured that educational policy would be determined from the center. With the college's curriculum and examinations to be administered from without, and with its academic and administrative staff to be composed initially of expatriates, the Irvine Committee had created in the Caribbean a virtual subsidary of London University. The absence of broad public debate and participation in the founding of the university meant that the institutional form and the determination of educational content would remain in foreign hands.

The problems attendant upon external control were reflected in the proposal to admit only four to five hundred students from all West Indian territories. Although the Irvine Committee justified this figure with the facetious assertion that it ruled out "the possibility of 'academic unemployment',", both its recommendation on number of admissions and its insistence on residence at the college revealed what an exclusionary institution had been envisioned. The college would not recruit the merely intellectually talented; rather, it would cater to an exclusive coterie of exceptional students who could both meet the standards of the British elite colleges and afford to live away from home. As such, the low enrollment figure and the related insistence on residence at the college gave hints of a policy which dismissed the issue of underutilization of resources and the hardship which mandatory residence might impose on some families. Fortunately, a visiting British fact-finding team subsequently identified these and other problems and called for substantial revisions in the original stipulations. The visiting team recommended the following in its 1954 report: a substantial increase in scholarships and financial aid; an increase in enrollment, because "with a total student number of only three to four hundred, [the college] is of necessity a very expensive institution"; changes in the entrance requirements; and greater flexibility in applying the residential rule. The visiting team remained silent, however, on the appropriateness of the curriculum, especially in the social sciences.[35]

Despite the daunting problems that elitism, external control, and foreign academic content would pose for inductees, the Irvine Committee succeeded in one of its primary purposes: creating an integrative regional center of higher learning. With political independence for the territories on the horizon, imperial policy belatedly sought to undo centuries of colonial policy by vigorously promoting the breakup of territorial parochialisms and insularities through the creation of a regional institution of higher education.

Notwithstanding this achievement, the unabashed promotion of pan-Caribbeanism from above was double edged, and not without a tinge of bad faith. For while the report expressed its concern with the necessity for West Indians to study their own problems and not be so much the "passive subjects of investigation by commissions and experts from outside," other motives, emanating from imperial concerns, also were evident. These were evident in Irvine's acknowledgment that new forms of *control* were needed in order to respond to the unfolding situation in the territories. Thus, in the committee's view:

> The forms of Imperial Control and even of influence are changing in response to the changing needs of today, and the time is coming for the Colonies, as it did for the Dominions, *when the bond of a common culture and the strengthening of ties of an unofficial and often invisible kind will assume greater importance than the forms of constitutional authority.* There could be no greater gift from Britain more rich in its future possibilites than that which we now recommend . . . The gift of this institution would both be a fitting and a logical climax of British policy toward this group of Colonies.[36] [Italics added]

In the context of this abiding desire to continue the sway of imperial culture and ideology at the point of higher education, the University College of the West Indies (UCWI) was founded in October 1946, with its first students entering two years later.[37] Thus, even though their attempt to create a political analogue to the university – the West Indies Federation – would later fail, the British did succeed, by preemptive action, in bequeathing an institution which eventually would undermine insularites bred by centuries of imperial rule. In time, the college would achieve something not even Irvine could have predicted: a rescue of the idea of pan-Caribbean unity from the ruins of the federation.[38] Ironically, where the British failed to forge either a political union among the territories or a regional identity among the native leaders, the creation of the university did lead, in an unexpected way, to a transnational sensibility among some parts of the intelligentsia.

In the early sixties, these intellectuals' interest in the pan-Caribbean idea found expression not in a desire to be part of a political union within an Imperial Commonwealth, but in the contrary sentiments of nationalism and anti-imperialism. Consequently Irvine's legacy, through the mediation of the intelligentsia, in time also would become the nemesis of the native postcolonial rulers. Indeed, the Irvine Committee alluded to precisely this outcome, when it remarked that "both directly and indirectly, this element of the population will have a wide influence for good or ill." At this late date, however, there was little that the British could do about the tendency of universities to produce defenders *and* opponents of the status quo. Impaled on the dilemma of wanting "responsible and well-informed leaders" and risking the possibility of radicalism at some future date, the British gambled on the "responsible" leaders and allowed the university to go forward.

The Emergence of the New World Group

This pan-Caribbean anti-imperial tendency was apparent at the Mona campus in Jamaica, which had established itself as the intellectual center in the region. By 1960, Mona not only had the largest contingent of faculty and students, but also was a pioneer in establishing a Faculty of Social Science with the important departments of economics and government, as well as the Institute of Social and Economic Research (ISER). Indeed, it was under the auspices of this institute that three West Indian scholars in 1960 produced the pathbreaking and controversial monograph of Rastafarianism.[39]

This study elicited criticism from the defenders of Exceptionalism, who sharply attacked the scholars, essentially for failing to reproduce the dominant ideology in their work. The monograph, after all, had implicitly but firmly rejected the contempt and hysteria which characterized the official attitude toward the Rastafarians. As early as 1960, then, a small but significant breach had opened between the state and a segment of the intelligentsia, over the latter's independence and lack of cooperation in elaborating prevailing values.

This rift would widen further in the postcolonial period, as various branches of the intelligentsia groped to define their roles in the unfolding politics of the region. The Cuban Revolution, the recent collapse of the West Indies Federation, decolonization, political crisis in British Guyana, and uncertainty in the region all demanded a response from the Caribbean intelligentsia. In fact, the mounting crisis in British Guyana late in 1962 led to the formation of a "New World" study group in Georgetown.[40] Within a year, the group had published the first number of *New World Quarterly*, a West Indian journal of opinion and debate on problems confronting the region. At the same time, the unfolding crisis in Jamaica drew some academics at Mona into limited forms of political activity. We have noted how the struggles of the unemployed affected reformist elements within the PNP, eventually resulting in the founding of the Young Socialist League in 1962 and the subsequent establishment of a YSL Area Council at the university. Composed of an ideologically diverse group, this Area Council provided much of the early theoretical guidance for the league, especially on the subject of development and underdevelopment.[41] In summer 1964, the attempt of these and other intellectuals to criticize JLP policies publicly, further heightened the anxieties of a regime already suspicious of the intelligentsia and wary of the university's role in promoting dissident ideas.

This wariness toward the university soon found expression in attacks on professors who were not West Indian natives but who nevertheless criticized the government. Spearheading this attack on "foreigners" on the university staff, Bustamante made it clear that criticism could bring expulsion. Replying to a critical column by a writer affiliated with the university, Bustamante warned that "an alien who has the audacity and impertinence not just to criticize but to write offensively against the Government or any of the ministers will be considered *persona non grata* and will be ordered out."[42] To avoid any misunderstanding about the intent of the regime's policies, the prime minister put native academics on notice by threatening that "those who cannot be deported because they are Jamaican citizens can be dealt with."[43] To make good these threats, the regime turned to a 1964 work permit act for authorization to expel non-Jamaican critics at the university.[44] At this juncture the regime clearly recognized that the university was failing to help cement the political power of the dominant classes. So far, no element among the academic staff had come forward publicly to champion the autocratic policies of the state, or to defend Exceptionalism.[45] Instead, a minority of the humanistic intelligentsia had adopted an adversarial posture toward the state.[46]

There are several reasons for this emergent opposition among the university intelligentsia. First, as a group with a guild interest in free speech, intellectuals could be expected to resist such encumbrances as censorship, state intervention in the routines of the university, and other official attempts to curtail their work. A second explanation for the dissident orientation has to do with the professors' training abroad. The bulk of those West Indians who advanced their education did so in universities in the metropolitan countries. Enrollment figures for the period 1946–54 (table 4) show the extent to which the Caribbean intelligentsia was being formed in a milieu outside the colonies. This pattern suggests that those who returned to lecture at the university were, on the whole, likely to be less reliable in their defense of the Jamaican status quo, having been cosmopolitanized and moved to a "critical state" by a sojourn abroad. (table 4).

A variant of this experience was also evident among certain expatriate faculty members. Having enjoyed a greater freedom in their home countries and being imbued with the tenets of liberalism and academic Marxism, some of them, "forgetting" that they were not in their own country, attempted critically to evaluate the policies of their host country. There remains one still more potent reason for the emergent adversarial orientation of the university intelligentsia: the his-

Table 4. Students from the West Indies in Universities in the United Kingdom and the Irish Republic, 1946–54*

	1946–47	1947–48	1948–49	1949–50	1950–51	1951–52	1952–53	1953–54
Bahamas	12	17	23	22	19	20	16	20
Barbados	64	72	73	80	78	87	91	112
British Guiana	124	142	166	155	169	180	210	235
British Honduras	19	25	25	19	13	12	13	10
Jamaica	308	380	391	387	448	533	659	864
Leeward Islands	13	18	27	27	30	32	36	30
Trinidad	118	175	214	224	274	306	340	370
Windward Islands	70	82	81	73	67	63	76	100

*Including those at the Inns of Courts, nonuniversity colleges, etc.

Source: Great Britain. Inter-University Council for Higher Education Overseas. *Report of the Visitor's Committee.* 1954. Appendix C, p. 63.

torical character of the world situation that shaped its members' consciousness. By the early sixties, the native academics had been swept up in a epoch marked by several ramifying events. These included the ascendancy of national liberation movements in Asia and Africa, the tottering of Britain's colonial empire, the explosive impact of the Cuban Revolution on the region, the onset of decolonization in the Caribbean, and the unfortunate events leading to the collapse of the West Indies Federation. Together with the visible poverty, unemployment, and economic backwardness evident throughout the region, these events forced the intelligentsia to engage in an intense scrutiny of their own societies.[47] As we shall see, the resulting attempt within the academy both to develop a critique of West Indian problems and to advance a format of opposition would be impeded by a high-minded but ultimately self-defeating idealism on the part of those who, early on, came to address these issues.

The incongruity of an awakened but militantly idealistic intelligentsia was manifested clearly in the circle of West Indian economists who referred to themselves as the New World Group. Initially organized in late 1962 as a study circle in Georgetown, British Guiana, the group quickly emerged on the Caribbean intellectual scene as a powerful ideological movement. In March 1963, the group published the first issue of the *New World Quarterly*, a journal which would become the primary forum for its ideas. Responding to developments in the late fifties and early sixties, the group elaborated positions on some of the key issues presented by them.

One such issue was the lack of public awareness of problems besetting the region. In an early statement on this question, the group noted its "dissatisfaction with the existing channels for public debate" and argued that by publishing the *Quarterly* and other materials, it hoped "to democratize the process of public discussion." Here the collective was expressing its acute awareness of the constricted scope of discussion on pressing regional problems, since this debate was largely confined to a few politicians, academics, and other experts. To remedy this deficiency, the group called for the creation of new forums of public opinion and identified itself as an agency that would act both as a clearinghouse for fresh ideas and as an expert collective seeking a popular audience. As an editorial in the *Quarterly* put it:

> The overriding need [is] to develop agencies of discrimination. Ideally, the task of selecting what is really desirable from among all the external influences makes a considerable demand on the collective wisdom of the whole community; and the necessary preconditions for it are, first that an abundance of helpful facts be made readily available *to the population at large,* and next, that there should be agencies stimulating and encouraging reasoned discussion of important issues.[48]

There was, then, a preoccupation with creating both a broader arena of public discourse and an alternative public opinion in an emergent postcolonial setting where media and print communication were as stunted as other aspects of these societies.[49] This commitment to the value of a broader public opinion and to its creation was a major innovation. Yet there were problems with New World's approach to opinion formation, premised as it was on the idea of a single homogeneous, literate, print-based public. New World's conception of public opinion contained the erroneous assumption that there was a single public in each of the islands, formed on the basis of an imagined commonality of experience, which could be appealed to through print communication.[50]

On the contrary, in the territories there really were two public opinions, arising from two dissimilar publics. One was the "traditional" public opinion created by a print- and newspaper-reading community. Despite comparatively high rates of literacy in the Caribbean in the early sixties, this nonetheless was a limited public, confined to those classes and strata who were linked by print communication. In Jamaica, this public was rather restricted in the early sixties, hampered by the underdevelopment of mass communication technology and by continuing pockets of illiteracy. This public therefore consisted mainly of those groups dependent on print communication and the discourse which emanated from it. Necessarily dominant in this public were the urban intelligentsia, the middle and upper classes, and those members of the peasantry and working class who had sufficient education and leisure time.

There was, however, a rival public opinion which emerged from face-to-face communication among the subordinate classes. This public, also created on the basis of an imagined commonality of experience, was formed on the basis less of print technology than of oral communication. The links binding this public together were necessarily less impersonal and involved not only face-to-face talk but also the *shared* imagination of folk memories, religious beliefs and practices, and other popular community experiences. This public was not united by print communication.

The boundary between the two publics was permeable. As print capitalism expanded in the former colonies and was complemented by educational policies designed to reduce the literacy gap, the gulf between the two narrowed. Indeed, in Jamaica as elsewhere, the popular public had its own local *literati*. Such persons traversed both "public worlds" and, as intermediaries, brought back from the domestic and international scene news otherwise inaccessible. At various communication sites (sidewalks, storefronts, churches, verandahs, yards, shops, country roads, bars), these news events would be mingled with rumor, existing beliefs, and folk inventions to produce a popular public opinion.

As for the dissemination of these opinions on a wider scale, this public, instead of relying exclusively on print communication, adopted a dramaturgic mode of communication involving popular argumentation, songs, festivals, religious rites, and dances, to both create and renew the "technologies" linking both publics. For example, by the mid-sixties the recording industry had become a new medium of communication for the popular urban public, as the aural model of communication found new life in the vogue of popular songs describing the pathos and anger of life in poor urban communities.

From this brief sketch of the two publics it should be apparent that the New World Group did not set out to address our popular public; nor is there any indication that they had considered means of reaching it. As dissident but tradition-bound intellectuals committed to the power of ideas and to their specialized forms of presentation (the article, the lecture, the occasional pamphlet, and the book), members of the group initially sought to do what they best knew how to do: through writing, convince the limited print-reading public that a correct understanding of local realities and the development of alternatives to those realities were urgently needed.

Despite the constraints imposed by the New World's medium of communication, the group's attempted renewal of public opinion constituted a momentous innovation. On the one hand, the group's commitment to a critique of Caribbean societies and to the making of an informed public represented a marked political advance in the region. Not only did New World's advocacy signal the development of the growing social responsibility of the university intelligentsia; its insistence on critique and public education also implied an ideological subversion of the status quo which, up to the late fifties, never had been systematically interrogated by Caribbean intellectuals. Consequently, ideological critique, the problematization of public policy, and the posing of alternatives not only opened up debate on pressing problems, but also exposed the weaknesses of governments in the territories while giving substance to public unease. Thus, while New World's proposals on public opinion and debate in retrospect might have seemed harmless and certainly nonrevolutionary to its critics, in the newly emergent Caribbean, with its uneasy and defensive regimes, both criticism and intellectual independence were acutely subversive, and governments recognized this. At a time when the dominant political parties in places like Jamaica were busy celebrating the advent of political independence and carrying in tow the bulk of the Caribbean peoples, the New World

Group and other nationalist intellectuals made the university a significant outpost guarding against self-congratulation and recognizing independence as a flawed achievement.

Especially the intellectuals' analysis of the problems in Caribbean political leadership and their theorizing on the causes of the region's economic dependence stood out starkly. From the start, their preoccupation with Caribbean economic dependence heralded the flowering of an indigenous scholarship devoted almost exclusively to economic theorizing and presentation of case studies. These writings, the bulk of them published in the mid-sixties and after, were enormously influential in the region, exerting a powerful influence within the university and on the educated stratum outside it.[51] As one critic of the group acknowledged, the economists exercised "a deep influence on the thinking of the students, university lecturers, high school teachers, journalists, publishers, artists, lawyers and others who wanted to develop a better understanding of West Indian society in order to contribute to its 'progressive' transformation."[52] Two consequences of this theoretical engagement on the part of the New World Group now can be identified. First, it led to the emergence of a specific Caribbean school of political economy devoted to the successive description of the dependent character of Caribbean economies. Second, despite the targeting of a limited public, their intervention offered prospects for a renewal of public opinion in an environment which was inhospitable to the expression of independent political ideas.

In light of this contribution to the reinvigoration of political life, the New World outlook was especially attractive to a section of the Caribbean intelligentsia whose members felt that their skills, training, and expertise deserved greater recognition by the state and society. This confluence in the views of the economists and other sections of the Caribbean intelligentsia disclosed a subterranean, parallel impulse at work in New World's agitation for an alternative medium of communication and for dissemination of "helpful facts" by academics. This was the existence, among the reformist branch of the educated bourgeoisie, of a technocratic ideology promoting fuller recognition of an excluded expert grouping—the New World Group and their sympathizers.

Even as the group ostensibly was examining Caribbean societies and subjecting their leaders to criticism, then, New World writers also tacitly were making a case for a section of the intelligentsia and other professional strata whose members longed for a place in the new societies commensurate with their advanced training. The problem was that many of these aspirants were cut off, if not excluded, from influencing public affairs by the lack of available vehicles or because the establishment ignored them. The New World Group's assertion of an independent role for intellectuals in opinion formation was, in part, an attempt to elevate the status of this segment of the professional class.

In making the case for this disenfranchised stratum, Lloyd Best, a Trinidad-born development economist and a founder of the group, noted that "the few people with whom we do communicate through our publications are themselves strategically placed to inform opinion in their roles as school teachers, civil servants, journalists, trade union leaders and other influential members of the community."[53] To emphasize this point, Best quoted a telling communication from abroad, written by a member of this stratum:

> There is among so many of us who were at U.W.I. as well as among hundreds of other West Indians abroad a tremendous amount of energy, talent, and a passionate longing to be of some effective use at home. But the channels into which all this can be directed are obscured by so many things that we continue to float around these alien cities frustrated, unmotivated and so useless, that we have little respect for ourselves left . . . [The New World Group has] . . . helped to revive in me a vision and now I will play my part by returning to the only place where I have a function.[54]

Behind the Caribbean economists' ostensibly disinterested appeal for an open discussion of society's problems lay the unfulfilled status ambition of a branch of the educated petty bourgeoisie. Yet it would be unfair and incomplete to suggest that the difficulties posed by New World's politics were simply a matter of class ambition. Far more problematical was the group's position on two major issues which had fundamental importance for progressive political forces in the mid-sixties: obstacles to political change in the Caribbean and strategies for overcoming them. New World's response to these two issues, typified by the views of Lloyd Best, the group's nominal leader and theoretician, put it at odds with competing radical trends in Jamaica.

Anomalies of Theoretical Activism: Rationality and Anti Politics

It will be recalled that, prior to the advent of the New World Group, activist organizations such the socialist UWC and the YSL already were on the Jamaican political scene. Their orientation was to build on the legacy of the Old Left by aligning themselves with popular movements in an attempt to change the country's political direction. For these groups, world imperialism and the collaboration of dominant native classes were fundamental obstacles to political change. For the UWC and the YSL, the way forward lay in political education of workers, peasants, and the unemployed, and in the direct participation of activists in popular struggles.

For its part, the New World Group set its face firmly against this trend. In rejecting involvement in the politics of labor, New World was emphatic: "This group is not a political organization in the sense of being committed to or contemplating any direct political action."[55] Led by Lloyd Best, who was a research fellow at UWI's Institute of Social and Economic Research in Jamaica, the group maintained that it would leave political activism to others, while pursuing a rigorous, objective critique of society on the basis of ideological nonalignment. In an early statement reflecting this outlook, the group declared in October 1965:

> Our radicalism was at no point to be identified with any of the going political doctrines, be it Socialism or Liberalism, Communism or Radicalism . . . Rather we want our radicalism to be interpreted as nothing more nor less than the sustained application of thought to the matters that concern us deeply.[56]

In a rebuff to their activist peers, Best and his colleagues maintained that obstacles to change were not due merely to imperialism and collaborating leaders. Outworn ideas, a deficiency of new thinking, and the absence of means for public discussion were just as critical, if not more important. An important strategy for change, for New World, involved the elaboration of new ideas and the development of solutions appropriate to the problems of the Caribbean. New World intellectuals would assume this responsibility and leave political activism to others. By late 1965, as socialist intellectuals and others sought ways to deepen their activism, New World, at its zenith, was arguing strongly for distinctly separate roles for political activists and intellectuals. Given this position, a nodal point in the politics of the anti–status quo movement was reached.

The tension occasioned by contrary political positions intensified in the ensuing years. Under attack from activists in the Young Socialist League and their sympathizers at Mona, and facing a similar situation at the University of Guyana, the Caribbean economists took refuge in a militant objectivism. Indeed, their commitment to sheer thought, eschewing all political ideologies and partisanships, survived increased pressure in 1966 on leftist intellectuals at Mona and even on members of the New World collective itself. Within three months of the declaration on the nature of the group's activism, the Jamaican state, as part of its policy of preventing subversion, seized the passport of George Beckford, a university economist and leading member of the New World group, as he prepared to leave in January for a trip abroad.[57] Four months later, Bertell Ollman, an American lecturer in political theory at the university and advisor to the Young Socialist League, was fired for challenging the university administration.[58] Finally, in October, Jay Mandle, another American lecturer, was forced to leave the country when the state refused to renew his visa. Paradoxically, at a time when these developments were beginning to generate political shifts, such as the growth of student activism at the Mona campus[59] and the opening of a rift between the regime and some of its key supporters,[60] the ideological line of the New World group remained firm.[61] Embattled, unable to ignore the seriousness of the foregoing events, and pressed by critics to stop being a "talk shop," the editors of the *Quarterly* responded in 1967 with a sharp counterattack in which they reaffirmed the original tenets of the movement and shifted the debate to the larger question of the role of reason in politics.

Writing for the group, Lloyd Best, in a statement justly famous for its controversial position on the proper role of the Caribbean intellectual, affirmed the need for "independent thought" and a commitment to *theoretical production*, in contrast to active political engagement.[62] Obviously addressing himself to the Young Socialist League and the intellectuals associated with it, Best decried their insistence on activism and identified their adherence to Marxism as a form of intellectual dependency. Criticizing the tendency to "uncritically take over political doctrines from others," Best asked; "Are we not now adopting one which glorifies the masses, the workers and the farmers?"[63] For him, the activism of the leftist intellectual was nothing but an expression of "cheap populism," another variety of dependence on external political models. Contrasting the technical orientation of intellectuals in the bureaucracy, who busied themselves with planning and administration, with that of the leftist intelligentsia, Best struck at the latter group. This "other half," he wrote, "is clamouring to lead the people. Like so many brave Bustamantes, their burning ambition is to march before the masses. Confronted with the questions as to how, where, and when, their answer is a stony silence. They too, one fears, are merely idling their resources away in impractical rhetoric."[64] By associating this "rhetoric" with European Marxism, Best identified several of its substantive limitations in both theory and practice, and implied that radicals' dependence on Marxism was just as slavish as the uncritical reliance on liberal capitalist ideas.[65]

Since all external ideologies were foreign imports which placed limitations on the emergence of "independent Caribbean thought," this outlook resulted in a curious intellectual nonalignment which seemed to see no substantive difference between liberal and Marxist ideas. To accept either uncritically, Best seemed to argue, was to submit to the hegemony of a largely irrelevant outside intellectual force. It was not clear from Best's polemics what the new political theory he had in mind for the Caribbean would look like, since he avoided a discussion of its pedigree. On closer examination, it appears that Best was trying to articulate not a new political theory, but rather the *political conditions* for its emergence. In short, Best was alluding to a type of intellectual creativity which would end what the group regarded as mimicry of the "plantation mind."

In order to facilitate this creativity, Best thought that the Caribbean intellectual had to meet four conditions: (1) remain aloof from established ideologies; (2) examine Caribbean societies in their specificity; (3) commit themselves to theorizing; and (4) avoid political activism. On the last two, Best was particularly insistent. Noting that "action in the field . . . presupposes theory," he opined that, while others might become politically engaged, the role of the Caribbean intellectual was to produce indigenous theoretical knowledge in order to bring about a change in social relations. Insisting on this priority of local knowledge, Best argued that "if we devoted our attention to the production of books, pamphlets and journals, and if we did it well, that would be plenty. The political organizers might then arise with something to say—at least with something they did not simply fudge from *Monthly Review* or borrow from the (late) Jules Dubois."[66] Given this restrictive view, it is not surprising that Best could assert without apology that "social change in the Caribbean has to and can only begin in the minds of Caribbean men."[67] Determined to maintain this divide between "disinterested" theoreticians and committed activists, yet impelled to answer his critics, Best issued the slogan which captured the idealism of the group: "Thought is the action for us."[68]

This startling assertion disclosed an underlying, partially articulated concern in Best's political ideas: the role of reason in politics and the faulty presuppositions of the radicals' alternative model of government. The former concern was expressed in Best's attempt to protect intellectual inquiry from the pressure of "politics," which he believed existed outside the academy and inevitably was injurious to the pursuit of knowledge. As he subsequently argued in a significant elaboration of this idea, a clear demarcation existed between the "intellectual system" and political activity.[69] In the former, there was unrestrained discourse, freedom of inquiry, resolution of differences through persuasion and reason, and a mutual commitment to maintaining these norms in order to facilitate the production of knowledge. In the latter, there was only the search for political power, with its temptation to mobilize masses for narrow "elite" interests and to censor those who speak critically.

Direct political engagement by the intellectual, then, threatened the search for knowledge. Indeed, for Best, a fusion of the two activities inevitably corrupted the "intellectual system," since the risks of politics would silence dissidents and violate the norms of the community, which emphasized the right to articulate deviant ideas. Besides, in Best's view, active engagement by New World would tend to eliminate "person-to-person conversations" and substitute organizational routines.[70] The civility of interaction, the handling of disagreements, and the protocols of knowledge-generating debate would, in Best's view, be ruined by the cut and thrust of political engagement. Consistent with these principles, Best saw New World as an organizational experiment in "how democratically to treat with conflicting points of view, thereby avoiding the 'arrogance of the left.'"[71] Because of these dangers, Best insisted that New World remain an *intellectual* rather than a political movement. While political engagement would be necessary, that would not be the burden of the group, since it would devote itself to research and development of ideas. In the face of mounting criticisms of the group's lack of a politics, Best answered by advocating the disassociation of the intellectual from organized politics in the interest of knowledge, and he proposed that activist tendencies be displaced by theoretical practice.

Several aspects of these views need comment here. One is that Best's position was not without merit. His insistence on the development of theory, and his call for the examination of Caribbean societies in their specificity were important contributions to the flowering of an indigenous intellectual tradition in the region. His demand for research agendas which problematized existing Caribbean societies was a distinct marker in the advent of a national and regional scholarship whose evolution continues to this day. Furthermore, despite the scorn heaped on it by critics, Best's advocacy of ideas over action was not the straightforward case of idealism they portrayed it to be. Though plainly riddled with contradictions, his ideas on the relationship between theory and practice possessed a "rational kernel." That is, Best's understanding actually was a flawed recognition of the relatively autonomous role that theory must play in developing an understanding of any society. As such, Best can be read as insisting on the determinate role of theoretical production in a scientific understanding of society and in its possible change.

In his view, this role depends partly on the ability of theoretical workers to pursue projects and ideas without the constraints of following the "line" of political organizations and ideologies. Although his formulation was unmistakably polemical and obviously tainted by anti-Marxism, Best's injunction against the "borrowed construct," when viewed in the context of his agenda for critical thought, must be seen as a corrective to the tendency among Caribbean intellectuals to forget the specificity of their societies by employing inapplicable concepts from Marxism and Western social science. It is also important to note that Best did not reject the necessity of political activism and partisanship. He clearly reserved a role for activism in a project for social change involving both academics and political organizers, but he insisted that the university intelligentsia, and specifically New World members, should not organize social movements.[72]

Last, the binary "activism-nonactivism" formulation of the debate obscured Best's deeper concern for reason in politics and his interest in the political model for a new society. For example, in 1967 Best raised the following important questions: What are the general social and political preconditions of free inquiry? How should movements handle dissension and thus stay the murderous hand of power when disagreements surface? What should the new society do to restrain bureaucratization? And, finally, what principles should govern the political and ideological alignment of Third World states? Regrettably, in the heat of polemical exchanges and binary formulations, these vital, knotty issues failed to get the hearing they deserved.[73]

Notwithstanding New World's salutary appreciation of the nature of and conditions for intellectual activity, this argument for divorcing the intelligentsia from political activism reflected several illusions which permeated the New World movement's outlook. One of these was the idea that intellectuals' interests were confined solely to the search for knowledge and the development of theories. By portraying the intellectual as an objective figure above the fray, without an interest in political outcomes, the group in effect denied intellectuals the possibility of active political engagement in the struggles of the Caribbean peoples. While New World held that its ostensible goal was to challenge the status quo with new ideas, its self-imposed ban on activism among the Jamaican people actually reduced the prospect of an effective challenge to the status quo. If New World had a deeper understanding of the sources of conflicts and obstacles to change than other groups possessed, then a need for some political activity to remove these obstacles was implied. Merely proposing agendas for avoiding intellectual dependency and warning of the dangers of political engagement while an untenable political situation unfolded was bound to invite criticisms of the group's motives. New World thus found itself in the unenviable position of adopting an uncertain opposition to the status quo, while disapproving of others' attempts to challenge it.

This contradiction was a consequence of the reformist nature of the New World movement, for, although it spoke the language of social change, in rejecting activism and bypassing the popular public it suggested that it actually wanted to bring about this change from above.

Furthermore, despite its contention that it was concerned simply with ideas, the group *was* preoccupied with political power, but primarily in order to advantage those experts whose talents were neglected by the new men in power. Behind the cry for new ideas and the convening of a new public lay the educated petty bourgeoisie's search for a more prominent role in national affairs. While waving an anti-elitist banner and evoking the prospect of a more democratic Caribbean, the politics of the New World movement also entailed the pursuit of a narrow, elitist class project. As events ultimately demonstrated, by the late sixties the unnoticed provinciality in Lloyd Best's ideas had become so thoroughgoing that eventually it led to an open split. Thus a major surprise in New World's politics was that, despite its emergence in the name of progress, its demise began on a conservative and romantic note.

This note was evident in Best's formal withdrawal from the group in November 1968, in order to pursue a model of community restoration based on the creation of a small-scale political unit in which dialogue and face-to-face communication could take place without rancor. This search for an older form of community, undisturbed by the winds of politics and the turbulence of social change, disclosed an abiding impulse in Best's ideas: retreat from a changing, homogenizing global system which sought to form all localities and peoples in its image.

In these terms, Best's criticisms of bureaucratization revealed not so much a concern for protecting popular participation against an overarching bureaucracy, as a revulsion against the impersonality of large organizational units. A similar romanticism was evident in his perspective on the university and intellectuals. Whereas his claims for their autonomy represented a useful balance to the political pressures of the Left and the government, Best exaggerated this view to mean that neither the university nor intellectuals were to become involved in the conflicts of a class-divided society. The university and intellectual work ultimately became means to *escape* from both the contest of ideologies and the cut and thrust of politics.

Finally, the romanticism in Best's outlook stamped New World thought with a conservatism which was expressed most clearly in its conception of politics. Not only was the latter viewed as a direct threat to intellectual work, but also it was seen as a practice which simply replaced one form of domination with another. Hence, no qualitative distinctions could be drawn between different regimes, since in New World's view, political change simply involved the creation of new orthodoxies and the replacement of one venal elite with another.[74] Given this pessimistic conception of politics, in which the future promised only the permanence of domination, it is not surprising that the New World movement had little sympathy for the socialist Left, and imagined itself a selfless purveyor of dissenting opinion against an ever-renewing autocracy.

Throughout the remainder of 1967, and well into the following year, the New World Group pressed on with its project of stimulating articulate public opinion through pamphleteering, seminars, teach-ins, and public forums. Although a few of these activities elicited favorable public support, for the most part they tended to reinforce the very intra-elite dialogue the movement ostensibly wanted to abolish. The public events it sponsored, far from triggering a sense of national urgency and crisis, degenerated into sterile exchanges. As the dissatisfied chairman of the group observed in his 1968 report, the result was an absence of lay participation in these discussions, as "economists from the University argued with government economists, representatives of the business community and of the sugar interests, about the structure of the economy, in a way that left the population apparently unmoved."[75] The larger population isolated from the university intelligentsia and untouched by the preoccupations of the New World Group, continued in its traditional relations and beliefs. The militant Kingston poor, and particularly the Rastafarians, continued their opposition through the articulation of a black nationalist ideology of indigenous vintage. Their adoption of "culture" as a basis of conflict eventually captured the attention of a lone intellectual — an African historian at the university — whose subsequent intervention on behalf of the urban poor sent shock waves through the society. We turn next to an examination of these events.

CHAPTER 7

The Advent of Black Power and the State's Reaction

By the end of 1967, the Jamaican state had confronted a variety of political and ideological challenges. These challenges had been expressed in the most varied ways: as black nationalism and social banditry among the urban unemployed, as restiveness among workers, in a search for a political role among parts of the university intelligentsia, and in groping attempts by political activists to resurrect a socialists tradition. These anti–status quo tendencies were remarkable in that they converged on the political scene in the 1962–67 period. For example, the advent of a militant urban Rastafarianism in the early sixties was matched by the emergence of both the Unemployed Workers' Council and the Young Socialist League; concurrently, 1964 saw the onset of rebel youth outlawry; the latter's ascent to public awareness coincided with the advent of the New World Group. If we include the sprouting in December 1967 of a Kingston group calling itself the Jamaica Council for Human Rights (JCHR), then it is evident that no fewer than four distinct oppositional formations had surfaced alongside a spontaneous and irreverent upsurge among sections of the militant urban poor.

Lending additional significance to the conjunction of these forces in the same period is the fact that they appeared at precisely the moment in which the upper classes were attempting to consolidate their moral and political leadership. The convergence of these opposition groups, having diverse class components and ideologies, represented the advent of a popular-democratic movement in a context where the dominant ideology had only shakily been established. Rastafarian black consciousness, rude-boy nihilism, UWC-YSL socialism, and New World nationalism all comprised an emergent field of ideological opposition and practices which cumulatively signified a challenge to the dominant classes. By late 1967, the JLP found itself engaged on several ideological fronts, trying to shore up a "toppling hegemony" and attempting to rule through a variety of restrictive measures.

Much of the force of the regime's ideological offensive and preemptive edicts was directed at the Rastafarians. This was due to the corrosive effect their radical outlook had on the dominant political ideology and to the apparent readiness of a few Rastafarians to take up arms against the regime. In addition, Rastafarian ideology, with its messianic impulse and religious allusions, had particular resonance among the urban unemployed. As a major current in the native peasant resistance tradition, Rastafarian ideology retained many of the rituals in the "religions of the oppressed." For instance, it commingled biblical themes of suffering and redemption with vociferous protest against the black man's oppressed status in Jamaica. This ideology appropriated the travail of the biblical Jews, transforming it into a metaphor for the radical oppression of blacks, and even insisted that blacks *were* in fact the biblical Jews.[1] This identification of the black poor with a mythic and embattled biblical existence conformed to what might be called the racial domestication of prophesy.

In light of this religious motif, with its reciprocal allusions to an oppressive existence both mythic and real, it is not surprising that Rastafarian ideology exerted an influence on those elements of the peasantry that had been forced into the urban enclaves. As Ken Post reminds us, the Jamaican peasants long had been accustomed to seeking comfort by reading their Bibles and searching it for prophecies that would corroborate real world events.[2] Consequently, Rastafarianism, which attempted to discover confirming evidence of this-worldly occurrences through a textual interrogation of the Bible, was highly intelligible to the former peasants who were now part of the destitute urban population. This particular aspect of Rastafarianism, then, conformed to a mode of ideological defense which sections of the urban poor long had adopted to account for their oppressed condition.

Despite an apparent convergence in the outlook of Rastafarians and other sections of the urban poor, Rastafarian ideology went beyond merely displacing oppression onto a religious plane. Because of its assimilation of the cultural elements in Marcus Garvey's black nationalism — a nationalism that had exerted tremendous influence on broad sections of black Jamaicans in the twenties and thirties — Rastafarian ideology transcended a traditional religious response and became distinctive in its own right. The Rastafarians, while using a biblical discourse, had gone beyond the constraints of a simple spiritualist displacement to claim an African nationality. This deeply-felt identification with an African heritage, by way of such Garveyite themes as racial pride and appreciation of African civilization, stamped Rastafarian ideology with a distinctiveness that went beyond its affiliation with traditional religious forms of peasant protest against oppression. Consequently, by the mid-sixties, the introduction of a politically-charged black nationalism, using a religious idiom familiar to the lower strata, enabled the Rastafarians to stimulate popular remembrances and resentments in a way that others in the society could not.

This fealty to popular memories and to the "hailing" of the lower classes in racial terms put the Rastafarians in an enormously advantageous position in the postcolonial period, for it allowed them effectively to dominate the ideological terrain of popular protest. Indeed, by appropriating this ground, Rastafarian ideology became "national" in its social character, since it encapsulated the basic contradictions faced by the majority of poor blacks. Furthermore, by embodying the yearnings of the subordinate classes in both the form and the content of their discourse, the Rastafarians by late 1967 had become the hegemonic fraction among the opposition forces. No other ideology or group appeared capable of competing with them. As for the Left, although the UWC and YSL fought in their different ways for a socialist renewal, they were hampered by severe constraints. These included a hostile anticommunist environment, bourgeois leadership of the working class, and the recurring tendency for leftwing middle-class opposition to become absorbed within the PNP.

Equally important were deficiencies within the Left which reduced the influence of socialist ideology. Many early postcolonial exponents of socialism were politically underdeveloped. They had an uneven grasp of Marxist theory and politics, and their knowledge of the social history of the laboring classes was limited. In addition, because of ruptures and vicissitudes in the native socialist tradition between 1934 and 1962, it bequeathed the Left little in the way of theory which could be used to respond to the protest that surfaced in the sixties. This period therefore found leftists unprepared to respond creatively to the upsurge in black consciousness. Thrown back on their own resources, these socialists generally adhered to a pristine worker's ideology which glossed over and demoted the significance of the nationalist content within the Rastafarian protest. Furthermore, the overwhelming attention given to rectifying PNP past "betrayals" deflected the Left from involvement in the epic conflict between the ideology of the Rastafarians and that of the bourgeoisie. As a result, the Left was unable to contribute to the important class-rooted ideological "debate" on culture and identity, as the issue of the ideological construction of the Jamaican people was fought out.

This conflict between black nationalism and Exceptionalism revealed an important divide between two competing conceptions of "the people." One was based on the project of the dominant classes, which sought to construct the Jamaican people as law-abiding, deferential, and exceptional. This ideology attempted to represent the subordinate classes purely in the image of the native middle and upper classes, whose political orientation toward colonial subordination was defined largely by accommodation and conformism. The other antagonistic conception of "the people" hailed them as an *oppressed race* and as *African exiles* in a strange land, held there in captivity by black agents of a marauding white Europe. Rastafarian ideology therefore recruited "the people" in explicitly racial terms. Furthermore, in the Rastafarians' philosophy, blacks were not really Jamaicans — only *displaced Africans* who one day would be repatriated to the Continent.

On the one hand, this Garveyite hailing of the people as an oppressed race and as Africans in the diaspora, with obligations to a distant continent, naturally created serious problems for Jamaican leaders; they faced the twin tasks of instilling loyalty to the *territorial* unit, Jamaica, and winning popular allegiance to Exceptionalism. On the other hand, the appeal to race in Rastafarian ideology was not without its difficulties for other anti–status quo forces.

As we have seen, Rastafarian ideology was enigmatic. It challenged existing class inequalities by hailing the subordinate classes on the basis of their racial origins and expressed an anti-imperialism with its allusions to a historic antagonism between black Africa and the white West. These features of Rastafarian ideology gave it a progressive character and allowed the Left to find an identity of interest between labor's struggles and those of the urban unemployed.

At the same time, however, tendencies in Rastafarian ideology would confound radical political activists. These included: the Rastafarians' rejections of involvement in the island's political life; their insistence on repatriation; and their reliance on biblical forecasts to account for the ultimate resolution of unfolding events. To be sure, there were many Rastafarians who, because they held to traditional tenets and engaged in various forms of political activism, did not fit into this category. In the early to mid-sixties, however, they were the exceptions, a fact which allows us to identify the general tendencies above as characteristic of the movement as a whole.[3] In this respect, the elements characteristic of modal Rastafarian ideology differed significantly from conceptions held by other radical anti–status quo forces.

For example, the Rastafarians' emphasis on race consciousness and their interest in and knowledge of an ancestral Africa were matters which did not agitate activists in the UWC, the YSL, and the New World Group. For example, the latter's concern pertained to expanding the range of public opinion and describing the island's economic dependence in a capitalist world. This New World ideology could therefore be described as nationalist. As we have suggested, however, this was an economic nationalism that did not deal with cultural questions. Indeed, although the New World group was sharpy critical of the prior generation of nationalist politicians, intellectuals in this dissident movement shared with their nemeses a cultural alienation from the Jamaican masses and limited knowledge of their traditions. This shared impoverishment meant that, in addition to their other debilities, intellectuals in the New World movement were not in a position to promote black nationalism. Thus, where the Rastafarians drew attention to race and culture, both in identity formation and in the reproduction of class power, these themes found no echoes in New World's ideology.

This lacuna points to a phenomenon unique in the dissident movement: the parceling out of anti-status quo themes among groups, each of which articulated specific ideological fragments or their variants in a hermetic universe. If we again compare the Rastafarians and the New World Group, we notice that each articulated a distinct brand of nationalism. On the one hand, the black nationalism of the Rastafarians invoked a return to the past and tied this to appeals for racial solidarity. On the other hand, the nationalism of the New World Group opposed foreign control of the economy and based its appeal on a defense of national sovereignty. Although these competing ideologies echoed each other in their political critiques, they nonetheless articulated distinct themes, and their exponents operated in separate spheres.

This noncomplementarity similarly was evident in the ways in which various dissident groups conceived of politics. Socialists and New World activists subscribed to a modern conception. That is, they shared the idea of progress and challenged the status quo on the basis not of traditional values but rather of a belief in agency and voluntarism in politics. In this context, political mobilization and the application of secular social science theory to political problems broadly defined the approach of radical intellectuals. For their part, Rastafarians and elements of the urban poor took a largely rejectionist stance toward the status quo, which tempered agency and organization. In the case of the Rastafarians, many among them saw politics as a corrupting, contaminative activity. Given the powerful spiritualist impulse and the mystical orientation of this ideology, agency was tempered by the belief that unfolding political events represented divinely ordained plans. Change therefore required not so much the promethean interventionism of the intellectuals, but rather a stoic patience or vigilant watchfulness to see the unfolding of events foretold.

By the latter part of 1967, these rival nationalism and cosmologies, each with its attached social forces, evolved separately — each unable to encapsulate the other. To expand on the metaphor: it was as if these social forces were in the same solar system but with different and distant orbital paths. Since none of these formations possessed the means to change its orbit to attract the others, the impasse had to await developments which would nudge each "planet" into a closer, "attractive" orbit. In political terms, the impasse had to await circumstances which would impel the groups to reconcile differences and act in unison against a common adversary. The event facilitating this development was the government's barring of a lecturer who had made extensive contact with the Rastafarians. Equally important in moving both groups closer was the existence, at the international level, of a political crisis which put the metropolitan bourgeoisies on the defensive against popular challenges to their authority. The confluence of domestic and international events prepared the ground for the October 1968 riot in Jamaica, and with it, the onset of a Black Power movement in the Caribbean.

Black Power in Jamaica

The year 1968 brought no relief to the JLP, which continued to face mounting opposition. A new tack was taken by a section of the opposition, when a small group of lawyers founded an organization called the Jamaica Council for Human Rights (JCHR). Among the founding members was Dennis Daley, former PNP member and YSL activist.[4] Aware of the intimidation experienced by YSL members over the years and particularly concerned about the middle class's failure vigorously to defend civil liberties, Daley and others in the JCHR devoted themselves to the legal defense of basic rights. January of the new year thus found a section of the opposition introducing human rights as an issue in the conflict.[5] This theme quickly was picked up by others in an apparent attempt to isolate the regime, which was in the awkward position of chairing the United Nations committee that designated 1968 as the year of human rights. Notwithstanding its role in the international agency, the JLP continued pursuing its deterrent policies.

Beginning in January 1968, the government again targeted Claudius Henry, the ubiquitous "Repairer of the Breach." It will be recalled that Henry was the Rastafarian leader arrested in 1963 for his militant activities in Kingston. Now he apparently had organized his followers into a body called the New Creation Peacemakers Association (NCPA), with branches in Kingston, Kemps Hill in the Parish of Clarendon, and Brae's River in the parish of Saint Elizabeth. On 23 January, the riot police conducted a massive raid on the NCPA.[6] This was followed by similar raids on 5 May and 3 June, in which prohibited literature was seized.[7] Less than three weeks following this last raid, the regime imposed a ban on literature authored by Afro-American activists Malcolm X and Stokely Carmichael. This increased action against Henry's group and the extension of the list of "undesirable publications" to include literature by activists in the United States' black revolt signaled the regime's heightened sense of vulnerability in a turbulent domestic and international period.

After all, in this period between January and June 1968, the metropolitan countries themselves were experiencing an unprecedented challenge to the authority of their governments. Stimulated by widespread opposition to United States intervention in Vietnam, a protest movement precipitated a major crisis within the cultural and political institutions of the industrialized nations. This crisis reached its height with the students' revolt in the Western capitals during the months of March and April, and it culminated in the near-collapse of the French state in May. However, it was the U.S. black revolt which proved decisive in the Jamaican context; ironically, the spark that accelerated radical developments in the island came from neither Cuban nor Soviet influence but from political developments in a friendly country. As we have pointed out, throughout the early postcolonial years, the JLP tried to enforce a quarantine against both communist and black nationalist ideological imports. Until 1967, this prohibition had been very effective in isolating the Jamaican people from the ideological influence of the Cuban Revolution and the U.S. black revolt. By 1968, it was becoming more difficult to contain the influence of the Afro-American struggle for social justice. The black rebellion in American cities in the summer of 1967 already had centered international attention—and especially the attention of the black diaspora—on the racial crisis in the U.S.

Given its proximity to the American mainland, as well as its extensive commercial and communications links with the U.S., Jamaica was fully exposed to developments there. We can safely assume, because of the extensive air travel between the island and the American mainland, that many Jamaicans brought back personal accounts of this important challenge to U.S. racism. Compounding the difficulties created by this exposure to developments in the U.S., the Jamaican government's ban on the literature and leading personalities of the American Black Power movement called attention to the Afro-American struggle. Because of an ever-enlarging censorship, those in the island who wanted to read about that struggle were hampered in examining primary sources, and those who tried to enter the island with this literature no doubt were relieved of it at the major ports of entry. However, in the context of the island's openness to North American cultural trends, this censorship was futile. Where widely-available broadcast news accounts and the importation of U.S. newspapers and magazines did not undermine the quarantine, avid interest in the subject among the Jamaican public undoubtedly made the policy unenforceable.

An indication of the growing influence in the island of the U.S. black revolt came with initial stirrings among students at the University of the West Indies. There, in February 1968, the Guild of Undergraduates expressed solidarity with the U.S. black struggle by donating monies to the Student Nonviolent Coordinating Committee (SNCC) "to assist it in its struggle against U.S. racism."[8] This action hinted at a growing development in the political awareness of the UWI students, who generally had been known as politically apathetic and careerist in orientation. Several antecedent developments on the international and domestic fronts had caused a few students to bestir themselves to engage in limited forms of protest. In fact, April 1960 had found them engaging in an anti-apartheid rally in Kingston, led by Philip Sherlock, acting principal at the University College of the West Indies.[9]

By the end of 1964, there had been a discernable increase in activism among the UWI undergraduates. In November, for example, they quietly demonstrated on the campus against the Ian Smith regime in Rhodesia. The following year they protested Smith's Unilateral Declaration of Independence, with a petition to Britian signed by some six hundred students.[10] Two years later, students were protesting the university's dismissal of an American lecturer, Bertell Ollman, and criticizing the vice-chancellor for running a "militaristic" institution and failing to resist government pressures on the university.[11] Students' impatience with Vice-Chancellor Sherlock's refusal to appoint a committee to examine the matter put them in direct confrontation with the top administrator at the university. On 18 May 1966, four days after Ollman's dismissal, the self-styled "May 18th Movement" blocked the UWI Registry, locking in the vice-chancellor and other university personnel for some five hours.[12] Although this protest failed to get Ollman reinstated, it suggested that a minority among the students had moved, since 1960, beyond an exclusive preoccupation with academic work to engage in limited forms of political activism.[13]

The students' 1968 donation of monies to the American Black Power movement confirmed an intermittent but increasing involvement in political activity. At the same time, this action demonstrated that the U.S. racial crisis was being felt in the island, as social forces not previously concerned with U.S. racial issues moved toward closer identification with it. In their political evolution on these issues, the students received significant support from Walter Rodney, a young Guyanese lecturer in African history.

Having graduated from UWI, Rodney taught in Africa for some eighteen months and returned to the island in January 1968 to take up a teaching post. Within weeks of his arrival, he began giving public lectures at the university. In some of these talks, he discussed facets of African civilization, with particular emphasis on the achievements and the creativity of the African peoples. Although his talks focused on Africa's past, extensively treating Ethiopia's history and that of the ancient African kingdoms and empires, what distinguished Rodney's approach was his attempt to show the *contemporary significance* of African history.[14] His lectures stressed the connection between an accurate knowledge of Africa's history and the use of that knowledge as "a weapon in our struggle."[15] Similarly, he emphasized how inevitable it was that, in opposing oppression, blacks would resist by affirming their racial identity. In these lectures and public talks, then, Rodney boldly linked the cultural affirmation of blacks and their *political* liberation.

This approach to African history undoubtedly related to the political crisis gripping the country, since Rodney was expressing an idea already held by the Rastafarians: that blacks in Jamaica had an African heritage and could find, in an undistorted African history, knowledge which could be used to recover their own history in the diaspora. Rodney asserted that the results of this discovery would be a mental liberation and a new sense of dignity and self-respect among blacks.

Equally important was Rodney's understanding that this new consciousness entailed a reexamination of the historical experience of blacks in Jamaica and an appraisal of their *current* condition. For Rodney, the reexamination of African history was tied directly to scrutiny of the black experience in Jamaica. It was this novel treatment of the relationship between African history and the Jamaican experience, as well as his lectures on Black Power, that earned Rodney the students' respect and gave him a following among them.

For many students, Rodney's formulation must have offered a way out of the crisis of identity and alienation occasioned by the island's cultural framework and by their experience at the university. By discussing the cultural and political significance of African history for blacks, Rodney provided intellectual and moral support to those inside the academy who were opposed to the status quo but were unsure about how to convert this opposition into political activity. Rodney's talks on African history amounted to the initiation of a process whereby the attention of students and sections of the university intelligentsia was turned toward an appreciation of the role of *cultural resistance* in political struggle.

As if to underline the importance of this issue, Rodney undertook a major initiative. After work, he left the sedate suburban environs of the Mona campus to make contact with the Rastafarians and other strata of the urban poor—the social groups whose ideologies and practices embodied some of the ideas being taught by Rodney at the university.[16] Some Sundays, for example, found him discussing aspects of African history in working-class districts in Kingston.[17] On other occasions, he could be found at workers' sports clubs and among the unemployed in the ghettos of West Kingston, sharing with residents his ideas on African history and culture and on their connection with the contemporary Jamaican situation. Undoubtedly, his criticism of the Jamaican government encountered a highly receptive audience, since not only the Rastafarians were to be found here in some density, but also other militant layers of the unemployed. This contact with the urban poor broke new ground, because it was the first time that a member of the radical university intelligentsia became directly involved with that sector of the population which was most opposed to the regime. Prior to this, the extent of the radical intelligentsia's contact with either the urban unemployed or the laboring classes had been negligible.

For example, even though the New World Group represented the dominant expression of discontent among academics, it had assigned itself a highly circumscribed role as an agency for the dissemination of ideas and as sponsor of academic debates on public policy.[18] By the group's own admission, however, most of these forums — except for the teach-in on the British invasion of Anguilla,[19] which was attended by some five hundred persons and broadcast live on radio — tended to be formal presentations lacking the immediacy or the political conclusions appropriate in dealing with unfolding developments. As the chairman of the group noted in his 1968 report, these forums failed to draw radical conclusions and were, for the most part, "lacking in relevance."[20] With the possible exception of members of the Young Socialist League who belonged to the UWI Area Council and were involved in the practical activities of the league, members of the radical intelligentsia kept their distance from the masses and confined themselves to teaching and research.

By combining his classroom teaching with personal contact and discussion with popular sectors, Rodney not only surmounted the intellectuals' isolation by fusing theory and practice, but he also served notice that the knowlege of the intellectual could and would be put at the disposal of the masses. By early April, this voluntarism quickened, with the news from the U.S. that Dr. Martin Luther King, the civil rights leader, had been slain. This news was received with shock and dismay by Jamaicans familiar with King's nonviolent campaign. That King, who was highly regarded by all sectors of Jamaican society, should have met a violent death for peacefully organizing to attain civil rights for U.S. blacks, undoubtedly caused many Jamaicans to reflect on racism in the U.S. and on the violence inflicted on blacks trying to achieve political rights. Local dismay at this turn of events in the U.S., coupled with the news of the riots ensuing in that country between 4 and 11 April brought home to Jamaicans in a dramatic way the realities of

American racism and the black protest against it. At this juncture, Rodney, whose activities apparently had come to the attention of the authorities,[21] began addressing the politics of the U.S. Black Power movement and the meaning of Black Power for the West Indies.

In a public lecture on the campus, he reviewed the significance of Black Power in its global context.[22] In this talk, he offered the view that there was a correlation between color and power in the contemporary world. He maintained that blacks and other nonwhites were victims in an "imperialist world" dominated by whites and that, in this world, "black people" were relegated to a position of inferiority, poverty, and power-lessness. The phenomenon of the U.S. Black Power movement, he ex-plained, was a necessary reaction by Afro-Americans to their exclu-sion from power and their subjection to violence. On this latter subject, Rodney took care to distance himself from those who held that the resort to violence by blacks was "unjustified morally" because it was just as harmful in its consequences as the violence exercised against them. In rejecting this position, which saw an identity between the violence of the oppressed and that of the oppressor, Rodney maintained that "vio-lence aimed at the recovery of human dignity and at equality cannot be judged by the same yardstick as violence aimed at the maintenance of discrimination and oppression."[23]

But Rodney's perspective on black power went beyond defending the exercise of violence by the oppressed. He also saw the U.S. black revolt as only one expression of a larger worldwide revolt by nonblacks against a "white imperialist world."[24] Although the contemporary crisis had manifested itself in the form of a global conflict between the "black" Afro-Asian bloc and the white Euro-American world, for Rodney the conflict simultaneously pitted the rich white capitalist nations against the poor "black" underdeveloped world. This understanding informed his view that the "association of wealth with whites, and poverty with blacks is not accidental. It is the nature of the imperialist relationship that enriches the metropolis at the expense of the colony, i.e., it makes the whites richer and the blacks poorer."[25] In this talk, Rodney con-ceived of Black Power as more than just the expression of a racial con-flict between blacks and whites in the U.S. Rather, the racial upsurge in the U.S. was a manifestation of a broader international struggle by "nonwhites" against their subordination in a capitalist world. And the Black Power movement was to be understood as a means of challeng-ing blacks' position in a global system of class and racial stratification which kept "nonwhites" politically powerless and culturally subordinate.

Following this talk on Black Power in general, Rodney delivered another lecture, this time on the meaning of Black Power for the West Indies.[26] In this talk, he reviewed the experience of slavery and rebellion in the region and appraised the legacy of racial inferiority among the blacks. In addition, he drew attention to the past exploitation of East Indians who were brought to the islands as indentured laborers. Rodney maintained that they, too, had been denied power and so necessarily formed part of the movement for Black Power.[27] For Rodney, then, the two most exploited racial groups in the West Indies were the black majority and the East Indians.

Concerning the place of the coloreds—the group of mixed racial ancestry in the West Indies—Rodney had this to say:

> The West Indian brown man is characterized by ambiguity and ambivalence. He has in the past identified with the black masses when it suited his interests, and at the present time some browns are in the forefront of the movement towards black consciousness; but the vast majority have fallen to the bribes of white imperialism, often outdoing the whites in their hatred and oppression of blacks.[28]

This dialectical view of the coloreds showed Rodney's appreciation of their indeterminate social character and allowed him to conclude that they were not to be written off, since "nothing in the West Indian experience . . . suggests that browns are unacceptable when they choose to identify with blacks."[29] He was less sanguine, however, about the Europeans, Chinese, and Syrians, whom he regarded as members of the dominant group in the region. It is not surprising that Rodney's remarks on the meaning of Black Power in the West Indies were made with these latter groups in mind.

For example, Rodney argued that in Jamaica, the blacks were victims of the myth of multiracialism, because, even though they comprised the majority group, they were being exploited by these ethnic minorities whose cultural status in the society was elevated above Jamaicans of African descent. Calling for an end to this economic and cultural subordination, Rodeny asserted that Jamaica should be acknowledged as a "black society where Africans predominate." In general, Black Power in the West Indies meant the creation of a society in which the blacks were self-determining—culturally, politically, and economically. As Rodney defined it, Black Power in the West Indies meant "three closely related things: the break with imperialism which is historically white racist; the assumption of power by the black masses in the islands; [and] the cultural reconstruction of the society in the image of the blacks."[30] At the same time, Rodney cautioned that Black Power had nothing to do with "racial intolerance" and was not an attempt to replace white racism with "black supremacy." Rather, the new society would have room for its ethnic minorities, who would enjoy *"the basic rights of all individuals* but [have] no privileges to exploit Africans."[31]

These were controversial ideas in a society in which the dominant classes already were unsettled by the postindependence upsurge in black nationalism. In the racially-neutered ideology of these classes, it was difficult to "think" the concept "Black Power" as it was defined by Rodney.[32] For them, open promotion of the outlook of any one racial group was anathema. Victor Grant, the attorney general, expressed this view best when he asserted that "we shall have *neither* white power nor black power."[33] Given this insistence on a racially neutered definition of "Jamaican-ness," the Guyanese historian's political intervention and revivifying of the Black Power concept — no matter how obvious its inclusion of non-African sectors of the population — was bound to ruffle the cultural sensibilities of the dominant groups.

Not only was Rodney expounding his ideas at the university and associating with the unemployed and working poor, but, to make matters worse, because of Rodney's activities, an emerging alliance was being fashioned among students, the intelligentsia, and sections of the urban unemployed. Indeed, sections of the urban unemployed were becoming frequent visitors to the campus, invited by Rodney to attend public lectures and discussions on Black Power. In fact, within four months of his arrival, the student publication *Scope* was reporting that a "Black Power Movement" had been formed on the campus.[34]

From the JLP's standpoint, the situation was threatening to get out of hand. Unlike earlier expressions of race consciousness among the urban lower class, whose members could be dismissed as "hooligans" and "troublemakers," this latest expression of black consciousness came from a traditionally admired stratum — the educated class. The growing alliance among intellectuals, students, and the unemployed shattered the official perception that only the disgruntled poor could find an identity in militant forms of black nationalism.

Rodney's radical coupling of cultural protest to anti-imperialist goals, a linkage long ignored by intellectuals, created a major political breakthrough for the opposition to the government, since it fused the two dominant ideological currents in postcolonial protest: socialism and cultural nationalism. As an exponent of this new synthesis, Rodney initiated what thus far had eluded most intellectuals: the absorption, secularization, and relative decontamination of spontaneous resistance ideologies.

This act of absorption and purification benefitted from the "play" of Rodney's secular and dialectical sensibility. Where, for example, the Rastasfarians and rebellious youths enveloped their critique of the status quo in a web of mystical and rejectionist formulations, Rodney initiated a reconciliation of their ideologies through the creative application of the intellectual's global perspectivism and anti-imperialism. Consequently,

Rodney's articulation of Black Power expressed both global-and local-level critiques of *class* rule and antagonistic racial themes — and this without falling into the illusions of popular ideologies or the orthodoxies of an automatic Marxist outlook. The overall effectiveness of this formulation of Black Power rested on its absorption of core opposition themes, while severely constraining any simple instrumentalist appropriation of Black Power ideas by either the JLP or by partisans of a crude black nationalism. In short, Rodney's activism was remarkable not for his founding of a political organization, since he created none; but for his twofold contribution: he transcended the barriers which hitherto had prevented the alliance of radical intellectuals and the militant unemployed, and he reconciled the previously estranged ideologies of socialism and cultural nationalism in Jamaica.

In response to this new alliance and ideological synthesis, the regime sought Rodney's ouster from the university. In mid-August 1968, the minister of home affairs summoned the vice chancellor of the university to protest Rodney's activities.[35] Apparently this meeting proved inconclusive, as Sherlock failed to give assurances that the university would put a stop to Rodney's activism. By mid-October, the regime had lost patience with the lecturer but still lacked a sound legal basis for taking action against him. It therefore tried to push the university into withdrawing Rodney's contract. On Monday, 14 October, the vice-chancellor was invited to an extraordinary meeting of the national cabinet, at which he was asked to terminate Rodney's contract.[36] Balking at this undisguised attempt to turn the university into a tool of the government, the vice-chancellor declined to make this political decision in the absence of any professional misconduct by Rodney. Sherlock therefore asked for more time to discuss the issue with the university's Appointments Committee.[37]

Sherlock's unwillingness to suspend university governance in favor of state security concerns was unacceptable to a regime determined to put a stop to Rodney's activism. The government therefore ignored the vice-chancellor's plea for more time, and took decisive action the next day. On 15 October, as Rodney returned to the island after attending a Black Writers' Conference in Montreal, Canada,[38] he was declared *personal non grata* and prevented from disembarking. This exclusion stirred students and sympathetic faculty, who assembled on the campus late that evening to consider what action to take.[39] Although the record of what transpired at this meeting is not available, a document issued on 16 October by a "Student-Staff Action Committee" suggest that a major issue was how to protest the exclusion and still heed regulations prohibiting marches without a permit.[40]

That careful attention was being given at this point to legal obligations to the state indicates the extent to which the government's "law and order" posture had influenced the students' deliberations. They and some members of the faculty apparently were not unmindful of the real physical dangers inherent in a confrontation with the riot police; a pamphlet produced by the students urged caution and nonprovocative behavior. Among other things, it warned students that

> This is a serious demonstration. It challenges the Government of this country and consequently places us all in danger. If we wish to make this protest for Dr. Rodney effective and if it is important that discipline and order be maintained throughout, each student is asked to pay very strict attention to . . . instructions.[41]

The concern for order and legality reflected a prudence born of fears for their safety, should the riot police be deployed to break up an illegal demonstration. This was a primary consideration which informed the type of action eventually decided on by the students for Wednesday, 16 October. In a plan to circumvent the restrictions against marches, buses would be used to transport the students to the city. There they would be dropped off in groups which could converge on the offices of the prime minister and the minister of home affairs to deliver two petitions.[42] The organizers of the march, still mindful of security forces and the risks involved, after seeking legal advice, on the day of the march issued the pamphlet described above, to the students exhorting them to be orderly and disciplined in their behavior.[43]

Despite these elaborate preparations to avoid trouble by staying within the confines of the law, an unforeseen factor intervened, as buses did not arrive at the university as planned. This unexpected development forced the students to abandon their concern for legalities and impelled them reluctantly to engage in an illegal march. No sooner had the students departed the campus on foot and moved down the adjoining Mona Road than they encountered riot police not only armed with the standard tear-gas cannisters, rifles, and batons, but also bearing an ominous machine gun mounted atop an aqueduct above the road.[44]

Refusing to be intimidated by this show of force but all the while maintaining a peaceable demeanor, some students managed to breach this barrier by coaxing the police to let them through. But as others tried to slip through the police lines undetected, one student was felled by an exploding tear-gas canister thrown in his direction. Despite this incident, it appeared at this point in the march, that the students' decorum and avoidance of bluster had confounded the police, and this allowed most of the protesters to get beyond Mona Road. As additional riot police were encountered further along the route, the students for the most part eluded them, using a number of stratagems. They hailed passing motorists, boarded public transportation, and dispersed to head for the destination of the march on foot. By the time the march reached the city and the office of the minister of home affairs on Duke Street, it had swept in its wake members of the unemployed and lumpenproletariat who had been roused by news of the banning. They now added a combustible force to the mass of demonstrating faculty and students milling outside the minister of home affairs' office. At this stage, a meeting with the minister, Roy McNeil, was requested. This was denied, and, instead, representatives of the protesters were permitted to see the permanent secretary, who stated that the prime minister had agreed to a meeting on Friday, two days thence.

This concession, marked by a lack of urgency in responding to the marchers, now determined the evolution of the demonstration. After pausing to consider their next move, the protestors decided to continue the march to the nearby George VI Memorial Park. On their way, the marchers passed the BITU offices on Duke Street. There JLP partisans awaited the demonstrators and stoned them as they tried to pass. As the students and others took cover, the irrepressible lumpenproletariat members, who had remained calm so far, now became greatly agitated by this provocation, and they began stoning the union headquarters and vehicles parked nearby. The introduction of this partisan political violence into the demonstration began to shift the balance against the university lecturers, who were trying to keep the demonstration peaceful. Indeed, by the time the assemblage had given up using this route to the park and had regrouped to take a longer detour through the main commercial district, it was evident that the volatility of the unemployed elements was increasing and becoming difficult to contain. Seasoned by years of combat with the riot police and already hostile toward the JLP, these elements in the march stood poised to defy the authorities. Inasmuch as the detour taken by the march brought it even closer to the areas frequented by the militant urban poor, their numbers among the marchers at this point probably increased significantly. The march wound its way through the crowded shopping area, becoming more turbulent as the unemployed turned increasingly restive, boisterously chanted slogans, and "bang[ed] on the sides of buses and cars."[45]

Although the marchers eventually found their way to the park without serious incident, the massing of riot police near the demonstration and the readiness of the militant poor to engage them finally tipped the balance. Despite plaintive pleas by the faculty for calm, the march came to an abrupt end as the police, firing tear gas, charged the protesters. In the ensuing melee, several of the marchers, including students and at least one faculty member, were beaten. Routed by this attack, the students and their professors fled and later returned to the university.

Commenting later on this incident, an organizer of the march said of the rout: "This signaled the end of the student march."[46]

As the students retreated in disarray, the pentup passions of the militant poor exploded. They hurled rocks at the police and stoned passing vehicles. Scattered from the park by the police, these rebels became separated from the students and retreated to nearby roadways. Others, in an evident attempt to exploit the disturbance, withdrew to the heart of the Kingston commerical district to wreak vengeance. There, vulnerable state-run buses awaiting passengers were attacked and set ablaze. Cars were overturned, and several stores were looted. In addition, the rebels directed their fury at government buildings and commerical establishments, damaging several of them, including some of the largest foreign banks and insurance companies in the city. By the time order had been restored, some ninety buildings had been damaged, along with over one hundred buses — thirty of which were completely gutted — and two insurgents had been shot dead. Thus, what had begun as a peaceful march to protest Rodney's expulsion had swiftly escalated into a serious but localized riot. For all its fury, however, the disturbance hardly threatened to become a frontal assault on the regime. The riot was limited in duration, lasting no more than a few hours, and was confined to a small part of the capital city. Moreover, the day's events failed to trigger any defiance among the working class or peasantry, and by the next day the disorder had subsided.

As for the students, a massive show of force at the university by the army and police, and a ban by the vice-chancellor on meetings on campus, effectively aborted attempts to sustain the protest. So the significance of the riot did not lie in its capacity to detonate an uprising against the regime. Apart from providing the militant urban poor with another opportunity to display antipathy toward a regime which sanctioned their status as pariahs in the society, the events of 15–16 October confirmed two important developments. First, the dynamics of unfolding events disclosed an emergent political alliance among students, intellectuals, the unemployed, and sections of the working class — a relationship which was nonexistent prior to 1968 and only tentatively established during Rodney's tenure. The longstanding lack of relation between the intelligentsia and the militant poor finally had collapsed in the heat of political activism and joint exposure to repressive state power.

Second, Rodney's banning and the subsequent attack on the university confirmed the JLP's persisting political vulnerability, its shaky legitimacy, and its increasing reliance on force to maintain its rule. Both its panicky responses to Rodney's activism and the *Gleaner*'s authoritarian denunciations disclosed how isolated and cut off from popular sentiment the regime and its closest supporters had become. Unable to reach out either politically or ideologically to the protesters, and determinedly pursuing increasingly ineffective policies, the JLP responded to critics with an unyielding authoritarianism.

The Authoritarian Counteroffensive:
The Regime and the Daily Gleaner Respond

Despite the government's quick suppression and containment of the riot and its easy demobilization of the students, the regime and the *Gleaner*, its main ideological supporter, continued nearly a decade of identifying the university with political subversion. Whereas the political independence of academic work and activity earlier had elicited criticisms, threats, nonrenewal of visas, and passport seizures, the protest against Rodney's expulsion now met heightened authoritarian rhetoric and more illiberal measures. In a broadcast to the nation from the House of Representatives, the prime minister enunciated three basic themes: the subversive nature of Rodney's activities, the students' participation in destruction of property, and the radicalizing of Jamaican students by "non-Jamaicans" from other islands.

Drawing on intelligence reports on Rodney, Shearer depicted him as a Communist who "actively engaged in organizing groups of semi-literates and unemployed for avowed revolutionary purposes."[47] Unable to cite evidence of a conspiracy or armed plot to overthrow the government, the prime minister relied instead on Rodney's openly stated opinions of Black Power, and particularly his association with the Rastafarians and the lumpenproletariat.[48] Evidently, having criticized the Jamaican government, Rodney was excluded for exercising two fundamental rights which capitalist democracies generally recognize: freedom of opinion and freedom of association. Although criticisms of the state and discussions with others opposed to it were not crimes under the Jamaican Constitution, the government, in the context of its abiding vulnerability on racial matters, once again made opinion and association illegal offenses. Unable to find evidence of treason, the government eventually suggested that it barred Rodney for meeting "with Claudius Henry who was convicted in 1960 of Treason Felony" and having discussions involving the "condemnation of the democratic system of Government in Jamaica."[49] Once again, an intellectual's assertion of independent political opinion and his association with traditionally despised sectors of the population had provided the occasion for sharp government curbs.

Protesting students faced a similarly exaggerated response. Ignoring their decorous attempts to remain within the law, the prime minister falsely accused them of "hooliganism" and wanton destruction of property. Reaching for maximum rhetorical effect and ignoring distinctions between the dignified, even timid, protest of the students and the ready militancy of the unemployed, Shearer charged, "the students and their friends" with engaging in "a campaign of pillage, looting, destruction of cars, filthy abuse, and stoning of decent citizens and arson."[50] Thus the nation was led to believe that the students had planned and participated in the destructive activities of the militant unemployed.

Finally, the prime minister wondered openly about "foreigners" and "non-Jamaicans" at the university, whom he declared were responsible for fomenting dissidence among "our sons and daughters."[51] This ominous note, which echoed the JLP's abiding belief that its troubles stemmed from the activities of foreigners at the university, eventually was to lead to the reintroduction of security measures barring "nondesirable" Commonwealth citizens from the island. Indeed, holding to this theory that naive Jamaican students were being "inflamed by fanatics and . . . corrupt agitators," the regime not only targeted foreign nationals at the university for sharp criticism, but also ignored the diminishing popularity of its policies among many Jamaicans inside and outside the university.[52]

In its turn, the *Daily Gleaner* emerged as the government's firm ally and as the vigorous proponent of a hard line toward the university and the protestors. In a series of editorials, the newspaper repeated the government's position on non-Jamaican provocateurs. In an editorial entitled "Cave Mona," the newspaper warned, "The country had better learn quickly that it will be disastrous to practice a policy of fatal conceit by thinking it can keep open bosom for international serpents. If the Jamaican students at Mona knew the facts . . . they would not only be ashamed of themselves, but also would be gravely alarmed."[53] The newspaper demanded that students "obey the law or accept the consequences" and declared ominously that "when next they march illegally they will not have the excuse of first time folly."[54]

The *Gleaner* made a similarly bitter denunciation of the intellectuals. They were dismissed as idle pot smokers, busily "indoctrinating as many students as possible in the historical inevitability of Communism." In the sensational prose of its editorial writers, the newspaper struck back at academic critics of the status quo with the observation, "It seems to be a common belief in the West Indies that to be an intellectual is to sit around and smoke pot and to hold views of extreme left politics, and to plot to overthrow any system of Government . . . in the interest of 'changing society.'"[55]

This anti-intellectualism in defense of national security inevitably extended its reach to the administration of the university. In what would become an open expression of dissatisfaciton with the vice-chancellor's leadership, the *Gleaner* sharply criticized his response to the crisis. Intimating that he was indecisive and not up to the job of firmly expunging dissent, the newspaper, on the day following the riot, hinted at the end of Sherlock's tenure by observing that "heavy work is cut out for his successor."[56] Less than a month later, the paper returned to this theme, observing that Sherlock's "recent failure to place the nation's needs at least as equal to the university's pride has been a sore disappointment to many of his secular admirers." The paper continued, "It seems that somewhere along the line it was forgotten at Mona that there is such a thing as Jamaica whose interest, safety and progress should be given a priority."[57]

In similar remarks in Parliament, Edward Seaga, a JLP member, also noted his dismay at the vice-chancellor's resistance to government pressures to have Rodney transferred to another campus. As Seaga observed:

> I must report to Parliament that I am perplexed at the posture of the Vice-Chancellor when confronted with the record of Mr. Rodney. When told that Mr. Rodney was a grave security risk, he did not venture to say what was possible to transfer Mr. Rodney . . . to another Campus although at the request of the Head of another Government he recently transferred a Jamaican lecturer from the St. Augustine Campus . . . back here to Mona.[58]

This ideological counteroffensive against the university and the rise of Black Power continued until the end of the year, with various officials articulating different themes and concerns. For the most part these revolved around such issues as the "un-Jamaican" character of Black Power, the need for a Jamaican university, and reassurances, such as those offered by Norman Manley, that no matter how serious the local situation appeared, the U.S. would never tolerate a hostile revolution in its sphere of influence.[59] In retrospect, official fears of an imminent insurrection seem exaggerated. No organized Black Power movement existed in Kingston. Nor was Black Power a national phenomenon reaching a broad range of classes. There was never a threat to the armed power of the state, since organized armed activity was not even on the minds of the students and intellectuals.

Finally, the protest was localized and confined to students, academics, workers, and a riotous group of unemployed protesters. They were participants in an isolated activity anchored around the very narrow issue of exclusion of a single, albeit highly admired, lecturer. The protest hardly constituted the dire revolutionary threat depicted by the regime. In this context of exaggerated fears and overblown claims, additional steps to impose curbs on the university did not meet with unqualified approval. Indications of the shaky support for the government's latest round of curbs were evident in several places.

First, far from marking the highpoint of Shearer's tenure, the JLP's annual meeting in November 1968 became an occasion for defensive resolutions defending the prime minister against critics. Thus, among the five resolutions moved at this conference, two were fulsome and self-conscious votes of confidence in Shearer's handling of the recent crisis.[60] Second, the appearance of public diffidence concerning his actions caused Shearer to demand public support. Criticizing the "neutrality" of the public, Shearer called on it to come to his defense and not allow "the hot heads and the extremists" to monopolize public debate.[61]

Apart from this hint of uneasiness about his actions, the prime minister's appeal overestimated the degree to which the students' views reached a wider public. After all, for several weeks after the event, the official government position, exaggerted and distorted, had enjoyed a monopoly in the country's only daily newspaper, the *Gleaner*. As we have observed, the newspaper firmly backed the government and led the ideological counteroffensive with sensational stories of plots and subversion. Only once — five weeks after the riot — did the *Gleaner* open its pages to allow the students to tell their side. Despite this media advantage, the prime minister apparently faced a noncommittal public verdict on his actions.

Finally, the reimposition of work permits for lecturers once again polarized the society around the issue of human rights.[62] Even after invoking fears about Rodney's intentions, only a tiny group of organizations, whose members traditionally were opposed by class and ideology to changes in the status quo, supported the policy.[63] Thus narrowly supported, the regime found itself opposed by a wider, more diverse group of organizations such as the Jamaica Teachers Association, the West Indies Group of University Teachers, and the Bar Council. In sum, although efforts to curb this latest expression of dissent certainly were comparatively mild, by the end of the year it appeared that the cumulative illiberal measures and their threat to democratic government had begun to erode the regime's support.

That such relatively modest curbs could prove unpopular with the public evidently was due to popular restiveness at the regime's inability to resolve the country's pressing social and economic problems and its growing tendency to rely on autocratic measures to deal with critics. After all, unemployment remained high, the crisis in agriculture persisted, and a recent government study had shown that even the better-off sections of the Kingston poor lived in extreme conditions.[64] Moreover, despite the formal exoneration of the prime minister from charges of corruption, public perception of official malfeasance was not allayed by findings that there was improper government interference in the investigation.

To be sure, the emergence of discontent among professional sectors of the society suggested neither an unambiguous vote for the claims of Black Power nor a desire for Communist solutions. However, the slight but evident shift among some sectors of "respectable society" seemed to indicate impatience with a regime which both appeared incapable of resolving urgent social problems and increasingly relied on autocratic interventions to preserve social order. The threat which this latter reliance posed to human rights and democracy in time would widen popular democratic opposition. For the next three years, however, the florescence of Black Power ideology among the intelligentsia was to provide an important context for the deepening isolation and eventual decomposition of the JLP. The next chapter examines how the dissident movement evolved in these years.

CHAPTER 8

The Apogee of Black Power Ideology:
The Abeng Newspaper Movement

October 1968 was a turning point in the Caribbean. On the government side, the JLP had increased its preemptive curbs. Not since the 1966 state of emergency had it taken such strong action to deal with opposition to its policies. Obviously the JLP hoped its tough response would weaken activism and create disarray among its critics. For the students, the events certainly marked a painful loss of innocence; they had come face-to-face with the armed power of the state, and many no doubt found the experience terrifying. The confrontation challenged them to transcend the confusion, fear, and uncertainty that followed the decapitation of their protest in October.[1] Most important, perhaps, the "Rodney Affair" was a watershed event for the radical intelligentsia. The government's response had presented them with a stark choice: retreat or maintain their activism and risk further curbs. This chapter argues that they bravely chose the latter course, leading to creative departures in the form of political activism. These departures, however, were attended by the turbulence of internal divisions and the gradual winnowing out of comrades who earlier had initiated opposition to the status quo.

The first indication of innovative forms of activism among the intellegentsia emerged not in Jamaica, but in Trinidad. Within two weeks of Rodney's expulsion, a branch of the New World Group there launched, on 28 October, the first issue of *Moko*, a radical newspaper. Devoted entirely to the recent events in Jamaica, this first issue broke through the censorship of the Jamaican press and presented the students' side of the story in Trinidad.[2] In an apparent reference to the *Gleaner*'s distortions and censorship of the protestors' views, the editors of *Moko* noted that they were attempting to establish "a genuinely independent newspaper, . . . an honest and truthful newspaper," free of the biases of the dominant regional media.[3] Once again, social conflict and radical intellectuals' opposition to censorship and the media's news ideology had spawned attempts to create alternative means of communication.

The appearance of *Moko* suggested a new departure in political activism. The premier issue of the newspaper, launched by radical academics in Trinidad, indicated that *Moko* would be neither a scholarly journal nor a highbrow paper catering to a limited audience of intellectuals. Rather, the first number of *Moko* was unambiguous in asserting that it wanted to be a *popular* newspaper – a paper for those whose views were not expressed in the established media. As its editors acknowledged, with a hint of apology, the idea for the paper was "conceived at the University." However, they noted, *Moko* was "not a University newspaper, nor do we wish it to be. Several of us are connected with the University but we are not only University people. We are anxious that we shall not be alone in this endeavour."[4] *Moko* constituted a new strategy for expanding links with popular forces in the Caribbean: the development of the agitational newspaper.

It was not entirely fortuitous that a popular press emerged in Trinidad. It will be recalled that the New World Groups on the various campuses had been under intense attack for their isolationist policy. Next to the Jamaican outpost, perhaps the most militant demand for increased engagement had come from activists at the Saint Augustine campus in Trinidad. There Lloyd Best, leader of the New World movement, over the years had faced insistent criticism for New World's narrow definition of intellectual responsibility. That definition finally had been challenged by Rodney's activism in Jamaica. Now the appearance of *Moko* seemed to signal an attempt to continue that tradition by promoting the cause of Black Power and intellectual activism through the medium of a popular press.

Because of his well-known position on this issue, this development was anathema to Best, who openly opposed the idea of Black Power in the West Indies, as well as direct action by the radical intelligentsia. Following *Moko's* appearance, Best's sharply critical assessment of Black Power was published in the 10 November issue of the *Gleaner*.[5] In it, the Trinidadian economist argued that Black Power was inapplicable to social relations in the Caribbean. Advancing a perspective that corresponded in part to views held by defenders of the Jamaican status quo, Best challenged Rodney's nuanced interpretation of Black Power:

> There is already much loose talk about black power when clearly there can be no simple division between black and white, where it makes little sense to advocate organized violence or even to provoke confrontation with the police. The blacks already are in control of the political system in the Caribbean. If anything prevents them from creating an economy appropriate to their own needs, it is the state of their own consciousness, their self-imposed unwillingness to stop being intimidated by the Marines.[6]

This condemnation of resistance to the status quo from one who had been not only a leading opponent of Caribbean regimes but also

the founder of an intellectual renaisssance in the region, signaled a retreat and a parting of the ways for Best. Ironically, the very nationalist
position which had launched the New World movement, with its insistence on the specificity of the Caribbean, now assumed a reactionary
form in relation to Black Power-as-ideology. This ideology now should
be opposed, in Best's view, because it was simply another foreign import which threatened the cultural autonomy of Caribbean peoples.

In a startling application of the hitherto valuable defense of the indigenous over the foreign, Best attacked Black Power ideology for what
he saw as its external, Afro-American provenance. In doing so, Best
tragically retreated to a chauvinism now directed at an imagined *Afro-
American* ideological domination of the Caribbean. Applying a logic
in which his particularistic localism triumphed over the larger unity of
the black experience in the diaspora, Best maintained:

> The needs of blacks in the rest of the world may be subordinated to those
> of blacks in the American metropole. Paris tends always to dominate the
> provinces as it were. It would be a very fine irony if the imperial pattern
> reasserts itself in the form of a domination of blacks in the Caribbean,
> Latin America and Africa by the interests of Negro America. The symbols
> and preoccupations of the Civil Rights movement in the U.S.A. may well
> take on a spurious universalism of the kind which led Marxism outside of
> Western Europe to ride rough-shod over local sentiment, to ignore local pos-
> sibilities and local limitations, and in the end to inhibit rather than to pro-
> mote radical reform.[7]

Whereas New World's nationalism earlier had launched a vital political
and intellectual renaissance, in the hands of Lloyd Best – the leading
exponent of the movement's political positions – this defense of the local became an instrument of reaction against *any* ideology not of local
vintage. In what must have been a sharp surprise to admirers of his earlier
dissidence, Best's unyielding opposition to any subordination of the
particular to the universal had brought his brand of "independent
thought" to its ultimate political destination: a provincialism verging
on a defense of the status quo. In the context of a heightened awareness
in the Third World of the commonality and unity of the "black" experience in a capitalist world, this paean to the singularity and exceptionalism of the Caribbean could only further antagonize Best's critics.
Coming in the wake of the Jamaican upheaval and converging with
similar formulations by defenders of the status quo, Best's critique of
Black Power was inflammatory and disruptive of the tenuous unity
which existed within the New World movement.

Within days of this published capitulation, Best had withdrawn from
the Trinidad group to form the small-scale, intermediate community

of rational persons he had envisioned. As the *Trinidad Guardian* reported on 18 November, rebellious members of the Trinidad New World Group had rebuffed his attempts to reorganize the faltering movement. In his turn, Best acknowledged that his departure was caused by protracted conflicts over "different conceptions of how change is to be induced" and repeated his longstanding criticism of those "obsessed with the idea of taking political power," even though they had "no discernable program, . . . organization, . . . [or] direction."[8] Since the dissidents already had seized the initiative in late October with the publication of *Moko*, it appears that Best's subsequent attack on Black Power and his farewell rejoinder in mid-November merely formalized the finality of this split in the New World movement.

Although this rupture in Trinidad initiated a gradual decline in the vigor of all branches of the New World movement, this development, far from dimming the intellectuals' political involvement, spurred their activism. In fact, the fortnightly publication of *Moko* in Trinidad spawned a similar effort by Mona activists. Having felt the batons of the riot police and having been stung by JLP and *Gleaner* criticisms, the intellectuals struck back by creating a popular press.[9] Ironically, it was the Jamaica branch of the New World Group which led this departure in Kingston. Despite the defection of their leader and the ensuing disorganization of the New World movement, members of the Jamaica group ignored Best's political example and put their weight behind the initiative to establish a newspaper. By the beginning of the new year, an advisory committee had been created to explore publication of a popular newspaper.[10] In a remarkable show of unity, radical socialists, New World activists, students, progressive academics, and others opposed to the Shearer regime now collaborated in the effort to launch the paper and with it another social movement.

Despite this momentum in Jamaica, the new unity represented a marriage of convenience. Substantive ideological differences on a range of political issues existed among these forces. For example, despite the unity imposed on the Jamaican intelligentsia in the wake of October's events, ideological tensions between radical socialists and moderate New World nationalists persisted. Common opposition to the Shearer regime had caused groups to set aside, for the moment, secondary contradictions among various tendencies in the founding group. Alluding to this unity-amid-differences, the editors observed: "We have one thing in common. We are concerned about the state of this country. About the fantastic amount of unemployment. About the poverty. Poor housing. Poor education and schooling. And above all, about our status as squatters in our own land."[11]

Practical considerations contributed to this enforced unity; the radical intelligentsia lacked expertise concerning how to publish and distribute a newspaper and assure that it spoke authentically to its intended audience. Under these circumstances, ideological differences readily gave way to a division of labor based on political experience, technical capacities, and preparedness for political engagement. These exigencies fostered a political cooperation which brought to the paper the intellectual, organizational, and editorial expertise of Norman Girvan and George Beckford, both university economists and leading members of the Jamaican branch of the New World Group. Similarly, radical socialist and former YSL activist Robert Hill—and later Trevor Munroe—brought to the effort intellectual energy and experience of activism among the Jamaican people. Apart from this political group at the core of an ever-changing editorial committee, an even more heterogeneous group of intellectuals—lawyers, academics, journalists, and writers—played a role in the initial stages of the paper's development.

Given this "mixed marriage" of politically diverse personnel, it is not surprising that there were difficulties in settling on a political identity and an ideological focus for the newspaper. Apparently, while moderates in the founding group were inclined to pursue the general idea of an alternative press which would address the national interest and include lively debate among differing perspectives, others contended that the paper could be more radical and instead should build on Rodney's legacy. That legacy called for the intellectuals' close involvement with the people, the promotion of black political empowerment, the defense of the people's culture, and a challenge to imperialism. Such a radical legacy had little in common with a wish that the paper merely reflect a plurality of ideas.

Robert Hill and the UWI lecturer Horace Levy were given the responsibility of drawing up a statement of "aims and objectives." Bearing in mind this legacy, they produced what turned out to be too radical a formulation, incorporating Black Power and anti-imperialist themes. Commenting on this early battle over the paper's ideological direction, Glenville Hinds, a participant in the movement, observed that the initial statement "was gone through with a fine-tooth comb by the National Newspaper Committee . . . and amended in critical sections so that it would not offend."[12] Ironically, despite the political gains won for the Left by Rodney's activism and the popularity of Marcus Garvey among sections of the urban unemployed and independent peasantry, Garvey's ideas found no ready acceptance among some serving on the National Newspaper Committee, the body supervising the founding of an alternative press.[13] Fortunately, the important assemblies held in various parts of the island to launch the paper indicated that popular sentiment—particularly among the lumpenproletariat—was strongly in favor not simply of an alternative press, but of a Black Power paper faithful to the ideas bequeathed by Rodney.[14] Given this pressure from below, the paper's orientation drew, albeit gingerly, somewhat closer to a Black Power perspective.

With this reluctant endorsement of a slightly more radical orientation than that preferred by sections of the founding group, the first issue of the weekly newspaper—the *Abeng*—was published on 1 February 1969.[15] Despite innocuous statements of its goals and purposes, which reflected the initial desire to remain noncontroversial,[16] the first issues nonetheless showed the *Abeng* to be a genuinely popular paper articulating the cause of black "sufferers"—that vast majority of poor Jamaicans whose social condition was marked by landlessness, poor housing, unemployment, exposure to police brutality, and political victimization. Despite the ideological timidity of its statements of goals and purposes, early issues of the *Abeng* managed to make *racial* uplift and a defense of the black "sufferer" its main causes.

A direct consequence of this orientation was that the paper echoed all the anti-*status quo* themes that had emerged in the postcolonial period. Two of these were police brutality and the functioning of a judicial system which was widely perceived to be biased against the poor. These poor, and particularly the urban unemployed, for years had complained bitterly of injustices suffered at the hands of Jamaican judges and the court system. Responding to this grievance, the paper promptly printed several indictments of the legal system. For example, in the very first issue, Hugh Small, the activist lawyer and former YSL president, pinpointed one of the most glaring problems of the judicial system: mandatory sentencing and floggings for crimes committed largely by the poor. Noting the connection between crime and social and economic conditions, Small called for major reforms and challenged the legal profession to speak out. Two weeks later, the paper reiterated the theme, linking crime and police abuses to an official policy of turning a blind eye to the social conditions of the black poor. Maintaining that the youth were "condemned" to scrambling "like dogs for scraps and leftovers from the tables of the rich," the paper drew attention to the frightening consequences which had already appeared in the society:

> Where this condition exists, there will be anger, hatred, crime and violence. The privileged can only survive by suspecting everyone who is black and badly dressed, by sleeping with one ear open and a gun beneath the pillow and by keeping savage dogs. The Government can only survive by arming and increasing the police and encouraging them to drop colonial niceties; by expanding the army and using it in frequent shows of naked force.[17]

In a novel move which allowed victims of the legal system to air their complaints, the paper created a regular column—the "Sufferer's Diary"—

that reported a litany of abuses encountered by the poor.[18] Thus, at a time when middle-class opinion-makers and many in the legal profession were reneging on their responsibilities on the justice issue, the *Abeng* took up the lonely battle to get a better shake for the poor with trenchant editorials, exposés, and new reports on inequalities in the judicial system.[19]

Another unmistakable focus which emerged early in the life of the paper was the affirmation of popular culture, particularly the celebration of the legitimacy of Rastafarian and other popular ideologies. Obviously trying to conform to one of Rodney's several injunctions, the intellectuals who edited the paper gave the unemployed broad opportunity to state their views in the *Abeng*. This resulted in an unprecedented evolution in the postcolonial media, as a weekly newspaper allowed the Jamaican poor to speak with an authentic, uncensored voice in its pages. Not surprisingly, black cultural nationalism surged to the fore. Spurred by the editors' publication of terse quotations and lengthy extracts of Marcus Garvey's speeches, variations on cultural nationalism became the vogue. For instance, Rastafarian expressions yielded discourses ranging from affirmation of pride of race, to praises for "His Majesty," the Ethiopian Emperor Haile Selassie. At the same time, Rastafarian social commentaries and trenchant political slogans directed against the Shearer regime ("Pharoah Share Out"), counterbalanced the Rastafarians' celebration of cultural nationalism and religious beliefs.[20]

Other cultural nationalists also found an ideological home in the *Abeng*. For example, the Nation of Islam's representative in Jamaica, Minister Cecil X, in a repudiation of the term "Negro," instructed the uninitiated in the ideology of his organization: "A negro is one who has no knowlege of himself or his kind, one who has lost his name, his language, his culture, his religion, and knows nothing whatsoever about his God. A negro is a robot or a walking dead who responds to the whip of the white slave master."[21]

For those more inclined to listen to a native voice which spoke without religious allusions and had the glamour of the Garvey name, Marcus Garvey, Jr., provided his understanding of Black Power. The younger Garvey affirmed, in addition to the need for unity and pride of race, the importance of creating political, cultural, and social organizations controlled by blacks. Echoing his father's views, he arged that "the goals of these institutions must be black ownership, black economic power, efficient black industry, science and technology, and, of course, black military power."[22] Aside from these emphases, which challenged the disadvantages of the black poor before the law and endorsed the legitimacy of their cultural self-assertion, a third dominant focus in the paper was hostility to the JLP and particularly to the tenure of Prime

Minister Hugh Shearer. Article after article accused "Pharoah's Government" of abuses, including human rights violations, political corruption, and censorship.[23]

The paper also took up the perennial postcolonial opposition theme that Jamaican governments, in their haste to industrialize, were much too lenient in offering incentives to foreign corporations, without adequate consideration of the nation's welfare. Lamenting the negative effects of the postwar laissez-faire economic policy on ownership of the national economy, New World economists warned that the government was coming dangerously close to selling out the national patrimony to foreign investors. Writing on the "History of Our Dispossession," George Beckford, the UWI economist, reiterated the view that a drastic change in economic policy was required to stem extensive foreign ownership of the economy. Complementing accusations thrown up by the sufferers in their biting slogan, "Pharoah Share Out," Beckford criticized the JLP for pursuing a policy which permitted "foreign white people . . . [to] own our basic resources."[24]

Throughout the month of February and the first weeks of March, this insistent expression of popular grievances showed the nearly-unrivaled hegemony of popular ideology within the paper. Although the New World view was evident in the paper's economic analyses and certainly was enshrined in the founding dictum that the paper existed to solicit "the widest possible participation of ideas from the people," it was obvious after several issues that Rastafarian and "lumpen" ideology now defined the paper's ideological orientation.

This influence was so pervasive that the two groups' phraseology and something of their world view steadily seeped into the outlook and formulations of *Abeng* intellectuals. Where these academics hitherto had maintained an innocuous identity largely rooted in their disciplines and professionalization, by 1969 they no longer could do so. As we observed, the year 1968, with its global upheavals, revivification of popular culture, and renaissance of Black Power ideology, had acted as a powerful cultural compression chamber, rapidly transmitting to sections of the intelligentsia a new racial identity as "blackman."[25] Operating in the era's cultural and political presssure cooker, *Abeng* intellectuals borrowed freely from the ensemble of popular slogans and epithets. Such terms as "sufferers," "pharoah," "black people," and "black man time come" all slipped into the language of the intellectuals. Swept up by this wave of black cultural nationalism, some among the intelligentsia not only sought the roots of their own identity, but also engaged in a fruitful archeology of black political culture. This scholarship yielded informative articles on several topics ranging from the newspaper work of activists such as Edward Jordan and Robert Love[26] to the significance of the 1938 workers' rebellion. In sum, from a position of ideological diffidence, not only had the *Abeng* steadily evolved into an authentic mouthpiece of the militant urban poor, but also the intelligentsia had become newly racially conscious, captured by the vogue in black cultural nationalism.

By the first weeks of March 1969, this dominance in the paper of popular ideological positions was being challenged by a nascent socialist outlook, which shifted the emphasis slightly in favor of workers' issues. Thus, an editorial on 1 March remarked that the current wave of workers' strikes had far-reaching significance. "We are seeing," the paper argued, "the birth of a new Working Class. Confused, partially hidden, complex, all the signs point to the Jamaican Worker retesting his strength, experimenting with new forms of action, and bringing his fellow workers a discovery of their power for too long suppressed."[27]

This important bow to the neglected role of the working class coincided with two significant developments. One was the formal appearance of Trevor Munroe as a member of the paper's editorial committee. Having completed his graduate work abroad on a Rhodes Scholarship, the former YSL activist and student organizer had returned to the Mona campus to take up an appointment as lecturer in the Department of Government. Coming to the *Abeng* relatively unhampered by a vested interest in New World thought, and retaining a grip on his old workerist position amid the growth of black cultural nationalism among radical academics, Munroe provided an independent political perspective which would nudge the *Abeng* away from the ideology of the lumpenproletariat.

By mid-March, a second and more important political development spurred this incipient challenge to cultural nationalism in the paper. This was the landing of British troops on the tiny island of Anguilla on 19 March, to put down an independence movement and attempted secession from the three-state confederation of St. Kitts–Nevis–Anguilla, all of which were under colonial rule. Coming at the height of the Black Power movement in the Caribbean and less than a decade after the larger islands had won their independence, this invasion brought back painful memories of British suppression of social movements under colonialism.[28] For leftists who hoped that the *Abeng* movement would take an even more revolutionary line and fashion an alternative for the sufferers, the suppression of the Anguillan protest fueled their determination to move beyond the celebration of black culture, to a firmer anti-imperialist position.[29]

For the moment, however, this radical anti-imperialism remained a minority tendency in an unapologetically populist newspaper movement. Just the same, the defenders of the nationalist perspective on the editorial committee were impelled to respond to criticisms that the paper lacked direction and had failed to suggest a coherent political alternative.[30] Articulating a position remarkably similar to that previously held by the New World Group, the cultural nationalists rejected calls for "a plan" and argued that not enough knowledge of Jamaican society existed to draw up firm alternatives. Besides, they argued, planning should not be "our business," because "our duty is to help create the environment which will bring forward proposals and actions from the people of this country when the time comes. Our present task must be to mobilize the people of this country for the struggle ahead."[31]

By maintaining that intellectuals should limit themselves to creating an environment in which popular initiatives could flourish, the exponents of this position reasoned that out of a dynamic interplay between intellectuals' insights and popular demands would come new ideas for the movement's direction. As an editorial defending this position put it, "The strategy of *Abeng* is — from the people to the paper; from the paper to the people and back again."[32] Any attempt unilaterally to impose direction from above merely smacked of middle-class arrogance and its antecedent, the old slave-master mentality. After all, these populists argued, "Plans involve telling people what to do. That is the way slave owners, colonial officials and local political agents of American capitalists behave."[33]

This polemic, with its defensive position that change and the movement's direction should be guided from below, disclosed immanent contradictions which now bubbled to the surface. These involved three interrelated nodal issues: (1) the disparity between the bourgeois social origins of the editors and the lowly, deprived status of the lumpenproletariat, the *Abeng's* social base; (2) the divergent perspectives among *Abeng* intellectuals on appropriate strategies for change; and (3) differing conceptions of the responsibilities of intellectuals in social movements. As these tensions matured over time, they contributed to an increasing turbulence inside the *Abeng* movement.

In early April, for example, the untimely death of the lawyer Denis Sloly[34] — one of the *Abeng's* most valued organizers — elicited eulogies which sought to deal with one of the criticisms voiced by sections of the urban poor. Apparently "some Rasta youths" and others had voiced their distrust of bourgeois intellectuals who championed the radicalism of the poor while continuing to enjoy the benefits of their privileged class positions. These intellectuals, the critics charged, were "opportunists" who risked little, while hoping to benefit from the struggles of the poor.

Seeking to answer this accusation, eulogists called attention to Sloly's self-sacrifice, capacity for work — evidenced by his attention to myriad organizational details — and commitment to the cause of Black Power.

Indeed, some intellectuals went further, challenging the lumpenproetariat's abiding distrust of light-skinned persons and noting the anomaly of a "Jamaican white man" from the Saint Andrew suburbs who nonetheless had become "intimately involved with a black man's newspaper."[35] Adding credibility to this rejoinder from the intellectuals, Ras Negus, a poet and contributor to the newspaper, defended the participation of committed members of the colored middle class in the Black Power movement and scolded critics who impugned Sloly's contribution simply because of his color: "We know he is black but some of us do not believe so. They do not think because he has come from the oppressive society that he would be able to shoulder the responsibility of playing an important part in the struggle."[36] This flurry of charges and countercharges, suggestive of the internal rattling in the movement around the three issues listed above, gave notice of a rift that later was to shake the movement and winnow its personnel. For the first half of the summer, however, these tensions were submerged by urgent concerns pertaining to the paper's survival.

In addition to the shock of losing Denis Sloly,[37] the paper was hit by a financial crisis and by incidents of political intimidation. In part, the basis of the financial crisis lay in the fact that the paper, consistent with its independent, anticapitalist position, refused to run advertisements. As the editors acknowledged, this decision meant that the paper survived "almost entirely upon revenues received from sales, with occasional assistance from close friends."[38] Although other funds probably came from sections of the middle class alienated by the JLP, their contributions dried up as the paper drifted steadily toward chauvinistic expressions of Black Power and eventually toward open Marxist positions.[39] Although the paper had reached a peak circulation of some fourteen thousand copies in early April, by the summer this figure had dwindled, as dissatisfaction with the paper's contents was openly expressed. Apart from the predictable sniping from hostile critics who argued that the paper was patently "racist," more sympathetic middle-class elements complained that it was becoming "boring" and repetitive, harping on the same themes without posing a viable alternative. Moreover, the publication of materials such as a picture of a black man carrying a fat white tourist on his shoulders and the racist comments of Marcus Garvey, Jr.,[40] gave credibility to the accusation that the *Abeng* not merely had exhausted the ideas which had made it popular, but had, in effect, lost its way. At any rate, this emergent financial crisis had a discernable effect on the paper's offerings. As of 10 May, the pioneering column, "Sufferer's Diary," was withdrawn. On 21 June the regular list of members of the editorial committee stopped appearing, the size of the paper was reduced, and, by the end of the month, the columns on

African news and the Nation of Islam also had been dropped.[41] As if things were not bad enough, a suspicious fire razed the *Abeng* printery in late June, and the paper reported that several of its vendors had been harassed and beaten by the police.

Despite the demoralization produced by its difficulties, the paper survived through the summer in a reduced form and continued reporting on allegations of police brutality, abuses by the dominant unions and political parties, and disclosures of JLP efforts to extend its censorship to programming on the airwaves. Yet the desire to expose the "seamy side" of Jamaican democracy could not contain the internal tensions which rocked the paper, pitting cultural nationalists against resurgent Marxists, and the lumpenproletariat against them both.

As we have observed, *Abeng* intellectuals of a revolutionary persuasion, earlier in March, formally had asserted their claim that the newspaper movement lacked direction at the top and was avoiding a revolutionary anti-imperialism. We argued that this position gained strength from a set of circumstances beginning with the Anguillan invasion and culminating with criticisms from several quarters that the paper was becoming irrelevant because of its refusal to pose a political alternative. Having been weakened by political events, a financial crisis, and increasing dissatisfaction with the paper's content, the cultural nationalists in the editorial group gradually found themselves outflanked by resurgent leftists whose positions became increasingly dominant by midsummer. For example, their proworker position was reflected in the 24 May issue, devoted to the celebration of Labor Day. In that issue, Trevor Munroe, who had emerged as the theoretician of the Left and the leading force pressing for a change in the paper's outlook, contributed a long article on the 1938 rebellion.

Writing under the pseudonym "Historian," Munroe analyzed the revolt and discussed the internal differentiation of the working class at that time. In subsequent weeks, the paper printed trenchant critiques of the dominant unions' role in throttling workers' activism, offered clear-eyed analyses of existing weaknesses in the independent labor movement, and criticized "American imperialism" on the occasion of Nelson Rockefeller's July 1969 visit to the island.

This ascendancy of laborist and anti-imperialist positions was attended by a corresponding decline in the quality of the defense of the cultural nationalist position. Whether its exponents on the editorial committee lacked the inclination to put forward their views or simply had capitulated to the Marxists is not clear. At any rate, no programmatic statements or editorials reflecting their position appeared in response to this challenge from the revolutionary Left. In the absence of formal statements from cultural nationalists among the *Abeng* intellectuals, criticism of the Marxists did come from others who defended black cultural nationalism, albeit in a politically irresponsible way.

Taking up the burden of those who felt the paper ought to retain its nationalist position, Marcus Garvey, Jr., denounced the advent of class analysis in the paper as "just another white man's doctrine" being injected into the black struggle. In a demagogic attack on the Left, Garvey slid into a fit of chauvinism and anticommunism:

> *Abeng* ought to be stimulating African consciousness and should emphasize Africanism rather than this attempt at creating class struggle in Jamaica. I believe that the attempt at class struggle is simply playing into the hands of the Communist infiltrator who I am certain is in our midst. I detest Communists as much as I detest capitalists. A white man is a white man and no amount of frothy talk from his mouth will change my opinion of him. I know the beast.[42]

With this counterattack, the line between the two camps was clearly drawn. Indeed, behind the crudity of Garvey's formulations lay an ideological orientation shared by many cultural nationalists in the *Abeng* movement. For example, in their heyday, New World intellectuals had evinced a similar anticommunism and hostility to class analysis, albeit couched in more sophisticated language. Inevitably, New World members had imported this political position into the *Abeng*. Likewise, Garvey, Jr.'s views resonated among all those cultural nationalists of different class backgrounds who, in one form or another, held a racially separatist outlook and believed in the fundamental incompatibility of "black thought" and white ideology. Orthodox Rastafarians, nihilistic youths, traditional Garveyites in the working class, and bourgeois middle-class nationalists all shared, in varying degrees of sophistication, Garvey, Jr.'s ideological outlook. Hence, in their effort to arrest the paper's ideological drift, the leftists had to deal not only with the nodal sources of tension identified previously, but also with this obscurantist impulse in black cultural nationalism. The daunting task of doing so fell to Trevor Munroe, who, in a series of articles diagnosing the myriad problems besetting the paper, argued for theoretical leadership by intellectuals, to combat the political and ideological weaknesses among the Jamaican people.

Writing under a new pseudonym ("Blackman"), Munroe observed that criticisms leveled at the paper no longer could be ignored as merely "coming from the enemy."[43] Accusations of ideological confusion, middle-class opportunism, political timidity, and the like had a *real* basis in contradictions which had arisen in the movement. One of these, of course, was the anomaly which saw poor and chronically unemployed people being led by privileged middle-class intellectuals. In Munroe's view, this contradiciton had grown inside the movement as a direct result of the Black Power upsurge, since this latter had, as one of its targets, the very social class from which the radical intelligentsia was drawn. It had become obvious to the poor that *Abeng* intellectuals, despite genuine attempts to shed their class identity and align themselves with the poor, were not prepared to give up the perquisites of their class position. For comfortable intellectuals to champion popular resistance when they had no experience of what it was like to go hungry for days on end, or to feel the lash of the cat-o-nine-tails, necessarily aroused the suspicion of the lumpenproletariat.[44]

In Munroe's view, the intellectuals' flirtation with radical politics, while holding secure positions in the society, was a serious threat to the Black Power movement, since it suggested that bourgeois radicals really were not prepared to risk their social positions. Furthermore, this posture not only bred distrust among the poor, but also imported into the anti–*status quo* movement the black poor's cynicism toward *all* members of the middle class, whether anglicized or newly radicalized by Marxist ideology. For the intellectual, the way out of this contradiction was to face the harsh facts: it was no longer possible, Munroe argued, "to be a bourgeois in social life and a 'revolutionary' in politics." Moreover, Munroe maintained that intellectuals should avoid being pulled under by the class and racial vortex of the society. Rather than becoming immobilized by their own as well as the society's "class-colour consciousness," radical intellectuals, Munroe maintained, ought to "move forward to a higher stage" from which they could provide the labor movement with sorely needed leadership. With these recommendations on how intellectuals might negotiate their way out of the contradictions of bourgeois leadership of popular movements, Munroe turned to disputes over strategies for change and the responsibilties of intellectuals in social movements.

These disputes had arisen partly because the then-ascendant cultural nationalists had refused to propose a strategy for change and instead had argued for a policy of learning from the people. This stance had resulted in the airing of every conceivable ideological tendency within the anti–status quo movement. The result had been a cacophony of ideologies, in which Rastafarianism, Black Muslim nationalism, rebel-youth nihilism, New World economic nationalism, Marxist anti-imperialism, and unabashed black chauvinism had had unrestrained play in the paper. This jostling of ideologies, far from being being regarded as a liability, actually had been encouraged. This policy and its implications were now challenged by Munroe.

Such a policy, he implied, represented an intolerable surrender of intellectual leadership. For intellectuals to draw back from presenting a systematic political line, in favor of printing the spontaneous ideologies of the people, was not to strengthen the movement but rather to endanger it. Alluding to the concerns of leftists, Munroe observed:

> Certain forces need to be sure the paper stands for something rather than everything before coming in. The line which treats everything from the mouth of the people as gospel is no line at all. Yet it is doubtful whether the paper could have become such a social force without being the mouthpiece of the people. The point is . . . that indiscriminate populism has served its purpose . . . to perpetuate it any longer is not possible — the paper will pass away if it does not meet the need of revolutionary analysis in more of what it prints.[45]

Instead of populism, what was needed was "revolutionary guidance" from the intellectuals on the paper's editorial committee.[46] For Black Power to have any meaning for the Jamaican people, Munroe argued, theoretical leadership had to be exercised at the top, to demonstrate the antagonism between "black exploitation and white imperialism." To get out of its political cul-de-sac, the *Abeng* had to point out the unmistakable implication of Black Power: that it "must inevitably come up against the ultimate enemy — the ruling class of the U.S. and their local houseslaves."[47] In short, Munroe argued that the surrender of intellectual leadership and the presence of a concatenation of ideologies in the paper threatened to divert the people from the real nature of their predicament.

Despite the usefulness of this intervention, Munroe's subsequent contribution fell short on the major issue of what was to be done. Contrary to the logic of his analysis, which suggested the formation of an independent working-class movement, Munroe retreated into a pessimistic assessment of political obstacles. Having helped to mobilize the militant poor against the state, he now emphasized the latter's overweening power and the durability of its institutions and supporting classes.[48] He rejected the idea that radicals might play a positive role inside one of the main parties ("putting a few conscious Brothers in . . . would hardly be worth it") and dismissed the possiblity of a "third party majority." In his view, even if this party managed to win an election, it still would face the determined opposition of entrenched interests. By mid-September, when the last of his contributions was printed, "Blackman" still was unable to describe the political alternative which the Marxist Left so insistently had demanded. Instead of providing an answer to the question on everybody's mind, Munroe had only repeated the leftist position that the structure of oppression in the country was due to a "new imperialism" in which "local capitalists" and American multinationals were joined.[49]

Munroe's inability to draw up an independent alternative hinted at an exhaustion of ideas within the newspaper movement. Although this malaise was not to become a permanent condition, since the leftists later joined the independent-trade-union movement as political tacticians, for the moment it pushed the *Abeng* movement toward its demise. As the movement faltered, the longstanding disillusionment of the nationalist poor broke through onto the pages of the newspaper. In one short but extremely revealing contribution, the sufferers in effect rang down the curtain on this political movement.

Writing in response to the "Blackman" series of articles, "Marcus," an anonymous writer, delivered the poor people's first major indictment of the *Abeng*; this was the charge that the paper's contents generally were unintelligible to its intended audience. Apparently in response to the increasing injection of academic social theory into the paper, Marcus complained:

> Like most of what is written in *Abeng*, I have a hard time to follow what he is saying because of the whole heap of big words and high-sounding phrases used. For the majority of us black people who just barely pass through primary school, the *Abeng* is hard to read. Too much big word for us the half-blind that this country make so. If *Abeng* is for the people, it must write so that the people can easily understand. Words like "bourgeois, monopoly," . . . to name a few and phrases like "archaic power structure", . . . [and] "arbitrary police action" confuse me and only make me feel to put down the paper.[50]

In one of the real ironies of the newspaper movement, much of its basic information, not to mention its sophisticated ideological pronouncements, was unavailable to the poor, since illiteracy barred the effective transmission of *Abeng* news ideology. Indeed, Marcus' assertion that "the way the paper is written, makes me feel like it is written for educated people alone," was eloquent testimony to a major handicap of popular movements like the *Abeng*: the inadequacy of print communication to influence groups outside the literate classes.

Continuing this powerful indictment of the paper, Marcus next raised the lumpenproletariat's other concerns. How was it, he asked, that a movement ostensibly defending the cause of Rastafarians had no room for one of its important leaders, Claudius Henry? Observing that black organizations in which Henry had no part would "have a hard time reaching anywhere," Marcus demanded that the *Abeng* intellectuals cease isolating themselves and draw closer to the people and to authentic community leaders like Henry.

Finally, in a reflection of the capacity among social outcasts for penetrating social insight, Marcus put the intellectuals on notice by calling attention to their unstable ideological orientation and contradictory postures.

I know some of the leaders are people with big words and no action, some don't really want change because change would shake their pockets or their parents and friends big deep thread-bags. Some only want changes so that they can be tomorrow's Manley and Busta and some merely floating with the tide . . . some are really with black sufferers, . . . Hail to them.[51]

From these remarks, it is clear that the unemployed poor had had enough of the *Abeng* movement. The impasse created by the paper's ideological crisis, the absence of notable representatives from poor communities on its editorial board, the vacillation of its intellectuals, and the daunting problems of illiteracy frustrated the lower class and increased its cynicism toward politics and the leadership of intellectuals. Hence, a social movement which had begun with high hopes of building on the political opening created by Rodney's activism ultimately was unable to move beyond political mobilization to organization, and finally broke up amid acrimonious disputes. The following chapter discusses the renewal of activism in the context of the JLP's political decomposition and the corresponding PNP resurgence and electoral victory.

CHAPTER 9

Activism and Political Change, 1969-72

Despite success in championing anti-status quo ideologies and the grievances of the poor, the *Abeng* newspaper folded after ten months of publication. Internal conflicts over ideology and strategy eventually overcame the newspaper movement's opposition to social injustice, and highlighted the need for new initiatives. Although its popularity among workers, youths, academics, and the unemployed was undisputed, and despite the political yield from its defense of the people's cause,[1] this initiative had exhausted itself. Challenged by leftists to transcend its limitations, the *Abeng* remained mired, promoting conflicting ideologies and articulating repetitive critiques. Unwilling until the last moment to confront its inherent contradictions, the paper folded amid calls that it go beyond populism to revolutionary analysis.

The demise of the *Abeng* did not signal a retreat from popular protest and activism, however. Indeed, the disintegration of the *Abeng* movement really was the latest permutation in the evolution of postcolonial radical activism. In discussing the aftermath of the *Abeng* movement, then, this chapter examines the JLP's continuing crisis and the emergence of new forms of political dissidence. The latter forms include the advent of an independent-trade-union movement, to which former *Abeng* activists attached themselves, and an increase in student protests against government and university curbs on the intelligentsia. The chapter concludes with a discussion of the JLP's political decomposition and the PNP's return to power in February 1972.

The Advent of Independent Workers' Unions: The ITAC

In the postcolonial years, the Jamaican working class played a minor role in the protests against the authoritarian state. Politically divided by the dominant unions, subject to the vagaries of an underdeveloped labor market, and constrained from seeking left wing alternatives until the mid-sixties, the working class remained largely outside the orbit of radical political activity. Despite this isolation from the anti-status quo political movement, workers nonetheless repeatedly demonstrated their dissatisfaction with wages and working conditions through a variety of job actions. Between 1967 and 1969 alone, over 900 disputes – not including work stoppages – were referred to the Ministry of Labour.[2] Throughout the sixties, unauthorized strikes, "go-slows," and demonstrations were typical responses by labor to unsatisfactory working conditions. Indeed, at the height of the strike movement in 1967–68, some 138 work stoppages were recorded, as workers grew increasingly restive.[3]

Coming in a period of increased political and social crisis, this heightened activism in the workplace revealed workers' growing dissatisfaction with their economic situation and increasing readiness to create disorder in the workplace to fulfill their demands. Thus even though labor did not spearhead the political opposition, its persistent job actions seriously undermined the JLP's attempt to maintain political order and industrial stability.[4] From 1966 to 1968, this restiveness in the workplace led workers to found independent unions and to unify them in October 1968 under a federal body, the Independent Trade Union Advisory Council (ITAC). Perennial dissatisfaction with antidemocratic and bureaucratic tendencies in the established trade unions, and labor's desire to be effective decision makers in their unions' affairs, produced this latest challenge to the status quo.

In this move toward self-management, Chris Lawrence, the veteran trade unionist, played a pivotal role. As a member of the black working class, Lawrence had participated in the leftwing trade-union activism of the forties and fifties.[5] However, in the wake of the 1952 PNP split and the ensuing disputes within the ex-PNP Left over political tactics, Lawrence – much like his contemporary Ben Monroe of the UWC – emerged from the period a committed socialist, opposed to political unionism of whatever political coloration. By the mid-sixties, Lawrence had risen to the position of assistant general secretary within the Trade Union Congress (TUC), an independent union which had degenerated into a form of business unionism not unlike that of the dominant BITU and NWU. No doubt chafing at this development, Lawrence eventually challenged TUC leader Hopeton Caven, accusing the union of corruption and the misuse of funds. Lawrence was summarily fired in January 1966, but he and several other workers formed the Jamaica Congress of Labour (JCL) and won legal recognition for the union in March of that year.[6] With the formation of the JCL, workers at long last had a union over whose affairs they exercised direct control. By the end of the decade, five more independent unions led by workers had emerged in various sectors of the economy. In September 1967, the Jamaica Maritime Union, an organization representing Jamaican seamen, was formed by activist Milton Scott and two associates. Within a few years, the JMU was representing fishermen and dockers.[7]

In addition to the major political upheaval of that year, 1968 saw the advent of other independent unions: the Printers and Allied Workers Association (PAWA), the Public Cleansing Workers Union (PCWU), the Jamaica Omnibus Services Workers Association (JOSWA), and the Service Stations Attendants Union (SSAU). By the late sixties, therefore, municipal workers, service station employees, printers, and public transport workers had turned their backs on the established unions and joined these newly-formed unions under working-class leadership. Representing some of the lowest-paid and least-organized members of the working class, these unions defended workers' basic rights in industries where such rights long had been ignored. The independent unions disputed wrongful dismissals, demanded better wages, and challenged employers' cavalier attitude toward the payment of overtime and back pay. Despite labor regulations requiring additional payments for overtime, these rules were often ignored by employers, including those in the public sector. As a result, the PCWU, and the JCL were forced to challenge the municipal government in 1968 to secure back pay for workers, because regulations requiring double-time pay for weekends and holidays had been ignored.[8]

Even as they scored important victories for workers, the power and effectiveness of these unions were hampered by deficiencies which put them at a disadvantage against employers. Prior to October 1968, for instance, the independent unions were sorely lacking in personnel and resources to pursue their objectives. They were also deficient in internal education, ideological leadership, and overall unity. Notwithstanding Lawrence's assistance through the JCL, these fledgling unions also had difficulties with internal organization, rank-and-file participation, and ideological development. Rather than becoming an expansive movement which combined the political development of its members with every-day trade-union concerns, the new unions confined themselves largely to bread-and-butter issues.

Given such shortcomings, it is not surprising that employers often held the upper hand in negotiations. As the ITAC itself noted, some employers flatly rejected these unions' wage demands; other refused to recognize the groups as legitimate bargaining agents and negotiated with other unions.[9] Consequently, despite the fact that workers gained political experience, administrative skills, and self-respect from creating their own unions, these advances were offset by continuing difficulties. It was partly to remedy these shortcomings that the leaders of the independent unions formed the ITAC in October 1968. Acting as a federal body for the several unions, ITAC sought to strengthen the unity of the affiliated unions, deepen workers' participation in them, and protect each union's autonomy.

Carefully avoiding the dominant unions' blanket approach to organization, in which workers in different trades were united in a single body and subordinated to a dominant leader, ITAC insisted on the distinctiveness of the separate unions and promoted their right to self-organization. Thus, unity and autonomy were twin goals in the founding of ITAC. At the same time, ITAC sought to remedy the deficiencies of the independent unions. These shortcomings included a low level of political information among the leadership and the rank and file, and a general absence of a strategic view of the connection between workers' struggles against employers and the continuing fight for national liberation.

Here Chris Lawrence, as a carrier of the earlier anti-imperialist tradition within the labor movement, assumed responsibility for political education in the ITAC. Both before and after the founding of the organization, Lawrence tried to cope, almost singlehandedly, with the problem of political education and the issue of the strategic direction of the independent unions. Drawing on his organizational experience, knowledge of the Jamaican working class, and familiarity with Marxism, Lawrence helped organize classes and study groups for workers and their leaders, initially at the JCL's office and later at the ITAC headquarters. In these classes, workers were exposed to Marxist literature and writings on the Jamaican labor movement.[10] In contributing to these discussions, Lawrence reviewed the development of the Jamaican socialist tradition, explained the causes of the 1952 split and its consequences, and in general tried to show the workers the political logic of their activism as it related to both the struggle for national liberation in Jamaica, and the international labor movement's challenge to imperialism.

Lawrence found his audience mostly receptive to this leftwing tutelage, even though several union leaders were non-Marxists. In fact, despite their unity on the question of workers' rights, the working-class leaders of the ITAC unions subscribed to contrasting ideologies. For example, Milton Scott of the JMU was a black nationalist and occasional chauvinist who, when it suited his purposes, paid "lip service to being a socialist."[11] On the other hand, Clement Sinclair of the SSAU, after a stint with Americans and Cubans at the Guantánamo Naval Base in Cuba, had returned to Jamaica with a marked antipathy toward the Cuban Revolution. Reginald Burke of JOSWA combined his role as a trade unionist with other responsibilities as a churchman. Finally, Sidney Da Silva of the PCWU was a Rastafarian, while Winston Pusey of PAWA was the only other Marxist in the movement besides Lawrence.

Not unlike the intellectuals on the *Abeng,* the working-class ITAC leadership was comprised of individuals who subscribed to incompatible ideologies while sharing a common defense of labor. Unlike relations on the *Abeng,* however, ideological disagreements within the ITAC did not prove to be cause for a breakup. Solidarity and a search for a common ground, overcame a weak sense of class struggle and working-class consciousness among the affiliates.[12] Chris Lawrence's care in not making Marxism a criterion for membership, the other leaders' genuine respect and affection for him as one of their own, and their common interest as trade unionists held these disparate personalities together in the first year of the ITAC.[13]

Still, if ITAC were to live up to its objectives of securing "just and proper rates of wages, hours of work and other conditions of labour," as well as supporting "all national and international anti-imperialist forces in defending the welfare of workers," the ITAC had to transform itself into a dynamic organization capable of realizing ambitious goals. In the area of labor research, these goals required accurate data on wages and salaries across various industries, up-to-date information on labor legislation, employment contracts, employers' profits, and the like. Given the independent unions' limited funds and lack of resources and personnel, this information was largely unavailable to them. Similarly, if the ITAC were to be effective, it had to expand its influence among the mass of disgruntled workers who were yet to be unionized. Here again, a coherent organizational strategy for expanding the ITAC base was lacking, as were fulltime cadres and skilled organizers.

This lack of trained organizers who could apply the strategies and tactics necessary to secure labor's victories against employers would prove costly in summer 1969, as JOWSA attempted to dislodge the BITU and NWU by demanding a representation poll of the transport workers. With the bus company's dismissal of Reginald Burke, president of JOSWA, the task of organizing workers for the poll fell to vice-president Milton Scott, with unfortunate results. Instead of drawing on ITAC's resources and Lawrence's experience in labor tactics, Scott in July 1969 contested the poll in a haphazard, personalist manner. Rather than easing the fledgling union into battle with the more powerful unions by first securing representational rights, Burke contested the poll by demanding full bargaining rights for all the workers. Given JOSWA's weaknesses and the dominant unions' entrenched positions, seasoned organizers, and party-linked largesse, this winner-take-all strategy was destined to fail. As results of the poll showed, JOSWA was unsuccessful in drawing workers to its cause, as some 60 percent of the eligible workers stayed away.[14] Despite this low turnout, the poll handily gave JOSWA the minimum 30 percent of the total membership required for it to represent some of these workers. However, because of

Burke's winner-take-all demand, this vital right was put in jeopardy. Thus, even with important strides in its first year, ITAC suffered from serious problems of organization and leadership. As one of its publications later acknowledged, "For the first year . . . things carried on almost as before," and the organization's goals "were not achieved because of the weakness of ITAC's executive."[15]

Compounding these weaknesses was the unavailability of radical intellectuals who might have provided some of the skills and resources needed by the fledgling union movement.[16] It will be recalled that, at the moment of ITAC's birth, radical intellectuals had just emerged from a prolonged isolation. Their advent on the political scene in the sixties had not yet brought them into sustained contact with the working class. As we saw in the case of the New World Group, the intellectuals' activism had put them into contact with disaffected members of the educated middle class, while the *Abeng* movement had brought other intellectuals closer to the militant urban unemployed. Not only were the intellectuals cut off from the independent labor movement in this period, but the resources which were poured into publishing popular journals and newspapers were denied to the struggling independent unions. For much of its existence, the *Abeng* provided no assistance to ITAC, and hardly any news about the union movement was carried in its columns.

With the demise of the *Abeng,* this situation changed significantly. Fed up with the populism of the *Abeng,* three leftwingers from its staff — Trevor Munroe, Horace Levy, and Rupert Lewis, all of the UWI — joined ITAC, at its invitation. By the first months of 1970, both Munroe and Levy were sitting on ITAC's Executive Council, while heading up the organization's research committee. All three also participated in the organization's political activities, by forming a separate collective which they named the Abeng Group. The presence of members of the Abeng Group on the ITAC executive brought new vigor to the organization. In expressing their commmitment to the political and economic advance of workers in a way that would strengthen the alliance between intellectuals and workers, these activists had found an ideal outlet for their energies.

As socialist members of the intelligentsia with advanced training in the social sciences, the *Abeng* activists' skills matched ITAC's current needs. On the organization's research committee, they brought skills sorely needed to unearth and interpret information relevant to the labor movement. Referring to the significance of their involvement in this area, these intellectuals observed appropriately that "intellectuals can learn from workers the conditions of struggle and in deepening this struggle find the point of their research. Workers can benefit from the information provided by the intellectual, information, for example, about an industry's profits, an employer's alliance with the politician, the inadequacy of wages offset by rising prices, and the international connections of management."[17]

In addition to handling ITAC's labor research, these socialists strengthened the union movement in other ways. For example, they assisted with the nagging problem of worker education and leadership training, while developing publications and agitational literature.[18] Moreover, as intellectuals and activists with experience derived from other radical organizations, they undoubtedly brought to the ITAC executive a theoretical leadership and strategic outlook for labor's forward movement in alignment with other anti-imperialist struggles. Where the ITAC so far had been unsuccessful in infusing its affiliates with a strong antiimperialist perspective, these academics, seasoned by their struggles elsewhere, injected a new emphasis on militant actions and initiatives by labor.

Several developments testified to this increased vigor inside the ITAC. After holding an Annual Conference on 25 January 1970, the organization sponsored a General Conference two weeks later. This meeting on 8 February elected new officers, formally coopted members of the Abeng Group, and adopted resolutions relevant to ongoing labor disputes.[19] The General Conference gave a "warm reception" to Trevor Munroe, officially a political scientist at the university, who spoke on the topic, "Conditions for Social Revolution."[20]

Over the next five months, as the domestic and international Black Power movement triggered student demonstrations and other political developments, ITAC broadened its political involvement by expressing its solidarity with these actions.[21] At the same time, the organization drew up a carefully-crafted new constitution and launched an important national organizational program to expand its membership. Several fulltime organizers were appointed in Kingston and the country parts to meet workers' increasing demands for independent representation. With these joint actions in mid-1970, a rejuvenated ITAC served notice to its members that trade-union activism and broader political concerns were an indivisible part of the independent union movement.

The Crisis Deepens at Mona:
The Expansion of Student Protests

With the JLP's suppression of the 1968 demonstration, the increase in student political activism was deflated. The immediate aftermath of the October events left them demoralized and badly divided.[22] Despite attempts by a few to counter the barrage of government criticisms, the political tide had shifted in the JLP's favor. This reversal created an opening for students who wanted to restore the *status quo ante,* and they took the offensive in an unsuccessful effort to oust the president of the Guild of Undergraduates.[23] With this turn of events, it appeared that the JLP's desire to see the campus return to its earlier political orthodoxy was being realized in a conservative drift within the student body. Such skirmishes among students, however, led to neither quiescence nor reaction. Rather, continued government pressure on the university, coupled with the appointment of a new vice-chancellor who was even more of a disciplinarian than his predecessor, paved the way for another wave of student protests.

It will be recalled that, after the October 1968 demonstration, critics of the university had suggested that a firmer hand was needed to run the institution. Vice-Chancellor Philip Sherlock had become a target of these critics, as his tentative effort to balance the university's independence against the state's security claims dismayed both government officials and *Gleaner* editorialist. Backed by a chorus of charges that the leadership at Mona was weak and indecisive, the supporting governments brought in Roy O. Marshall, a white Barbadian professor of law, as the new vice-chancellor replacing Sherlock, who already had been scheduled to retire.

Taking up his duties in early 1969, Marshall inherited an institution severely weakened by internal divisions and buffeted by government pressures. The latest of these pressures included security checks for all new appointments to the Mona campus and demands for a code of conduct for students and faculty. Indeed, blatant threats to disrupt the functioning of the university had become part of this campaign, as the *Gleaner* reported the government's intention to reimpose work permits for all non-Jamaicans working at the institution, should administrators fail to cooperate.[24] With Marshall's appointment, it appeared that the Jamaican government had found an administrator prepared to respond affirmatively to its security concerns.

In the first months of his tenure, the new vice-chancellor presided over the approval of the controversial "Code of Conduct" for academics that had been demanded by the JLP.[25] As a document designed to curb political activism, the Code of Conduct was remarkable for its subservience to the government's wishes. In the three important areas of staff-student relations, extra-university activity, and participation in politics, the document hewed to positions taken by the Jamaican government. In the first area, the university, reflecting the official theory that students were being duped by their teachers, warned academics not "to manipulate the policy of student organizations" or use their relationship with students "for the purpose of religious, political or racial propaganda."[26]

The UWI administration adopted a similar position on intellectuals' off-campus activities. Echoing the official view, which regarded dissident intellectuals as ideological fanatics, the university called on academics to display in their extra-university involvements "the same attributes that mark the discharge of their University functions, namely: objectivity, impartiality in assessing evidence, logical reasoning and integrity."[27] The university apparently was prepared to punish academics who violated these strictures, as it noted that the "quality" of these outside activities would be used "in assessing their performance and their claims for advancement."[28]

Finally, the UWI administration made it clear that radical faculty and staff would find little support for their controversial politics. While acknowledging that staffers were "free to seek political office," the university suggested that where such activities brought staffers into conflict with the state, the university could not "guarantee support to any of its members for consequences which flow from their political activity."[29] In short, at a time when dissident opinion and political activism were increasingly under official attack, the UWI administration had little to say in defense of unpopular ideas in a democratic society. Instead, the university had thrown its support to those who would curb unpopular speech and activism. With the approval of the Code of Conduct in September 1969, the "get-tough" policy against JLP critics increased, with the cooperation of the Marshall administration. Among its first victims[30] were Clive Thomas, a Guyanese lecturer in economics, who was banned from the island; and Eric Frater, an assistant registrar and PNP activist, whom Marshall had reassigned because of the activist's involvement in political campaigning.

These actions prompted sharp student protests against the government and the Marshall administration. Alluding to the possible "ruin" of the university, the graduate student body decried arbitrary curbs based on mere differences in political opinion,[31] and the undergraduates pointed up the UWI administration's bias in penalizing Frater even as it allowed his JLP counterparts on campus to engage in active politics.[32]

In the ensuing weeks, opposition to Marshall increased dramatically. As students' impatience with his inaction on the Thomas banning grew, the Frater issue became embroiled in national politics, with the PNP criticizing the vice-chancellor's action.[33] Rejecting Marshall's claim that Frater's political activities were incompatible with his position as an administrator, the PNP reminded Marshall of his responsibilities:

> Unlike the Civil Service, the University is not an instrument to carry out the policy of the government of the day. Its duty is to carry out the functions set out in its Charter and also to bear witness to those fundamental demo-

cratic principles enshrined in the constititution of all the countries which it serves. Those principles include freedom of speech and the unimpeded right to engage in lawful political activities.[34]

In other words, political participation was Frater's constitutional right as a citizen and so was not subject to restrictive administrative edicts.

The PNP's statement on Frater brought into focus another issue at the heart of the controversy — namely, the propriety of academics' political activism. In a firm rebuttal to those who saw such activities as improper, the PNP went to the heart of the matter by observing that "the idea that political activity is something disreputable and semi-legal — to be tolerated within limits but not encouraged — is a hangover from our neo-colonial past. It has no place in an independent country, and the university of all places should play a leading part in destroying such a notion."[35] With this intervention, the PNP did two things: it spoke for those who were opposed to the colonial character of the university and the JLP's attempt to keep it that way, and it became a powerful political ally of embattled academics, beleaguered students, and demoralized staffers.

Confronted with these pressures and the growing national concern with human rights, civil liberties, and abuses of authority, Marshall responded with a weak, bureaucratic defense of free speech while emphasizing the need for guidelines in political bannings.[36] Citing the demoralization of faculty, the vice-chancellor initially questioned the arbitrariness of Thomas' exclusion, and asked the government to explain its action. After being rebuffed by the security minister, who refused to provide answers, Marshall returned to an uncompromising defense of the state's authority to deal, where it saw fit, with "illegal activities which aim at bringing about a change in the constitution or in the government of the day."[37] Thus, at a time when voices were being raised against abuses of civil liberties, the vice-chancellor seemed intent on offering justifications for continued curbs.[38]

With Marshall adopting a position almost indistinguishable from that of the government, the students stepped up their protest. They called for a "commission of inquiry" into the operations of the university and demanded that the vice-chancellor act to reappoint Thomas to his post by 13 October — the date for graduation exercises — or they would be forced to take "positive action." When Marshall failed to act on this ultimatum, the students took the action they had promised. As graduation exercises proceeded and the vice-chancellor began addressing the assembly, more than half the students walked out.[39] Moreover, as the first anniversary of Walter Rodney's expulsion approached, students marked the occasion by boycotting classes and barring entry to the registry building for several days.

By the end of the month, student protests had spread to the Saint Augustine campus, as Trinidadian students challenged the nonrenewal of another faculty member's contract by surrounding the pro-vice chancellor's residence and occupying the bursary and the administration building. At the same time, in an apparent show of intercampus solidarity, Mona students reportedly were planning to take direct action to support their peers in Trinidad.[40] Almost exactly a year after their forced retreat and the subsequent appointment of a vice-chancellor sympathetic to the government, then, the students had rallied with renewed protests against both the state and the authoritarian UWI administration.

This revivification of campus protest continued into the new year, as Caribbean governments sought to protect themselves against an ever-encroaching Black Power movement. After all, the Caribbean Black Power movement had drawn its ideological inspiration from the Afro-American struggle for social and economic justice but domesticated its themes to address class and racial inequalities in the region. The demand for Black Power in the Caribbean was an expression of the black majority's unfulfilled desire for a better life — one which would see an end to the poverty, social injustice, and cultural discrimination prevailing in the region. As a rallying slogan, "Black Power" condensed the black majority's historical grievances against the rule of hegemonic classes at the local and international levels. The Black Power movement represented a serious threat to the ensemble of relations which had emerged from the colonial period and to the Caribbean regimes that presided over them.

Given this antagonism between the anti-imperialism of the Black Power movement and the political conservatism of the regional governments, it is not surprising that in 1970 these regimes grew increasingly defensive, as they became the targets of Black Power advocates. Indeed, between February and May of that year, the Black Power movement reached its apogee, as popular demands for change became more insistent and as links among the unemployed, students, workers, and intellectuals strengthened. As ever, this rising demand for change was initiated by students and their supporters at the Mona campus in Jamaica. On 2 February, students occupied the Creative Arts Center — a venue on campus which many regarded as a bastion for the promotion of European culture. The continuing neglect of the indigenous cultures of the Caribbean in the center's offerings had outraged sections of the student population, who saw this policy as yet another denial of the legitimacy of the islands' national arts and culture. As the campus newspaper recalled approvingly, the students

> were protesting against many things: the highbrow arrogance of its staff; its programmes of cultural elitism and exclusivity; its presentations — Eurocentric,

prestigious and patronizing when not contemptuous of W[est] I[ndian] Folk
Culture. The Center, it seemed, had no space for the work of non-
professionals, or Rastafarian artists or W[est] I[ndian] playwrights. Its function was that of a Musuem, where *Culture*—the higher things, for the gifted
and the cultivated, not the cultists!—would thrive in its necessary walled-in
silence.[41]

While students, faculty, and independent artists attempted to remedy
this neglect by holding teach-ins and staging their own productions over
several weeks, the vice-chancellor acted to break up the occupation of
the Center. Citing the threat to the "maintenance of order" posed by
the students' "unlawful occupation," Marshall suspended four of them
and sought an injunction from the courts to end the occupation.[42]

Even as Marshall's actions and the exigencies of upcoming exams
eventually forced the students to end their occupation, in Trinidad Black
Power protests were endangering the Williams government. Five days
after the occupation of the Creative Arts Center began in Jamaica,
students from the Saint Augustine campus marched on the Canadian
High Commission and the Royal Bank of Canada to protest the trial
in Canada of West Indian students charged with destroying computer
facilities. On 4 March, this action was followed by a massive Black Power
march of thousands from Woodford Square to Shanty Town in Trinidad,
where the demonstrators denounced the Williams regime's indifference
to the needs of the black majority.

Over the next six weeks, the protestors kept the pressure on the
Williams government with more marches and demonstrations. However,
as this protest took a new turn, with the convergence of workers' demands with those of the Black Power groups, Williams recognized the
danger and on 21 April declared a state of emergency. Despite a subsequent mutiny by a section of the Trinidadian Defense Force, the spontaneous "February Revolution" petered out, as the Coast Guard put down
the mutineers.

This close call for the Williams regime, coupled with missteps by
some Black Power advocates, gave frightened forces in the region another opportunity to discredit the protestors. For example, at a news
conference in Guyana, Stokely Carmichael—who had been invited by
Ratoon, the Guyana Black Power group—exasperated his hosts by
speaking casually about the use of violence and declaring that the
Caribbean Black Power movement specifically excluded coloreds and
Indians. This misstatement of the movement's purposes and Carmichael's ignorance of Ratoon's position of Afro-Indian solidarity gave
detractors ammunition for their counteroffensive. Not only did governments compete to bar Trinidadian Black Power figures from their territories, but some, like Barbados, prepared legislation to criminalize

the advocacy of Black Power ideas. In Jamaica, the government and its allies repeated their characteristic refrains. For its part, the JLP showed its continuing inability to address the issue of black nationality in terms which would take into account the popular desire for social justice and the recognition of a new cultural orientation and subjectivity. The regime stuck to its bureacratic, racially-neutered definition of Black Power as black dignity and black economic mobility, ambition, and self-respect.

In its turn, the *Gleaner's* response to Carmichael's racially exclusivist formulations was to offer up the ideology of Jamaican Exceptionalism. Labeling Carmichael a "racist," the newspaper asserted that "since probably more than a million of the West Indian people are neither black nor white, the doctrines preached by Mr. Carmichael are just plain nonsense on the West Indian scene, where black and coloured people have advanced to greater status and freedom than anywhere else in the world."[43] In the aftermath of the "February Revolution" and the continuing crisis at the university, this reaffirmation of the ideological tenets of Exceptionalism hinted at a shaky renewal of confidence among defenders of the status quo. With the diminution of the Black Power movement in Trinidad and its exhaustion in Jamaica, Caribbean regimes had come through the upheaval largely intact, albeit compromised by their opposition to it. The *Gleaner's* apparent confidence in the permanence of the ideological status quo failed to acknowledge subtle changes which had begun to emerge after some eight years of protracted political challenge.

To appreciate these developments, one need only point to the character of the political scene in the region during 1970-71. A variegated opposition movement, comprised initially of a narrow range of social forces, had succeeded in calling attention to the fundamental problems of Jamaican society. In an epoch in which popular revolts had become generalized on a global scale, the activism of these domestic movements and their popularization of anti–status quo themes had succeeded in impugning the legitimacy of the regime, without having the capacity to dislodge it.

Having successfully withstood the often spontaneous popular-democratic protests, the regime still was burdened by its defense of increasingly unpopular policies. An apparent stalemate existed between the regime and its opposition. Given this impasse, a major question remained: Could the political system accommodate the popular demand for social and economic justice, or would social relations deteriorate further? As it turned out, Jamaica's authoritarian democracy, with its system of party competition and electoral rivalry, defused the political crisis and created the opening within which political renovations might emerge.

The JLP's Political Decline

In our analysis of the JLP's politics, emphasis has been put on its authoritarianism. When faced with political challenges, the JLP employed strategies of containment and preemptive curbs. Such defensive responses owed much to the particular historical background of Caribbean political leaders, who had had a dual apprenticeship in authoritarian and democratic political practices. On the one hand, the political leaders' exclusion from power under colonial authoritarianism had given them a familiarity with dictatorial rule; on the other, their extended apprenticeship under the semidemocratic system of internal self-government had exposed them to the merits of capitalist democratic rule.

This double ideological formation under colonialism was carried over into postcolonial practices. In combatting the political opposition, the JLP, not unlike the colonial state, was moved to rely on both restrictive laws and unilateral, nonreviewable edicts to maintain its rule, but it refrained from liquidating the political forms or all the procedures of bourgeois democracy. Unfortunately, on those occasions where the JLP thought it had secured legal legitimacy for its illiberal policies, the actual effect was a subversion of law, and with it, subversion of aspects of liberal democratic government. Perhaps recognizing that neither an exclusively authoritarian use of the law nor the promotion of an enforced civic morality would extricate it from its political crisis, the JLP did make hesitant, unconvincing efforts to respond to some popular demands, combining certain positive initiatives with restrictive policies.

For example, in response to early expressions of black nationalism, in 1964 the JLP had Marcus Garvey's body exhumed in England and returned to the island. Two years later, in an attempt to placate the Rastafarians, it hosted Ethiopian Emperor Haile Selassie's visit to the island. And almost a decade after independence, the JLP belatedly introduced a system of national honors and awards. In the regime's view, this latter was necessary "to overcome the inferiority complex resulting from centuries of colonial status, and to reinforce and reflect desirable social conduct and attitudes."[44] However, as the student protests and increasingly militant Black Power movement showed, these defensive measures did little to change popular perceptions, since other policies indicated that black nationalism was anathema to the regime.

On other controversial issues, such as foreign ownership of the national economy, and the unemployment and marginalization of youth, the JLP developed responses which proved unconvincing.[45] For instance, in dealing with the growing demand for a larger domestic share in the ownership of the national economy, the JLP and its allies were able to articulate only a weak policy of "Jamaicanization." In fact, this policy was notable more for its reassurances to capital than for its defense of the principle of national ownership. In announcing a 2 percent tax on foreign financial institutions, the prime minister took care to note that the companies could avoid paying the full tax by permitting Jamaicans to own 51 percent of the companies' shares. Indeed, the government further weakened this measure by reassuring the corporations that compliance was not a matter of urgency. In a remarkable address to representatives of foreign capital, the prime minister told them that "the changes to be made do not have to be made instantly. Companies are working on programmes which involve gradual movement over a six to seven year period from total foreign control to Jamaican control. This period will give us ample time to enable adaptations to be made and to deal with the problems which inevitably take place when change comes out."[46]

Why would the government announce a policy of nationalizaiton of the financial sector of the economy and then proceed to water it down? Part of the answer lies in capital's distaste for state ownership of the economy and the JLP's determination not to be perceived as the agent of a policy directed toward state ownership. Having become fearful when the PNP proposed land reform and public ownership of the national economy in 1964, foreign capital was decidedly edgy about this JLP attempt to appease popular sentiment. It was therefore left to Neville Ashenheim, a leading representative of domestic capital and leader of government business in the Senate, to set the record straight. Reassuring capital about the government's intention, Ashenheim noted:

> It is not impossible that the phrase "Jamaicanization" might be misunderstood by persons abroad . . . we do not, and I repeat we do not, mean the nationalization of our industries and our means of production. There may be appropriate occasions for nationalization of industries . . . but that is not what people understand by Jamaicanization . . . we have not got a programme of nationalization. We have a programme of Jamaicanization; and, in so far as the foreign sector is concerned, Jamaicanization means not nationalization, it means not confiscation, it simply means an invitation to go into partnership with the people of Jamaica.[47]

Despite this reluctance to speak of nationalization and state ownership of the economy, circumstances in the sugar industry left the regime little alternative but to assume ownership of sugar lands. After presiding over an industry marked by inefficient production, declining output, and chronic worker dissatisfaction, the West Indies Sugar Company (WISCO), a subsidiary of the British firm Tate and Lyle, began its withdrawal from sugar production in the island.[48] Faced with the news of this corporate move in 1970, the government opted to sign an agreement in May 1971 to buy some sixty thousand acres of sugar lands from WISCO. Although the government tried to depict this transfer as part of its program of Jamaicanization,[49] this buy-out had less to do with an affirmative policy of reducing foreign control of an important national industry than with the *fait accompli* presented by WISCO's investment decision. In sum, the JLP's positive responses often were unconvincing and contradictory. Such steps, taken reluctantly and under duress, did little to convince the public that the regime was committed to change.

These half-hearted concessions to popular sentiment did not suggest that the regime's determination to continue its unpopular policies had weakened. Despite growing public opposition to its abuse of power and its bias in applying the law, the JLP maintained its unyielding law-and-order position.[50] In time, this policy alienated sections of the middle class and professional groups. The president of the prestigious Bar Association, for example, echoed broad public sentiment as he decried the erosion of civil liberties and called for a public inquiry into the administration of justice in the country.[51] A similar disaffection spread among the clergy. In 1967–68, this group vigorously had opposed legalized gambling, which came with the passage of a Lottery Act.[52] By 1968, lottery fever had spawned such an orgy of betting by large numbers of poor Jamaicans eager to end their poverty that the clergy was stirred to protest. Lamenting the dismal social consequences of this frenzied attempt to "get rich quick," church leaders called in vain for a ban on this state-sponsored activity. After turning a deaf ear to the clergy on the issue of gambling, the regime compounded its difficulties with the church by trying to muzzle clergymen who, in the aftermath of the October riot, had begun delivering sermons critical of the government. This effort to bar the church from exercising its traditional role as a moral witness within the society proved particularly objectionable, since the JLP went so far as to summon the heads of the major denominations, to warn them to curb "ministers who . . . use their pulpits for purposes other than religion."[53]

In spite of its overtures to black nationalists, the regime was adamant in excluding from its ideology themes thrown up by the opposition movement. Black consciousness, social justice, and economic nationalism, as ideas, all were shut out of JLP ideology. In the dymanics of Jamaica's postcolonial social relations, these ideas had become so closely identified with the radical opposition and its antagonism to the dominant classes that JLP absorption of these ideas would have required a significant ideological transformation of the party. In short, the JLP would have had to become a radical populist party, articulating the people's cause against capital and its hegemonic classes. In 1971, such a political shift was out of the question for the JLP. By this time, the conflicts between the regime and the popular-democratic movement had accumulated to the point where the JLP was broadly regarded by the people as being too closely identified with the interests of capital.

As if these problems were not enough, the economic difficulties of the middle to late sixties, and the JLP's inability to solve them, contributed to growing dissatisfaction. For example, in this period the sugar industry entered a major crisis, as its viability and legitimacy were called into question.[54] In response to an industry characterized by inefficient production, labor-management disputes, declining output, and calls for mechanization, the regime adopted ad hoc measures which did little to resolve the crisis or placate the contesting parties.[55] As noted above, a solution of sorts was imposed on the regime, with Tate and Lyle's partial withdrawal from the industry in 1971.

As the crisis in agriculture deepened, the 1970s saw a general worsening of the economic climate. For instance, overall unemployment increased significantly, despite large-scale emigration between 1960 and 1970. The official rate of unemployment shot up from 13 percent in 1960, to 24 percent a decade later. Similarly, the public perception of significant class inequality was confirmed by reports of unequal income distribution.[56] According to one estimate for 1970, some 5 percent of the population received 27 percent of all income, while another 20 percent of the population received a mere 5 percent of income.[57] If rising import prices, increased taxes on goods and services, and negligible government efforts to improve labor's standard of living are taken into account, it is evident that, by the early seventies, labor's increased economic hardship was intensifying popular dissatisfaction, already high because of authoritarian policies.

Given these liabilities and the imminence of national elections, it may be argued that all that was required to take advantage of the JLP's advancing political decomposition was the availability of an organization. The situation in fact demanded a legitimate political organization with ties to all the major classes in the society, an organization that could earn the support of the political opposition and could come to power electorally. Since not a single organization among the antisystemic forces possessed these characteristics, the PNP was in a position to fill the breach. As early as 1969, it began to do just that by associating itself with the ever-widening popular disaffection with the regime.

The Recuperation of the PNP

As the foregoing indicates, the JLP's autocratic policies and its inability to find solutions to the urgent problems of the society helped fuel political opposition. Indeed, shock waves from the October explosion sent tremors throughout the society, stirring a range of social forces impelling them into opposition against the regime. Inevitably, this wave swept the PNP in its path and forced it to define its relationship to the upsurge in black consciousness, the mounting protest against the abuse of power, and the pervasive sense in the society that the JLP's policies had polarized the country. An indication of the direction the PNP was likely to follow came in February 1969, with the accession of Michael Manley, Norman Manley's son, to party leadership. Although his father had delivered a bitter farewell speech the previous November criticizing Black Power and the new generation of political activists,[58] the younger Manley took a more conciliatory approach.

In his inaugural address to the party in February, Michael Manley showed sensitivity to the unfolding crisis, invoking a broad popular appeal designed to exploit the exigencies of the moment. Developing the themes of moral rejuvenation and political participation, the younger Manley called for a "restoration of justice," a "dialogue with the people," and a national effort to "heal the society and bring it back together in some sort of unity, inspiration and purpose."[59]

Consistent with political practice in a competitive two-party system, Manley repeated the litany of charges which had been leveled against the government. He emphasized the need for integrity in public life, called for an end to gerrymandering and political victimization, and warned of the possible eclipse of democratic institutions. By adopting a general appeal based on the moral reconstruction of the society and the inclusion of disaffected groups in political decision making, Manley began to fashion a role for the PNP as an advocate for popular aspirations against an abusive, antidemocratic regime. Interestingly, in taking this position Manley really did not mark a significant ideological departure for the PNP. Rather, he was merely continuing the party's tradition of ideological progressivism — a tradition that generally had found the PNP adopting more socially progressive positions on issues than those taken by the conservative and pragmatic JLP.

Despite the advantages of this continuity in the party's ideological outlook, the late sixties and early seventies posed new challenges for the PNP. For one thing, the political scene in Jamaica, ideologically, had altered sufficiently that the PNP no longer held a monopoly on the development and articulation of radical ideas. Nor was it the only organization employing popular appeals. As we have seen, a plethora of ideological competitors had arisen in the sixties. Movements espousing socialism vied with others championing cultural consciousness, economic nationalism, and black economic and political power. Their presence on the political scene introduced new themes and policy options which won support from a range of disaffected social classes.

In these circumstances, for the PNP's rhetoric to echo such ideas put it on the side of the popular opposition. At the same time, it left the party in the awkward role of ideological imitator and latecomer to 1960s radicalism. Moreover, with the dissident movement having all but preempted the ideological terrain with its anti-imperialist and anti-JLP positions, the PNP, as one of the main political parties, had to determine just where it would locate itself ideologically, so as not to alienate this potential base of radical support. The challenge for the PNP, then, was to adopt a position which would win over the radical opposition without alienating the ideologically moderate social classes which provided the party's traditional base of support.

If the lack of a pioneering ideological role for the PNP put it at an initial disadvantage, then the fact that youths, disaffected workers, intellectuals, and the urban unemployed regarded the party not as an agent of change but as part of the problem created additional difficulties for a PNP recovery. It should be recalled that the sixties had spawned a general crisis of the dominant political institutions, which weakened popular support for both the PNP and the JLP. After all, in this period there was not only opposition to the JLP but also a generalized disaffection with official politics and established institutions. Political cynicism and disillusionment with official politics were especially rampant among workers, youths, and the unemployed — not to mention the fact that oppositon to the existing system hardened among socialists and Rastafarians. In this setting where there was a general delegitimation of official politics and institutions, the PNP had the task not only of reviving interest in political affairs, but also of extricating the party from this wider malaise. In some respects, the party was in a position similar to that in which it had found itself in 1962, when it faced the challenge of rejuvenation and recuperation. Unlike the case in 1962, however, in 1969–71 the party's difficulties were compounded by a deepened anti-systemic disillusionment.

The PNP's rejuvenation was eased somewhat by the emergence of the younger Manley's leadership of the party, and by the fact that the PNP was the only viable alternative for those wishing to oust the JLP. This strategic position in the political system was all the more important since the opposition, despite its political importance, neither threatened to displace the established parties at the polls nor challenged power through extraconstitutional means. Under these circumstances, the anti-JLP forces had little alternative but to look to the PNP if they wanted to bring about political change. Evidently aware of its strategic position, the PNP began fashioning a broad, people-oriented campaign to isolate the government, revive interest in the PNP, and rebuild popular loyalty to the political system.

One early step in this direction was the creation of a youth organization in July 1969. In an obvious bid to win the support of disaffected youths, the party maintained that young people at the time had no political voice in the country, encouraged their participation in PNP affairs, and promised to familiarize itself with the problems of youths and addresss their concerns. With this early focus on youth, the party highlighted an issue that was to recur throughout its election campaign: the inclusion of social forces who were ignored by the political system. It came as no surprise that Manley emphasized the party's interest in the plight of the unemployed "sufferers." At the annual party conference in 1969, he addressed these people directly, declaring, "Wherever you are, know that you are my true constituency in this country. You are the first object of our concern and your case shall be at the heart of our planning for the furture."[60]

Complementing the reformist themes of moral regeneration of the society, political inclusion of neglected groups, and restoration of democratic rule, the party also broached the issues of ownership of the economy and the country's relations with the Third World. On the question of economic nationalism, the PNP adopted the cautious position of promoting increased local ownership of the economy, while avoiding demands for nationalization of foreign enterprises.[61] At the same time, the party hinted at the development of a new foreign policy in which strategic alliances with the Third World would assume increased importance. In sum, as a party seeking to revive its political fortunes, the PNP by 1970 had taken up positions widely discussed among opponents to the status quo.

Despite this imitation, the PNP was careful to avoid the more controversial positions of the opposition. In the politically charged atmosphere of the time, the party carefully avoided Black Power and anti-imperialist appeals, as well as specific proposals for economic reform. Instead, the party emphasized the rectification of JLP abuses and called for the moral reconstruction of society, in which all classes and groups would play a part. At a time when social and economic inequalities and established political institutions were being challenged by the radical demands of the Black Power movement, the PNP was groping its way toward a cautious, nonantagonistic opposition devoid of radical rhetoric.

As its electoral campaign showed, the PNP's strategy was devised to draw support from the widest possible ensemble of classes and groups. The party could be seen as attempting to fashion not only its own revival, but, indeed, a recomposition of the political order. National unity rather than class polarization became a central theme. In the prelude to the elections, the PNP continued its appeal to a broad alliance of classes, including the unemployed, youths, farmers, professionals, businessmen, workers, and academics.[62] At the same time, Manley persisted in his challenge to the clergy, asking it to help him reverse the "moral decline" of the nation, and projected himself as a secular redeemer come to save the people. Unlike any previous leader of a dominant party, Manley employed religious language and even assumed the name of the biblical prophet "Joshua," to draw the religiously devout to the PNP's program of political reconstruction.[63]

As election day approached, the larger themes of moral rehabilitation and restoration of democracy were expressed in the compelling popular slogans, "Better Must Come," and "It's Time for a Change."[64] At the same time, political rallies throughout the country invoked the language, symbols, and music of the masses. The party's open identification with Rastafarian culture, its unabashed promotion of reggae music, and Manley's close identification with popular aspirations all made the PNP an irresistible alternative to the JLP.

That party, facing widespread disillusionment with its policies and a general perception that it had presided over a gradual decline in the material wellbeing of all classes, responded to the PNP's electoral strategy with an unconvincing defense of the status quo. In contrast to the PNP's symbolically "hot" election campaign, the JLP conducted a "cold" bureaucratic campaign based on a defense of tradition and stability.[65] Unable to match the charisma of the younger Manley, hampered by its inability to incorporate popular aspirations, and saddled with the social and economic legacies of its decade-long tenure, the JLP went down to defeat in an electoral landslide in February 1972. The PNP won 56.4 percent of the vote and 36 seats in the House of Representatives, with the JLP getting the remaining 16 seats and 43.4 percent of the vote.

The Enigma of the PNP's Victory

That the PNP secured this victory with significant support from social forces associated with the dissident opposition, as well as from the working and capitalist classes, created a dilemma for many on the Left. The JLP had been ousted from political office, but not by the radical opposition. Instead, one of the established political parties, invoking the people's culture, had secured a major electoral victory by forging an alliance among farmers, workers, capitalists, members of the middle class, and the unemployed. Given the class division in Jamaican society and the polarization of the time, a legitimate question could be raised about the PNP's class orientation. What class did the party represent? Was it procapitalist, as some on the Left maintained? Or, in light of its legitimation of popular culture and defense of the people's cause, should it be regarded as a populist party?

As the socialist Abeng Group observed, the PNP's landslide was indeed enigmatic. In its view, the PNP's victory had "produced a sight most strange in times of heightened social struggles – the imperialists and local capitalists are celebrating the PNP victory at the same time as the masses whom they oppress and exploit."[66] Although the early remarks of the Abeng Group suggested that the PNP's political orientation was indeterminate, it may be argued that the party remained primarily procapitalist and certainly was not pursuing a strategy of left-wing populism.

Notwithstanding the party's use of religious symbolism, popular music, and unabashed overtures to the Rastafarian movement, the PNP conducted a political campaign familiar in the context of the Jamaican two-party system. That is, it concentrated on the misdeeds of the government, promised to rectify them, and sought support from all those classes alienated by the incumbent's policies. At one level, the party's ideologicial progressivism and its antigovernment orientation explain how the PNP succeeded in winning the 1972 elections. In these terms, the PNP's recuperation was not a paradigmatic case of a resort to leftwing populism, in which a party champions the cause of the downtrodden against an oppressive capitalist class. In the strictest sense, the PNP was not a leftwing populist party, since this form of populism requires the championing of the people's cause against either capital or the social classes associated with it. Neither appeal was present in the PNP's antigovernment campaign. How then to account for the overtures to the people? What was the significance of the apparent people-orientation of the party between 1969 and 1972?

There are two possible answers to these questions. The banal answer is that the PNP wanted to return to power and did what was necessary to achieve this outcome. In characteristic fashion, it exploited all the weaknesses of the incumbent regime, employed an ideological progressivism, and took advantage of the currency of popular culture to win the allegiance of social forces traditioanlly neglected by the political system. By legitimizing the culture and ideology of the people and articulating their aspirations, the party was able to return to political power. While this explanation alludes to certain realities of Jamaican politics, it concedes too much to political opportunism and neglects a wider field of political determinations.

A second and more appealing explanation is that Jamaican society and its ensemble of social relations had entered a period of crisis, whose attenuation required concessions to popular demands. As the foregoing has shown, popular aspirations found expression in three nodal impulses: the struggle for a new subjectivity, the demand for improvements in labor's standard of living, and the search for a newer, emancipatory politics. With the antisystemic movement as their vehicle, these impulses intensified the class-linked contradictions in Jamaican society, while the JLP's policies contributed immeasurably to the unfolding crisis of the social system. In the context of flourishing radical movements and a significant delegitimation of the social system, the PNP's national-unity campaign may be seem as an apparent effort to reconstitute the political order through a controlled transformation from above. The popular campaign leading to the PNP's 1972 victory must be seen as an example of crisis management from within the system. In sum, the political recuperation of the PNP was not a triumph of leftwing populism. Rather, the PNP's return to power, by way of multiclass appeals and support for popular aspirations, should be seen as an example of crisis management and political reconstruction from above. With this perspective in mind, in the next chapter we examine the contribution of the dissident opposition to this emergent reconstruction of the political order, and draw up the balance sheet of a decade of protest.

CHAPTER 10

The Dissident Movement and Social Change, 1960–72

In the postcolonial period, the JLP was constantly on the defensive, as it sought to ward off recurrent challenges and shore up its tottering political rule. The shakiness of the regime ultimately derived from its inability to surmount the colonial legacy of economic underdevelopment. Economic backwardness contributed to a growing crisis of unemployment, which eventually was transformed into a political crisis. As a growing proportion of the rural population was deposited into the capital city, they not only swelled the ranks of the unemployed, but also developed a militancy which spawned an expanding political opposition. It was this widening opposition which finally culminated in the PNP's electoral victory in 1972. Given the opposition's attempt to discredit the structure of competitive party politics, this outcome, in which the party system became the regulating mechanism in the conflict, raises the question of what the opposition actually achieved. After all, though the dissident movement had influenced the ouster of the JLP, it witnessed, immediately thereafter, the installation of the other established political party, the PNP. In other words, the decade-long protest saw neither the subversion of the existing political order and its replacement with an alternative from the Left, nor the dissolution of the longstanding party allegiance among the masses. Rather, the occasion of the PNP's victory disclosed the extent to which the Jamaican system of competitive party politics still commanded sufficient loyalty that citizens relied on it to resolve their discontent. What, then, in the face of this evident recuperation of the political order, was the significance of the opposition? What claims may be made for the movement's influence on politics and social relations in the 1960–72 period? In sum, what was the radical opposition's relative contribution to the changes which occurred in the period under discussion?

Three factors may be cited in assessing the significance of this decade of protest: the means possessed by the opposition which enabled it effectively to challenge the JLP, the contributing factors which permitted the opposition to exert its influence, and the balance between the opposition's achievements and its limitations. Of the several means possessed by the opposition, two were especially effective: its critique of official ideology and policy, and its efforts to make this criticism available to a larger audience. Criticism of ideology and exposure of state policies to wider *public* scrutiny were potent weapons in the hands of JLP detractors. Whether this criticism appeared in technical journals, occasional pamphlets, agitational newspapers, or mass protests, the opposition succeeded in problematizing state policy and expanding the number of participants in debates. Emphasis on ideology-critique and the public availability of criticism was decisive because it cast doubts on policies which either were not subject to broad public scrutiny or had yet to win wide public acceptance. In the early postcolonial years, the JLP was busy consolidating its rule and legitimizing its policies. Sharp and controversial critique at this moment caught the regime in its most vulnerable state, since the opposition simultaneously disputed various policies, proposed alternatives, and sought to create the basis for independent, popular opinion-formation in the island.

For a regime that wished to limit discussion of its policies, this intervention was a serious challenge. The JLP rejected the idea that dissenting individuals, organizations, and movements could have an autonomous and legitimate role in politics. Official hostility to the development of an independent popular public opinion, distrust of intellectuals, censorship of "unacceptable" ideas and political views, and curbs on radical movements revealed a marked uneasiness with political tendencies not endorsed by dominant politicians and established institutions. For the JLP, then, the major worry was potential subversion of the status quo, through the creation of independent sites for opinion formation.

Against this background, the opposition's activism and advocacy of independent ideas began the important work of legitimizing dissent and developing alternative policies for public consideration. Whether in the Rastafarians' assertion of an alternative conception of nationality and their belief in the capabilities of the unemployed, or the New World Group's defense of intellectual activism and new ideas, the dissident movement acted as an incubator of neglected, often villified social and economic alternatives. In precipitating, with its repeated interventions, an intense debate on society, politics, and the economy, the opposition pushed back the constraints on ideas in political discourse, broadened the scope of conceivable political alternatives, and expanded the participation of excluded groups. In circumventing censorship, the opposition introduced new ideas into public debate and invigorated the democracy the JLP had weakened. While the JLP justified its censorship of opinion in the name of protecting political liberties, the dissident movement defended the freedom to think unacceptable opinions and to promote them through political activism. By pursuing the critique of official ideology and policy, the expansion of public debate, and the mobilization of politically excluded groups, the opposition introduced important criteria by which postcolonial regimes would be evaluated.

A second factor which made the radical opposition particularly effective was the persistence and expanding scope of its activism and elaboration of tactics. Political opposition in Jamaica showed a remarkable continuity of protest, sustained for more than a decade. In this time, myriad dissident tendencies made their appearance on the political scene. The period saw a serial unfolding of political organizations and social movements whose ideologies and demands created an aura of crisis and challenge inside the country. The sixties saw the sustained permutation of protest, beginning with Rastafarian black nationalism and urban youth outlawry. That development coincided with the New World Group's dissidence, which in turn gave way to the *Abeng* newspaper movement and its political tributaries. This sequential unfolding of organizations and movements extended the life of the protest and made the dissident movement more difficult to suppress.

At the same time, the opposition employed several tactics which kept the regime off balance. Dissidents created community organizations as bases of anti-JLP activism. Protesters marched on government buildings, sugar estates, and construction sites, and Rastafarian protestors and rebellious youths invented new identities and codes of morality. Activist intellectuals also maintained vigorous criticism of the regime. Some prepared agitational literature and mobilized the poor, while others raked the regime with nationalist criticisms in journals, pamphlets, and public forums. If demonstrations and a rebellion by the riotous poor are included, this repertoire of tactics helped to undermine the official view that Jamaica was an exceptionally stable and harmonious society.

Finally, the expansion of the dissident movement, from a small group of protesters into a broader opposition encompassing a range of social classes, gave radical critics another important source of leverage to use against the regime. From its beginnings in the plaintive protest of the lumpenproletariat, the opposition grew to include urban youth, academics, community activists, workers, students, professionals, the clergy, and, under Michael Manley's leadership, eventually the PNP itself. This expansion of the movement demonstrated the popular-democratic orientation of the opposition and disclosed the JLP's growing political isolation. At the same time, the spread of dissent beyond the initial vanguard suggests that, after a period of isolation, the radical pioneers saw their positions adopted by moderate political forces. As a result, the JLP no longer could target leftwing critics or the rebellious urban unemployed as the sole repositories of political dissidence.

Such leverage as the opposition possessed would have been less effective without the presence of certain contributing factors. For example, dissidents in the sixties had the benefit of a favorable confluence of events, including the advent of the American Civil Rights and Black Power movements, the struggle against neocolonialism in the Third World, and the development of antistate and antiwar movements in Europe and North America. These international events, with their anti-imperialist and cultural-nationalist themes, had resonance and appeal in Jamaica. The domestication of these themes by political activists, and their mirroring at the local level international class and ethnic inequalities, complicated the JLP's attempt to consolidate its rule.

The existence of a significant space for protest in the society was a second factor which permitted the opposition to exert an influence over political events. Notwithstanding official attempts to curtail the civil liberties of dissidents, substantial political freedoms were retained under the JLP. Although dissident intellectuals met with political intimidation, passport seizures, political bannings, and censorship, none was ever arrested, imprisoned, murdered, or subjected to internal exile for political views. Few, if any, clandestine organizations were formed because of government harassment. Most dissenting organizations generally were able to publish their views and to demonstrate their opposition openly without fear of imprisonment, retaliation by death squads, or systematic harassment by the security forces. While colonial-inspired laws had a particularly grave effect on the political liberties and economic fortunes of the unemployed and militant poor, the JLP's authoritarian rule was remarkably free of systematic and draconian abuses of human rights.

It may well be that the country was spared such abuses because of the powerful grip of liberal democratic ideology on the capitalist classes and the political leadership. Paradoxically, the anglophilia of these classes, which had such an ambiguous effect on the transition to independence, now permitted extensive space for "lawful" political opposition, sparing dissidents the worst experiences of authoritarian rule. Compared to the fortunes of dissidents under highly authoritarian regimes elsewhere in the Third World, then, the Jamaican opposition enjoyed broad freedoms and exercised these to maximum effect. In fact, it was precisely the JLP's encroachments on political freedoms taken for granted in Jamaica that contributed to the alienation of large sections of the public and eventually led to that regime's electoral defeat.

The policies of the incumbent regime also were a contributing factor which permitted the opposition to exert its influence. In the area of political liberties, the regime's authoritarian rule and disciplinarian morality, while popular among sections of the capitalist class, eventually became a liability. As the JLP resorted to preemptive measures and infringed on the liberties of its opponents, it alienated important groups in the society. Increasingly, sections of the clergy, the educational establishment, and the legal profession defected to the opposition, strengthening the demand for an end to abuses of civil liberties.

The regime's affirmation of a nonracial ideology which barely concealed its repudiation of black nationalism also put the opposition in an advantageous position to influence events. At a time when anti-imperialist cultural nationalisms were in vogue in both the Third and the First Worlds, the JLP's rejection of the meaning of this cultural renaissance for Jamaica allowed its opponents to win important constituencies and to define the conflict as one of political, economic, and cultural subjection of blacks. By taking refuge in multiracialism and attacking black nationalism, the regime gave detractors such as the Rastafarians and the *Abeng* movement an opportunity to use a defense of black nationality and culture as weapons against it. Similarly, the regime's inability to resolve the country's economic policies fueled opposition and added credibility to the dissidents' critiques and proposals. Almost ten years of unrelieved double-digit unemployment, significant growth in inflation, increasing perceptions of income inequality, and negligible improvements in labor's standard of living led to the political weakening of the JLP. In short, without such glaring failures of the regime, the opposition almost certainly would have had even less political influence.

But where the regime's abuse of civil liberties, its anglophile cultural orientation, and its inability to resolve the country's economic problems were important determinants in its demise, such leverage as the opposition possessed by itself could not have brought about the JLP's ouster. The final factor which facilitated the opposition's effort to remove the JLP from power was the existence of a political party susceptible to the opposition's reformist appeals. The availability of the PNP as a party of reform and its readiness to draw on the opposition's themes made it the organization through which the dissidents indirectly exerted their political influence. Despite its cautious and nonantagonistic political campaign, the PNP did articulate several of the opposition's demands. Its ideologically-charged appeals for the restoration of democracy, its promise to include neglected groups, and its well-received assertion that "It's Time for a Change," were critical factors in securing the JLP's removal from office.

Having considered the resources possessed by the opposition and the conditions which augmented its leverage in a campaign against the state, we still must remember that this was a movement with serious deficiencies. These limitations produced conflicts and internal disunity which diluted the movement's effectiveness. In the political sphere, tensions existed within and between components comprising the movement. Among the lumpenproletariat, for example, ambiguity of motives abounded. Rastafarians wanted no truck with Jamaica's capitalist society and insisted on repatriation to the African continent. At the same time, they championed a petty entrepreneurial vision, in which they would be masters of their own economic destiny within a capitalist world. In their turn, the rebellious youths mimicked Rastafarian ideals but protested their condition by an outlawry which evinced a covert desire for political inclusion. Their role in party political warfare and their susceptibility to seduction by society's materialism highlight the contradictory orientations which existed in even the most rejectionist element of the opposition.

Other conflicts within the movement took their toll on unity. For the YSL, the struggle over the issue of autonomy from the PNP confused its cadres and disillusioned workers when the formation of the Workers Liberation Union had to be abandoned. A not-too-dissimilar ordeal was enacted within the New World and Abeng movements. While the former grappled with the issue of activism versus nonactivism for intellectuals, the latter became embroiled in conflicts over socialism and black nationalism. While these conflicts seasoned activists in ideological struggle and winnowed participants for a future vanguard, they distracted the opposition and shortened the lifespan of individual organizations. Since most organizations failed to survive beyond an early stage of development, they were prevented from playing a sustained, longterm oppositional role. Although this was not always true of *leaders* of these movements, the brief lives of individual groups meant that successor organizations had to start afresh clarifying ideologies, improving tactics, and attracting new recruits. Conflicts within individual units were reproduced *between* organizations. Ideological disagreements and disputes over tactics also hampered unity. The New World Group became a determined opponent of the Young Socialist League because of the latter's activism and socialist leanings, while the Unemployed Workers Council repeatedly attacked the YSL as a tool of the PNP.

This disunity was aggravated by a lack of effective leadership. It may be argued that those who were equipped to provide the movement with theoretical and political leadership — normally middle-class intellectuals — were ill-prepared to play this role. The younger generation of radical intellectuals was hampered by a limited knowledge of their country's history; those who subscribed to socialism had no firm grounding in Marxist politics; and others who turned to activism were themselves politically inexperienced. Moreover, many intellectuals who ventured into radical politics did so belatedly and only on a parttime basis. This involvement was parttime due to the fact that these intellectuals were busy being students, practicing attorneys, and university lecturers. At one level, therefore, the need to secure an education or a livelihood barred fulltime involvement.

At another level, a reformist orientation among the middle class led its members to seek solutions through existing bourgeois organizations. Hence, the middle-class intelligentsia's dissent, with its anti-JLP flavor, inclined this group toward the PNP rather than to the creation of independent antisystem organizations. The belated switch to radical antisystem politics occurred only when a few came to appreciate the limits to change that were imposed by both political parties. By the late sixties, this parttime involvement and PNP linkage had created such a political backlash from within the opposition movement, that dissident intellectuals reduced their involvement with the PNP and increased the time devoted to antisystem politics.

Instead of bringing focus and coherence to the opposition, this belated commitment raised doubts about the intellectuals' ability to provide effective political leadership, particularly in response to political and ideological tendencies of the militant poor. As I have shown, the political orientation of the latter was contradictory. On the one hand, the militant poor exhibited an antisystem orientation and a class-antagonistic morality. On the other, they displayed decidedly antisocial ideologies and practices. Among these were: nihilism and a celebration of outlawry-as-opposition; the invocation of mysticism to explain social relations; a reflexive distrust of the middle class; and a black nationalism which often slid into anti-Chinese racism.

The intellectuals' response to these orientations was ambiguous at best. The leaders of the UWC, YSL, and ITAC attempted albeit with mixed success, to moderate these negative tendencies by recruiting the unemployed into their organizations. In their turn, socialist intellectuals from the Abeng movement critiqued the people's populism and analyzed the contradictions which led unemployed workers to make political attacks on middle-class intellectuals. On the other hand, nationalist intellectuals, riding the wave of the people's protest, valorized the politics of the militant poor and championed their opposition to the system. Walter Rodney's intervention disclosed the power of this strategy. Despite his exemplary achievement, however, Rodney's intervention held one potential danger: it opened the door to the possible abdication of intellectual leadership, as activists allowed themselves to be "captured" ideologically by the popularity of black cultural nationalism. This is precisely what occurred inside the Abeng movement, as nationalist intellectuals surrendered to the politics of the militant unemployed in the name of solidarity with the oppressed.

Now, having considered the conditions facilitating the opposition's leverage against the state as well as the protesters' resources and limitations, we are in a position to appraise the significance of the opposition. The importance of the dissident movement may be found in its broad impact on state and society in the sixties. The radical opponents of the regime were pioneers in challenging the suspect foundations on which both political parties, but especially the JLP, sought to establish their legitimacy in the postcolonial period. By attacking the political, economic, and ideological conceptions of the country's leadership, the antisystem movement gradually undermined the cohesion of the state and the power of the dominant classes. Indeed, by establishing the terms of opposition — racial-class inequality, cultural domination, imperiled national sovereignty, abuse of civil liberties, and political disenfranchisement — the dissident movement helped set the agenda for a series of national "debates" and social struggles on public policy. An important consequence of these disputes was the defection of strategic social forces to the side of the opposition, a shift that eventually brought about an ouster of the JLP from political office. Protracted dissidence, then, not only played a vital role in triggering broad debate and struggle over the JLP's policy, but also promoted the decomposition of the regime by contributing to a shift in the alignment of forces after 1962.

There were several indications of this sea change. The upper and middle classes had emerged from the colonial period in a relatively confident and culturally preponderant position. By 1971, this assurance had given way to sharp fears and an inconstancy of mood in the face of increased social protest. The impact on the middle class was particularly acute. In 1960, it had experienced little internal division. Buoyed by its postwar economic gains and politically ascendant with the coming of decolonization, this stratum devoted itself to enjoying the perquisites of its status and showed minimal concern for the condition of the lower classes. A decade later, the middle class was torn by divisions, as the conflicts emanating from the social struggles made themselves felt. The most notable effect was that the class split into two fractions; one identified with socialism and with the causes and symbols of popular culture, while the other resolutely devoted itself to a defense of the status quo.

If we turn our attention to the university, the trend there suggests a similar break in the political development of students and intellectuals. Whereas both groups generally had remained aloof from social struggles in 1960, by the end of the decade, a significant segment had become leading political activists. A similar trend was to be discerned among other corporate groups, such as lawyers and the clergy. In sum, the dissident opposition unleashed a new moral and political consciousness which few in the society could ignore. The movement inspired increased attention to public affairs among all groups, and helped set lasting standards for the evaluation of public policy. A salutary effect of this opposition was a belated acceptance of its demands. Dissident ideas — effective political participation for the masses, increased attention to the issue of ownership of the local economy, and recognition of the island's African heritage — won increased respect and were grudgingly accepted by the political parties. Similarly, as a movement dedicated to exposing the "seamy side" of Jamaica's capitalist democracy, the opposition played a major role in stemming encroachments on basic freedoms. Here the opposition not only showed greater regard for the broad protection of such liberties than their official defenders, but it also secured increased legitimacy for leftwing and other radical participation in national politics. As an essentially reformist movement, the opposition acted as an incubator of alternative ideas and possibilities, in circumstances where the influence of the "colonial common sense" was still pervasive.

Beyond these broad influences, there was one other development of note: namely, the internal growth and maturation of the opposition itself. After years of protest, a fund of political awareness and a deeper knowledge of the problems of Jamaican society had accumulated inside the movement. Political struggles had provided invaluable political experience. Activists had learned to confront problems and challenges as they arose, and, although the protesters' responses sometimes could be confused, by 1972 the net result had been growth in the movement's capacity to produce creative responses to unfolding events. It even could be argued that, for all their shortcomings, the intelligentsia did make an important contribution to this development by disseminating radical ideas among disaffected social classes. Among the latter, the spread of ideas such as an end to political unionism, commonality of interest between employed and unemployed workers, and the possibility of self-organization by labor was due largely to the tutelage of the intelligentsia. These intellectuals brought a knowledge of working-class culture and radical developments in the outside world to the subordinated Jamaican classes. By introducing concepts, experiences, and theories from the heritage of the world's socialist and anti-imperialist movements, dissenting intellectuals transmitted to these local classes increased political confidence, a better understanding of their lives, and a sharper ideological focus for their radicalism.

There was, of course, a reciprocal tutelage of intellectuals by popular forces. The latter showed intellectuals the impossibility of combining parttime activism with the enjoyment of class privilege; intellectuals discovered both the political salience and the limits of cultural protest and, at first hand, learned of the hardships and discriminations endured by labor. This complementarity of dissent and reciprocal transfer of ideas gave the movement a capacity for self-renewal, even as they altered the terms of Jamaica's social and political relations. In these myriad ways, the political opposition in the sixties exerted a decisive influence on political and social events well beyond its limited means and minoritary status.

CHAPTER 11

Epilogue:
The Fate of the Opposition,
1972-88

In the aftermath of the 1972 PNP victory, the rhythm of Jamaican politics changed dramatically, and with it the fortunes of the nation and the Jamaican Left. In the sixteen years between 1972 and 1988, Jamaica experienced an unprecedented political and economic crisis which ushered in a massive reduction in the standard of living of all social classes except the wealthiest stratum. In this period the poor and the working class were hit particularly hard, as successive governments grappled with an intractable economic crisis induced by several related factors. These included the politics and economic strategies of the parties that governed the country between 1972 and 1988; the structural dependence of the island's economy, with its sensitivity to global political and economic trends; the imposition and failures of successive International Monetary Fund (IMF) austerity measures between 1977 and 1988; and the country's costly inability to diversify production and increase the output of the domestic economy. In the seventies and eighties, these interrelated determinants led to results unfortunate but predictable in a small dependent society: inflation, skyrocketing prices, shortages, layoffs, budget deficits, foreign exchange crises, and economic contraction. The centrality, intractability, and ajudicative impact of the economic crisis on political affairs in this period revealed definitively the limits of politics and ideology in solving the problems of an open, resource-poor, and dependent island economy in geographical proximity to the North American mainland. In fact, because neither the PNP, which articulated a socialist ideology in the years 1972–80, nor the JLP successor regime, which offered procapitalist policies between 1980 and 1989, could cushion the destructive effect of the economic crisis on the national economy nor halt erosion of the standard of living of Jamaicans, it became clear that objective constraints had narrowed the scope of policy options. This realization in the late eighties introduced a palpable chastening of expectations and a diminution of ideological fervor; as a result, political caution now is the defining temper among all political tendencies. This mood contrasts sharply with the mass mobilization and ideological polarization of the seventies and the high expectations for economic recovery evident in the early eighties. This epilogue charts the political fortunes of leftwing forces after 1980, discusses the sustained effects of the radical movements of the sixties on the seventies, and offers a perspective on an era marked by the leftwing quest for social change in the years 1960–88.

Ascent and Decline of the Left: 1972–80

With the PNP's return to power in 1972, the dissident opposition justifiably could feel that it had won a significant political victory. This movement's long years of struggle, in combination with other factors, had contributed to the electoral defeat of the authoritarian JLP government. Moreover, this victory had been achieved with the assistance of personnel from the opposition movement who accepted Michael Manley's invitation to join his election campaign. Despite some wariness and distrust of the PNP among radicals, several activists had responded to Manley's overtures in the 1969–71 period. Among the numerous young people who had responded to the PNP's appeal was a former Abeng activist and organizer from Saint Ann Parish, D.K. Duncan; he had been given the task of organizing the 1972 election effort. As the symbolic and organizational mobilization for the electoral contest affirmed, Duncan had proved to be a gifted organizer and tactician; he supervised the formation of hundreds of PNP party groups throughout the country.

This development, in which a few members of the dissident movement again were drawn to the PNP, was significant, as it pointed to the reentry of leftwing activists into a party that had been torn by factional strife in the early fifties and sixties. This rapprochement between the Left and the PNP in the late sixties and early seventies was not based on a transformation in either the ideology of the party or the class composition of its social base and leadership. Indeed, in 1972, the PNP remained fairly similar to what it had been in 1944: a political entity led by centrist politicians that drew popular support from a multiclass coalition of workers, peasants, and members of the middle class and the bourgeoisie. Notwithstanding this cross-class composition, anti-JLP sentiments and the PNP's progressivism and sympathy for the cause of the "sufferers" were enough to overcome skepticism among sections of the radical opposition. This return to the PNP by sections of the left-opposition pointed up a persistent fact of Jamaican political life in the modern period: the continuing dependence of socialist-oriented forces on the PNP. This fact, a function of the minority status of movements hoping to pose alternatives to the two dominant parties, and of the PNP's

ability to articulate a genuinely progressive alternative to the JLP's un-
diluted free-market orthodoxy, produced a recurring cycle in which
socialist-oriented activists fought to realize their ideas for even more
radical change by joining the PNP. This dynamic was reproduced in
the seventies, as a few leftwing activists who hitherto had been part of
the opposition movement, entered the new PNP administration.

Despite the fact that this ideological force-field drew some opposition activists to the PNP, segments of the dissident movement remained
openly suspicious, even hostile, to the new regime in the early seventies.
For these groups, the PNP victory was seen as the result of a skillful
manipulation of popular discontent by one of the capitalist parties. Certainly this position was taken by members of the Abeng Group. This
formation, in which Trevor Munroe and other UWI lecturers played a
leading role, had survived the bruising ideological battles of the sixties
between black nationalists, Marxists, and New World exponents of intellectual activism. Now, in the wake of the collapse of all the movements in which UWI intellectuals had been involved, the Abeng Group,
with its new and self-consciously Marxist outlook, emerged in 1972 as
the dominant organization of radical intellectuals outside the PNP.

Unlike members of the opposition who were drawn to the PNP
because of its legacy and its populist ideology, intellectuals in the Abeng
Group chose political independence and became sharp critics of the
Manley government, particularly during the first years of its rule. Like
many leftists in this period, the group approved of the changed policies
initiated by the PNP after 1972: lifting of the JLP ban on radical literature, the end to the harassment of dissidents, and other programs initiated by the new government in its first three years in office.[1] At the
same time, the Abeng Group found unacceptable and criticized the
PNP's attempt to satisfy the interests of both labor and capital. For
example, the group opposed several appointments given to members of
the business class during the PNP's first term in office.[2] Dissatisfaction
with a populist regime which sought to straddle the division of classes
by appealing to the mutual interests of patriotic capitalists, the middle
class, workers, and the poor led the Abeng Group to intensify its efforts
to defend the workers' interests. By December 1974, with the creation
of the Workers' Liberation League (WLL), the leaders of the group had
shifted to an openly communist position.

Even before Trevor Munroe and the other Abeng activists took advantage of the favorable political climate to launch a communist vanguard, the members of the Left who had joined the PNP were experiencing a rise in their political fortunes. As the PNP expanded its policies
of social reform, D.K. Duncan, who had helped to rebuild the party
organization, was appointed as PNP general secretary in June 1974. This

elevation of a leftist to a key party post occurred with the explicit approval of Michael Manley, the party leader. In this period, Duncan also enjoyed the support of the PNP Youth Organization (PNPYO)—a political organization of radical youths who increasingly came to be at odds with the party's multiclass orientation—and those inside and outside the party who shared Duncan's vision of a more egalitarian Jamaica.

By 1974, the situation of the Left inside the PNP was not too dissimilar from that of the YSL in 1962, when a benevolent, centrist party leader, seeking to reinvigorate the PNP, had identified the party with a small group of leftists. However, the recurrence of this phenomenon in the seventies was to have different consequences; although Michael Manley shared his father's commitment to ideological pluralism in the party, the younger Manley had been swept to power on a wave of popular sentiment in favor of changing the structure of inequality at home and the pattern of the country's economic dependence. By 1973, Michael Manley's ideological pronouncements and policy initiatives had designated him a champion of the poor and a spokesman for the underdeveloped nations.[3]

Notwithstanding popular domestic pressures for change and a new sense of ideological commitment in the PNP, the party's radicalism in the seventies should not be explained solely on the basis of ideology. External factors such as world inflation, the emergent Third-World demand for a new international economic order, and the nonaligned nations' rhetorical position that the big powers should stay out of their affairs were also relevant determinants in the PNP's move to the Left. The PNP's initiatives in the early seventies primarily reflected *domestic* political factors, while demonstrating the effect of external factors on local political dynamics. Coming in the context of such party initiatives as the 1974 bauxite levy, support for national liberation movements in the Third World, and development of friendly relations with Cuba, this PNP overture to a few radicals in the early seventies marked a discernable leftward drift. Indeed, this move was confirmed by the announcement in fall 1974 that the party was committed to the ideology of democratic socialism.[4]

This apparent radicalization of the regime by the end of 1974 benefitted the party Left. Despite ominous economic developments between 1973 and 1975,[5] the few leftists inside the party apparatus prospered, as Manley took increasingly anti-imperialist and populist positions at home and abroad.[6] Even as the deepening social crisis added to the Left's political influence inside the state, party, and society, however, the crisis brought major setbacks between 1973 and 1976. In this period, the economic situation worsened, domestic opposition to government policies increased dramatically, and urban political violence, a chronic feature of Jamaican politics, took many lives. A particularly bad year, 1976 saw clashes between urban political gangs, bombings, random criminal violence, and suspicious fires. Occurring in the context of mounting polarization between the regime and its detractors, the foregoing events produced a sense of chaos and fear in the society. Indeed, the social disorder had became so severe that on 19 June the PNP declared a state of emergency, amid claims that a coordinated effort was afoot to destabilize the government.[7]

With the emergency in force for several more months, the party mobilized its supporters for its annual conference. The September 1976 party meeting gave further evidence of the growing political influence of leftist cadres in the party, who produced a turnout in the tens of thousands at the National Stadium. Confronting sharp political attacks from the JLP, the *Gleaner,* and local entrepreneurs, Manley delivered a stinging denunciation of a "clique" opposed to his policies and announced to foreign capital that the country was "not for sale." This popular mobilization was repeated on 21 November at an even larger rally of more than one hundred thousand at Sam Sharpe Square in Montego Bay, where the PNP announced that general elections would be held on 12 December.

A Pyrrhic Electoral Victory, 1977-80

This massive show of popular support in November was converted into an electoral landslide for the PNP in December. Framed by both political parties as a contest between capitalism and socialism, the elections pitted a conservative JLP — which pointed out the persistence of the economic crisis and warned against a communist threat — against a confident PNP promising to continue policies benefitting the working class, small farmers, and the unemployed poor. Given the serious economic and political challenges of the previous four years, the PNP electoral victory was astonishing. The party won 56.8 percent of the popular vote — at this stage, the largest share in Jamaican political history — and forty-seven of the sixty seats in the House of Representatives. But even as this victory capped the achievements of leftist party cadres under the leadership of PNP General Secretary D.K. Duncan, the poll revealed an ominous shift in the party's support. Where 75 percent of white-collar workers and other professionals had given the PNP their support in 1972, this number had declined to approximately 57 percent in 1976. More significant was a precipitous slide in support by capitalists and wealthy professionals; only an estimated 20 percent backed the PNP in 1976, down from 60 percent in 1972. Reinforcing this sharpening social division, the party scored large increases among blue-collar workers and the unemployed poor, the two groups who gained most from the PNP's first term of office.[8] This increase in support of the manual working class and the poor, together with a clear majority among the middle class and farm workers, suggested that the party had won a mandate to continue its policies.

The Left certainly drew this conclusion, as members from its ranks — party General Secretary D.K. Duncan, former YSL member Hugh Small, and ex-Abeng activist Arnold Bertram — won seats in the House of Representatives. While this development was a major political breakthrough for leftwing members who had only recently entered the party, it was balanced by the fact that, up to 1976, none of them held positions in the Cabinet. This situation was to change in January 1977, with Duncan's appointment as minister of national mobilization and Hugh Small's promotion to minister of youth, sports, and community development. These radicals, together with housing minister Anthony Spaulding, became the small nucleus of leftwing influence in the Cabinet at this stage of the Left's revival. Although the Left carried significant political and ideological influence within the party secretariat, in the PNPYO, and among the rank and file, its members were a distinct minority inside the Cabinet, where political power was wielded by a majority fraction of moderate and center-right politicians.

This slight growth in the influence of radicals inside the Cabinet was balanced by an increase in the visibility of the Workers' Liberation League (WLL). As a group whose leadership was drawn almost exclusively from among young UWI social science lecturers, the WLL had become, by virtue of this provenance, the most militant and articulate voice of the non-PNP Left. By 1976, it had assumed a highly public role as a Marxist-Leninist vanguard, campaigning against what many on the Left saw as an attempt to destabilize the PNP, led by the U.S. Central Intelligence Agency (CIA). The year 1976 therefore found the WLL playing the roles of staunch ally of the PNP and inveterate critic of that party's detractors inside and outside the country. In adopting this position, the WLL had reversed its earlier hostility to the PNP and taken up a position of "critical support" for that party.[9]

This shift in position was the result of a 1975 meeting of Caribbean and Latin American Communist and Workers Parties in Havana, Cuba, that endorsed the policy of supporting regimes in the Third World identified as pursuing a "noncapitalist path."[10] Between 1975 and 1980, the WLL held to this "line" of the regional communist parties, notwithstanding criticisms from others on the Left that it was endorsing policies inimical to the interests of the working class. Over the next four years, the WLL — renamed the Workers Party of Jamaica (WPJ) in 1978 —

achieved greater national prominence, despite its negligible support among the population.[11] The WPJ's high visibility was complemented by a parallel expansion of the non-PNP Left. By the late 1970s, other socialist organizations — the Jamaica Communist Party (JCP), the National Union of Democratic Teachers, the WPJ-linked University and Allied Workers' Union (UAWU), and the Committee of Women for Progress (CWP) — had appeared on the scene and were active among workers and members of the lower middle class. The simultaneous creation of local community councils, neighborhood organizations, and grassroots bodies devoted to socialist values added to a florescence of independent activism reminiscent of similar developments a decade earlier.

This rise in the fortunes of the Left, both inside and outside the PNP, was threatened as a growing balance-of-payments crisis forced the PNP to seek relief from the International Monetary Fund (IMF). In the summer prior to the elections in December 1976 and unknown to many in the Cabinet, a negotiating team had met secretly with IMF officials to discuss possible terms for a loan. In January 1977, the party publicly rejected the IMF's terms as too harsh, since the fund had demanded, among other things, a 40-percent devaluation and sharp cutbacks in public spending. In early January, Manley registered his disgust with the fund in the following broadside: "This government, on behalf of our people, will not accept anybody anywhere in the world telling us what to do in our country. We are the masters in our house, and in our house there shall be no other master but ourselves. Above all we are not for sale."[12]

Cheered by this bracing polemic, members of the PNP Left proposed an alternative to the IMF's austerity measures. They argued for an alternative production plan, based on the growth of domestic agriculture, cuts in foreign exchange allocations to the manufacturing sector, and promotion of small business enterprises. If these measures could be matched by loans from the socialist bloc and from the Organization of Petroleum Exporting Countries (OPEC), then, the Left surmised, an escape from the IMF's austerity measures might be possible.[13] As leftwing university economists worked to draw up this alternative production plan in January, the Cabinet debated what to do about the immediate problem of a potentially disastrous shortage of foreign exchange. In a pragmatic move which rejected the Left's alternative plan, the Cabinet elected to seek an agreement with the IMF. By July this agreement was in place, and it momentarily eased the foreign-exchange crisis. This breather had been achieved, however, at the expense of party radicals. In addition to seeing their production plan jettisoned by the Cabinet, in the aftermath of the party's annual conference in September 1977, they saw a further reduction in their influence as D.K.

Duncan tendered his resignation as general secretary and minister of mobilization.

Despite this effort by party moderates to hold the line against a repudiation of the IMF, the agreement with the fund collapsed in December 1977, as the government failed one of the fund's quarterly performance tests.[14] The party secured a new agreement in May 1978, but its tough austerity measures exacted a heavy toll on the national economy; in fact, the IMF's stringent regime of budget cuts and devaluations failed to alleviate the economic crisis and cost the PNP political support.[15] By 1979, the economic situation could not have been worse. The economy was showing negative growth, inflation stood at 20 percent, unemployment soared to 31 percent in October, real wages for workers declined drastically, and, because of the contraction of demand, government revenues fell precipitously. These difficulties were compounded by declining foreign investment, as international firms hedged their bets in the face of mounting social strife: a popular riot protesting a gas price hike, JLP street demonstrations, and hysterical JLP and *Gleaner* charges of "mismanagement" and a turn to communism. The government's further failure to meet the IMF performance test in December 1979 only deepened this crisis and added to the disarray in the island.

The possibility of yet another IMF agreement, even more punishing in its requirements, gave PNP radicals another occasion to influence national policy. They opposed a new agreement with the fund. After extensive discussion and debate at the 1979 party conference, an Economic Commission was established to analyze current policy and make "recommendations concerning future economic strategy and policy with particular reference to the IMF."[16] This commission, which included radical economists from the UWI, recommended a break with the fund. This decision was endorsed by a meeting of some 2,500 delegates in January 1980.[17] Two months later, the National Executive Council (NEC), the party's policymaking body, rendered a sweeping endorsement of the commission's recommendation. Manley informed the nation of the party's decision and announced that elections would be held in October. Thus, in the aftermath of their setback in 1977, party radicals seemed to thrive in this latest crisis. Having been rebuffed in 1977 by moderates in the Cabinet, the Left was now at its zenith, as Manley, the NEC, and the rank and file all endorsed the bold bid for an alternative development path. To confirm the apogee of the Left's influence over economic strategy, Hugh Small was appointed minister of finance, and this gain was buttressed later in the year by Duncan's return as general secretary.[18]

This renaissance of the radicals in the party was matched by an escalation of WPJ activism. With Trevor Munroe at the helm, the party mounted an all-out attack on the IMF, foreign capital, and the JLP.

The WPJ organized political rallies, disseminated literature, and, through its activists in the CWP, UAWU, and the Jamaica Broadcasting Corporation, tried to mobilize popular support for the PNP. To this end, the WPJ announced that it would not field candidates in the upcoming elections but instead would campaign for the PNP's reelection. This attempted electoral alliance by the WPJ was rejected by senior members of the PNP, but there was no open repudiation of the communist party's support. In the ideologically heated campaign, which saw the JLP promising "deliverance" from the ruinous policies of the PNP and the communist threat, the tacit alliance between the WPJ and the PNP seemed to suggest that both parties shared a common ideology. In fact, this was merely an alliance of convenience.

At any rate, this mobilization for a leftwing alternative was largely a defensive rear-guard effort. Eight years of PNP rule had brought only a deepening social crisis and a steady erosion in the standard of living of the very classes from which the PNP drew its support. Moreover, with the exception of the years 1973 and 1978, which showed feeble rates of growth, Gross Domestic Product declined steadily between 1973 and 1980.[19] This negative growth, plunging real incomes, massive increases in the cost of living, and rising unemployment had defined the PNP's second term in office. Despite anti-imperialist mobilization and retrenchment efforts, the economic decline persisted. Indeed, the near-collapse of the economy and the inability of the regime to manage the economic crisis and the political tensions unleashed by its policies, eroded the party's popular support. The political consequence was a precedent-setting PNP defeat at the polls, as the JLP won almost 60 percent of the popular vote and fifty-one of the sixty seats in the House of Representatives.

Recriminations, Leftwing Disarray, and a PNP Revival: The Seaga Years, 1981–88

The margin of the JLP's triumph, surpassing the record set by the PNP in the 1976 elections, testified to the sense of exhaustion and mounting dissatisfaction with the PNP after 1976. Having conducted a successful campaign in which communist ideology and "mismanagement" were identified as the root cause of the country's problems, the JLP entered political office vowing to provide "deliverance" with its brand of free-enterprise policies. The new administration, headed by Prime Minister Edward Seaga, immediately changed the course of the country's foreign and domestic policies. On the international front, the administration moved immediately to establish a special relationship with the conservative Reagan administration in Washington. No doubt aware of the ideological profit to be reaped from association with an anticommunist, pro-American government which had just defeated a leftwing regime and American nemesis in the Caribbean, the Reagan administration designated the Jamaican prime minister the first foreign head of state to visit his White House. In the ensuing years, the Seaga administration would use this connection to win significant economic assistance for Jamaica, while unabashedly supporting the anticommunist Reagan policy in the Caribbean. The Seaga administration's adoption of uncritical support for American foreign policy objectives in Latin America and the Caribbean, and its willingness to draw the U.S. into the domestic affairs of the Caribbean, effectively closed the circle on the internationalization of the region's politics begun in the Manley years. Two results of this shift to an anticommunist and pro-American position were a severing of diplomatic relations with Cuba and a reversal of Jamaica's position as an advocate for the Third World in international forums. Finally, the Seaga administration's growing status as an American client in the region was strengthened when it promoted and participated in the October 1983 American invasion of Grenada, in the aftermath of factional strife within the Grenadian leadership and the killing of Maurice Bishop, Grenada's prime minister.

At home, the JLP's domestic policies stressed what it called the "freeing up of the economy." Consistent with its belief in foreign investment capital as the engine of economic growth in countries like Jamaica, the Seaga administration returned to the development strategy of the fifties and sixties. In the eighties, this meant the deregulation of the economy, divestiture of state-owned enterprises, promotion of foreign investment, creation of nontraditional markets, and increased borrowing from foreign lenders. Thus, where the Manley government had reserved a paramount place for the state in its economic strategy and had pursued a redistributive policy, the Seaga administration insisted on free-enterprise principles and made capital inflows a major priority in its economic strategy.

While Seaga pursued this course, the Left and the PNP were in disarray. The staggering PNP loss left both the party and its allies demoralized. The 1980 defeat held a glimmer of hope, in that the electorate largely had voted *against* the PNP than *for* the prescriptions of its opponents, but, from the leftists' standpoint, political prospects remained grim. For example, the JLP conducted a house cleaning at the JBC, purging many of the communist journalists who were linked to the WPJ. This move blocked that party's access to the airwaves and ended the leftwing slant of JBC news reports. In addition, the PNP suffered another crushing defeat in the March 1981 parish council elections to fill posts at the local administrative level. The JLP took 60 percent of the vote and 262 seats, leaving the PNP with the remaining 25. The WPJ fared no better in its first foray into electoral politics, as its two candidates in that election were soundly defeated in spite of running a close race with the PNP in the two constituencies.[20] Lastly, the Seaga administration's strategy of "playing the American card" seemed to validate the JLP's policies, as the economy returned to positive growth, paced by massive infusions of aid through the World Bank, the American government, and a more lenient IMF.[21]

To make matters worse, recriminations emerged on the Left, as the inevitable postelection assessments began. Some on the Left saw the WPJ policy of supporting the PNP as a distinct liability. For example, the Revolutionary Marxist League (RML), a small group even more marginal than the WPJ, advocated nonparticipation in the 1980 and 1983 elections. Holding fast to its position that the two major parties were tools of the capitalist class, the RML impugned the WPJ's alliance with the PNP. The RML's position echoed the post-1952 critique by sections of the Left, which argued that socialists should challenge the capitalist-influenced PNP instead of becoming its ally.

This leftwing critique of the WPJ's strategy was matched by an opposite criticism from the PNP, as that party took stock of its defeat. The PNP issued a firm repudiation of the WPJ's electoral support, which, party officials argued, had hurt the PNP's reelection bid by blurring the differences between the two parties. Michael Manley and others maintained that this confusion in the public mind helped the JLP smear the PNP with the charge of communism. This accusation, ostensibly directed at the WPJ, marked a shift toward the center by the PNP since the 1980 elections. Although the radicals D.K. Duncan and former Minister of Housing Anthony Spaulding won top party posts at the party's annual conference in September 1982, divisions persisted over the PNP's future course.[22] The moderate wing wanted the party to settle down to charting a new path and hoped to diminish the party's image as a far-left organization. But others, like Spaulding and D.K. Duncan, wanted to keep the party on its leftward course. As this division unfolded, Manley joined the moderates and rendered a verdict on the party's direction. In a rebuff to the communist party and those in the PNP who might share the WPJ's ideology, the party leader reassured the public that "the WPJ would be fought as resolutely as the JLP in gaining state power."[23]

This parting with the far Left was the latest move in the PNP leader's oscillation between leftists and party moderates. In his attempt to bring order to the PNP, Manley was not unmindful of political developments since 1981. Most significant was the astonishing fact that the JLP, after a moderately successful first year, was encountering new woes, as its recovery effort stalled. Despite a remarkable ability to attract foreign economic assistance, mostly in the form of loans, the JLP encountered several problems by the end of 1982, including a fall in domestic agricultural production, rising prices, high unemployment, a decline in the rate of economic growth, and, worst of all, an unexpected drop of some 30 percent in bauxite earnings.[24] Although the JLP tried to accentuate the positive and made optimistic forecasts about the rate of recovery, the electorate steadily was losing patience with a regime promising that economic management and infusion of foreign investment would ease the country's crisis significantly. The government itself made matters worse with its avid courtship of foreign investors and relaxation of import controls. On the one hand, the former policy antagonized local business interests while reinforcing working-class perceptions of the JLP as primarily the party of the "big man."[25] The latter measure, on the other hand, weakened management of the economy by allowing nonessential imports to consume scarce foreign exchange. The cumulative impact of these developments was a decline of popular support for the JLP and a small increase for the PNP between October 1980 and December 1981.[26] By October 1982, public-opinion polls showed the PNP ahead for the first time since its defeat. This startling turn of events increased the isolation of the Left and strengthened the hand of moderates in the PNP. One effect of this relative diminution of leftist influence was demoralization and loss of discipline in the Left. Rather than wait out this party retreat as they had done in 1977, prominent leftists succumbed to pressures designed to further marginalize them. Thus General Secretary Duncan and Vice-President Anthony Spaulding — only recently elected to their senior positions — quit the party at the end of 1982 in fits of personal pique.[27]

The years 1983–86 saw a continued decline for the JLP, as it suffered several major setbacks. The government failed two consecutive IMF performance tests in 1983, and the subsequent agreement with the fund led to layoffs, major price hikes, currency devaluations, and increased taxes. With polls showing a resurgent PNP and disillusionment with the JLP, Seaga grew desperate. In November 1983, he announced new elections for the following month. Coming on the heels of the killing of Prime Minister Maurice Bishop in Grenada and the JLP-supported American invasion of that country in October, this call for new elections, two years before they were constitutionally due, was a transparent effort to benefit from the Jamaican public's disgust with the murder of Bishop and from its qualified approval of the American invasion. However, instead of easing its woes, the JLP's action triggered a constitutional crisis, as the PNP boycotted these elections and left the government to win all sixty seats without an opposition in Parliament.[28]

The years 1984–86 were even worse, from the JLP's standpoint. In February 1984, the U.S. firm of Reynolds Metals and Kaiser Steel Corporation, which had been mining bauxite ore in the country for forty years, gave notice that it was closing its operations in Jamaica and would find cheaper bauxite elsewhere.[29] The economy returned to negative growth after 1984, and in 1985 debt payments consumed almost 50 percent of export earnings. The postelection social peace was broken by an islandwide demonstration against a major hike in the price of gasoline, while the 1986 budget hit hard at business activity with massive duties on imports.[30] In July 1986, the PNP swept the parish council elections, winning twelve of the thirteen contests in the local administrative districts and garnering 57 percent of the popular vote.[31]

In this harsh verdict on six years of JLP rule, the electorate reiterated the complex sentiments it had expressed since the 1980 elections: that, while it rejected communism, it nonetheless approved of policies which improved the lives of working people and was not prepared indefinitely to support governments whose policies resulted in a persistent disastrous erosion in their standard of living. The durability of this orientation within the mass public over the 1977–86 period transcended the ideological appeals of the political parties and led in the eighties to the JLP's crisis of credibility.

This rejection of communism and pragmatic concern with material improvements diminished the appeal of communist parties such as the WPJ. In the eighties, that party too went through its season of discontent. In addition to the aforementioned hostile JLP and PNP measures which weakened it, the WPJ's stunning apology for the actions which led to the murder of Maurice Bishop isolated it in the country at large and caused consternation among leftists. Likewise, the WPJ's crushing defeat in the 1986 parish council elections (it won no seats, of 128 being contested), confirmed polls showing its consistently negligible support among the electorate.[32] In responding to this "poor performance," the WPJ observed that it had set "unattainable targets" and had engaged in "wishful thinking." Continuing this self-assessment, the party also noted that "trying to do more than the situation allows politically can now kill the party . . . Drastic change must now be made to match what party members and the Jamaican working people can manage in a time when they have been taken up with survival and are placing some hope in reform."[33]

Finally, in the late eighties, the WPJ's own exercise in self-criticism brought a plethora of criticisms of its politics. Cadres accused the general secretary of conducting the party's affairs in an authoritarian, "Stalinist" style; others criticized the party's neglect of the inseparable link between socialism and freedom; and party women delivered sharp feminist cri-

tiques of the patriarchal "machismo" model of male vanguard leadership. With this disarray and scattering of the Left within and without
the PNP, another era of leftwing activism had ended in political impasse. Given the correlation of this development with continuing JLP
woes and with polls indicating that voters felt they would be better off
under a PNP administration, few in the country were surprised when
the PNP swept the February 1989 general elections in a landslide.[34]

Perspective on an Era: Social Movements and the Struggle for Change in Jamaica, 1960-88

The almost thirty-year quest for radical social change in Jamaica altered
the dynamics of Jamaican politics. The period saw radical movements
and activists progressively expand their influence over national politics
while engendering growing opposition from their detractors. This pattern was particularly evident in the seventies, with its tremendous political
mobilization and polarization of social forces. This era of radicalism
saw the country move from a period of restiveness in 1960 — typified
by localized street-corner Rastafarian protests against economic and
cultural discrimination — to a fullblown, multidimensional social crisis
defined by economic ruptures and sharply-drawn ideological lines. Radical intellectuals and their politics were centerpieces in this drama. Their
trajectory over almost three decades took them from the status of plaintive critics of power, to a position of ideological and political leadership in one of the major political parties. This ascendancy brought small
numbers of them into the corridors of power and exposed them to the
maelstrom of social and political upheaval.

In the same period, the domestic politics of the small island nation
shifted from muted concerns over inequalities between the "haves" and
"have nots" to open ideological warfare between antagonistic social
classes. This sharpening of social divisions led to the internationalization of Jamaican politics and to sharp oscillations in the pattern of its
foreign policy. Likewise, the country began its independence with an elite
consensus on a strategy for economic development which had put the
island in the forefront of nations experiencing impressive and sustained
rates of economic growth. Almost thirty years later, the country's economy lay in near-ruin, battered by inflation, weakened by years of negative
growth, and mortgaged to international financial institutions. Whereas
the quest for political office and the survival of elected regimes in the sixties had been governed solely by domestic politics, a decade later this
sovereignty was encroached on by the significant local influence of international lending agencies and the American government.

Table 5. Electoral Results in Jamaica, 1944–80

	Votes Cast	Voter Turnout %	JLP		PNP		Other	
			Vote %	Seats	Vote %	Seats	Vote %	Seats
1944	349,127	52.5	41.4	22	23.5	5	35.1	5
1949	467,179	63.8	42.7	17	43.5	13	13.8	2
1955	486,644	63.9	39.0	14	50.5	18	10.5	—
1959	557,794	65.4	44.3	16	54.8	29	.9	—
1962	575,779	72.3	50.0	26	48.6	19	1.4	—
1967	442,572	81.5	50.7	35	49.1	20	.3	—
1972	473,651	78.2	43.4	16	56.4	36	.2	—
1976	735,948	84.5	43.2	13	56.8	47	— —	—
1980	852,706	86.1	58.9	51	41.1	9	.1	—

Source: Michael Kaufman, *Jamaica Under Manley,* (Westport, Lawrence Hill, 1985), 51.

Notwithstanding these shifts, other elements of Jamaican politics remained unchanged. Remarkably, the two major political parties withstood the shocks and tremors of these developments. Neither twenty-
eight years of insistent leftwing effort to supplant them nor the pressures
of the collapsing economy undermined the two dominant parties' supremacy in national politics. They not only survived, but they tightened
their clientelist grip on the masses even as their hierarchical organizations and patrimonial styles persisted. Finally, despite Edward Seaga's
clumsy attempts to deny the electorate a voice in local elections in 1984
and 1985, the five-year cycle of general elections emerged largely intact[35]
(see table 5).

For their part, the 1960s radical movement and its associated activists
continued to shape the politics of the seventies and eighties. They did
so positively in the seventies, by helping to fashion the PNP's political
and ideological agenda. Indeed, some of the ideas for change which
had been debated at the university, in local communities, and within
leftwing organizations in the sixties, became policy during the PNP's
terms of office. In this respect, it may be argued that, while the PNP
came to be the effective organ of radical change, the social movement
of the sixties was the party's real tutor and intellectual font. The activists of the sixties also influenced national politics in later years, through
the reactions they elicited from detractors. The latter never tired of
mobilizing anticipatory fear by calling attention to the activists' political
influence in the PNP, their direct participation in the exercise of state
power, and the danger that they might carry out a leftwing coup.

By exaggerating the capacity and influence of the Left, its detractors
did it a disservice, for even at their zenith, the radicals in the PNP still

were under the suzerainty of that organization and its leader. All of the Left's initiatives — from their entry into the party to their promotion of the break with the IMF — had either the implicit or the explicit approval of Michael Manley. This patronage, while securing their presence in the party, seriously hampered them at critical points. In many ways the fate of the PNP radicals in the seventies resembled that of the YSL, their 1960s counterpart; survival depended largely on the benevolence of the party leader. Not unlike his father, Norman Manley, who finally sided with the center-right in the factional fights of the early sixties, Michael Manley, amost twenty years later, decided that his party's return to power was being jeopardized by recalcitrant leftwingers.

The travail of this indentureship within the PNP was reinforced by the radicals' overestimation of subjective factors. The excessive emphasis placed on ideology and voluntarism by leftwing groups inside and outside the PNP typified this weakness. In the seventies, radicals typically discounted the political facts of geopolitics, institutional legacies, and the structural constraints of an export-oriented island economy. For example, as the dominant actor in the non-PNP Left, the WPJ succumbed to this temptation. It turned a blind eye to geopolitical considerations with its fierce attacks on the United States; it ignored its miniscule support among the population in favor of a near-clientelist relationship with the PNP; it depicted the JLP as a party outside the ideological traditions of the country, ignoring the JLP's massive support among the electorate; and it posed the issue of the country's future in purely ideological terms. To make matters worse, the WPJ adopted the Leninist vanguard model of politics and organization, at a time when this orthodoxy had been repudiated within communist circles in Europe, the region of the model's provenance. Despite these shortcomings, the WPJ played a positive role in the 1970s with its patriotic agitation on behalf of the Jamaican workers. The task which now remains before it and all leftwing forces in the 1990s is the perennial one faced by socialists: how to develop a strategy of transition which secures both political freedom and material improvements for the laboring classes.

Notes

CHAPTER I

1. I am aware that there are differences of emphasis and even conflicting viewpoints within each of these approaches. Moreover, despite significant differences, Marxism and modernization theory have a common Eurocentric bias in their shared view that capitalism brought "progress" to non-Western societies. These considerations aside, there are certain "domain assumptions," paradigmatic themes, and influential statements which continue to define each perspective; I shall refer to these paradigmatic themes and influential statements in discussing each perspective.

2. See, for example, Lucian Pye and Sidney Verba, eds., *Political Culture and Political Development* (Princeton, N.J.: Princeton Univ. Press, 1965). This text was one in a series on the topic of political development sponsored by the Committee on Comparative Politics of the Social Science Research Council.

3. For a recent review of these issues, see Samuel P. Huntington, "Will More Countries Become Democratic?", *Political Science Quarterly* 99 (1984):193-218.

4. For an early statement which outlined these preconditions, see Seymour Martin Lipset, "Some Social Requisites of Democracy: Economic Development and Political Legitimacy," *American Political Science Review* 53 (1959):69-105.

5. For a recent version of this argument applied specifically to African states, see Goran Hyden, *No Shortcuts to Progress* (Berkeley: Univ. of California Press, 1983).

6. For Huntington, cultures which are consummatory in character are those in which "intermediate and ultimate ends are closely connected," making the prospect of democracy less likely. Huntington argues that such cultures generally are found in countries in which Islam, Confucianism, and Buddhism are the dominant religions. On the other hand, countries with Protestant and Catholic traditions, and other "instrumental cultures" — ones that do not link immediate concerns with destiny — are more likely to be democratic.

7. For a discussion of the theme of personalism in Africa, see Robert H. Jackson and Carl G. Rosberg eds., *Personal Rule in Black Africa* (Berkeley: Univ. of California Press, 1982).

8. Goran Hyden, *Beyond Ujamaa in Tanzania* (Berkeley: Univ. of California Press, 1980).

9. See Richard Sandbrook, *The Politics of Africa's Economic Stagnation* (New York: Cambridge Univ. Press, 1985).

10. Jeanne Kirkpatrick, "Dictatorships and Double Standards," *Commentary* 68 (Nov. 1979):34–45.

11. See Claude Ake, *Revolutionary Pressures in Africa* (London: Zed Press, 1978), 36–37.

12. Ibid., 37.

13. For a variation on this theme with respect to authoritarianism in Latin America, see Guillermo O'Donnell, "Tensions in the Bureaucratic-Authoritarian State and the Question of Democracy," in *The New Authoritarianism in Latin America*, ed. David Collier (Princeton, N.J.: Princeton Univ. Press, 1979), 285–318.

14. Goran Therborn, "The Rule of Capital and the Rise of Democracy," *New Left Review* 103 (May–June 1977):3–41.

15. Samuel Huntington, for example, has defined a democratic polity as one in which "the most powerful collective decision-makers are selected through periodic elections in which candidates freely compete for votes and in which virtually all the adult population is eligible to vote." Huntington, "Will More Countries Become Democratic?"

16. Carl Stone, *Democracy and Clientelism in Jamaica* (New Brunswick, N.J.: Transactions, 1980), 108.

17. Ibid., 109.

18. Ibid., 94.

19. Therborn, "The Travail of Latin American Democracy," *New Left Review* 113–14 (Jan.–Apr. 1979):73.

CHAPTER 2

1. See, for example: James Carnegie, *Some Aspects of Jamaica's Politics, 1918–1938* (Kingston: Institute of Jamaica, 1973); Trevor Munroe, *The Politics of Constitutional Decolonization* (Kingston: Institute of Social and Economic Research, 1972); Ken Post, *Arise Ye Starvelings: The Jamaica Labour Rebellion of 1938 and Its Aftermath* (The Hague: Martinus Nijoff, 1978); and George Eaton, *Alexander Bustamante and Modern Jamaica* (Kingston: Kingston Publishers, 1975).

2. For a discussion of anti-Chinese sentiment in this period, see Carnegie, *Some Aspects*, chs. 4 and 5.

3. Ibid., ch. 5.

4. Post, *Arise Ye Starvelings*, 206–212.

5. Ibid., 206.

6. Ibid., 98.

7. Ibid., 98–103.

8. Ibid., 98.

9. The frustrating experience of the black members of the middle class who were elected, on the basis of a limited franchise, to the colonial legislature between 1914 and 1938 is extensively documented in Carnegie, ch. 4. Remarking on their hapless status in the legislature, Carnegie appropriately refers to these electives as "an opposition which would never have a chance to govern."

10. See Trevor Munroe, "The People's National Party, 1939–1944: A View

of the Early Nationalist Movement in Jamaica" (M.Sc. thesis, Univ. of the West Indies, 1966), 8.

11. See "Forward March," Pamphlet (Kingston: PNP, 1941). Kingston, Jamaica, Institute of Jamaica, Hart Collection.

12. For a discussion of the organizational permutations and sheer drama characterizing the struggle of the middle class to adopt a nationalist position, see Post, *Arise Ye Starvelings*, 213–32; as well as Trevor Munroe, "People's National Party."

13. H.P. Jacobs, an Englishman who was political editor of the influential middle-class journal *Public Opinion*, had rejected the notion of utilizing the slave experience as a basis for a unifying culture. He argued instead for displacement of the slave culture by a more representative culture which could "be produced only by an educated class which is Jamaican at heart." Cited in Post, *Arise Ye Starvelings*, 217.

14. Ibid., ch. 5.

15. See Trevor Munroe, "The Bustamante Letters: 1935," *Jamaica Journal* 8 (Mar. 1974):2–15.

16. Post, *Arise Ye Starvelings*, 255.

17. Ibid., 261.

18. Eaton, *Bustamante and Modern Jamaica*, 37.

19. Ibid., 31–36.

20. Post, *Arise Ye Starvelings*, 238–61.

21. Here his biographer was prompted to observe that "Bustamante at that moment was, however, at odds with the temper of workers." Eaton, *Bustamante and Modern Jamaica*, 37.

22. Thus, in one of his earlier statements to workers Bustamante remarked: "It is your duty to organize against abuses and oppression but above all, respect yourselves, be courteous to everyone, to police, to government, to your employers and to your own fellow workmen; with discipline, order and comradeship we will compel cruel capitalists to repent and treat you justly and fairly." Cited in Post, *Arise Ye Starvelings*, 256.

23. Ibid., 221.

24. Ibid., 215.

25. Ibid., 220.

26. Eaton, *Bustamante and Modern Jamaica*, 38–39.

27. I am relying on both Post's and Eaton's accounts for the facts and interpretations of events surrounding the 1938 strike.

28. Eaton, *Bustamante and Modern Jamaica*, 40.

29. Post, *Arise Ye Starvelings*, 285.

30. Eaton, *Bustamante and Modern Jamaica*, 44.

31. See Post, *Arise Ye Starvelings*, 293–99, and Eaton, *Bustamante and Modern Jamaica*, 56.

32. Post, *Arise Ye Starvelings*, 292.

33. Ibid., 365.

34. Rex Nettleford, ed., *Norman Washington Manley and the New Jamaica: Selected Speeches and Writings, 1938–69* (New York: Africana Publishing, 1971), 12.

35. In one of his earliest anticommunist attacks on this contingent in the PNP, Bustamante asserted, "There is a communistic group working behind the scenes of the P.N.P. being formed . . . What they aim to do is bring about the fall of myself and Mr. Manley in turn, and then ride to Legislative Council power on the shoulders of a Labour Party they hope to control." Cited in Eaton, *Bustamante and Modern Jamaica,* 67.

36. Post, *Arise Ye Starvelings,* 401.

37. Trevor Munroe, "People's National Party," 64-65.

38. See "Report of the 2nd Annual Conference," Richard Hart Collection of PNP Papers, Institute of Jamaica, Kingston, Jamaica (hereafter cited as Hart Collection), p. 14.

39. Cited in John C. Gannon, "The Origins and Development of Jamaica's Two-Party System, 1930-1975," (Ph.D. diss., Washington Univ., 1976), 124.

40. Eaton, *Bustamante and Modern Jamaica,* 88.

41. For a discussion of the deficiencies of the constitution, see Trevor Munroe, *The Politics of Decolonization,* 45-55.

42. Every constitution is a ratification of the balance of power between classes in a society. For a review of Jamaican constitutional history which confirms this principle, see Lloyd Barnett, *The Constitutional Law of Jamaica* (London: Oxford Univ. Press, 1977).

43. This modification allowed the development of a Cabinet, headed by a chief minister. However, the "reserved powers" of the governor were retained.

44. For the fortunes of the leftists, see Trevor Munroe, "The Marxist 'Left' in Jamaica: 1940-50" (Kingston: Institute of Social and Economic Research, Working Paper no. 15, 1977).

45. Michael Kaufman, *Jamaica Under Manley* (Westport, Conn.: Lawrence Hill, 1985), 50.

46. In 1939-49, the PNP consistently called for the creation of an Industrial Development Corporation, ostensibly to assist *local* capital. By 1949, however, the party had gone beyond this stance, supporting a variety of incentives specifically designed to attract foreign investors. See Stacey Widdicombe, *The Performance of Industrial Development Corporations: The Case of Jamaica* (New York: Praeger, 1972), 78-79; Richard Hart, "Jamaica and Self-Determination, 1660-1970," *Race* 13 (1972):271-97.

47. For example, gross capital formation in 1954 was only 37.6 million Jamaican dollars and unemployment in 1953 was 17.5%. See Owen Jefferson, *The Post-War Economic Development of Jamaica* (Kingston: Institute of Social and Economic Research, 1972), 64, 28.

48. Much of the theoretical underpinning for the party's position and for the development strategy in the post-war years was provided by the West Indian economist Arthur Lewis. Lewis at the time was engaged in a polemic with the Bentham Committee on the question of creating a domestic manufacturing sector. In supporting the creation of an IDC and special incentives for capital, Lewis argued that the domestic bourgeoisie was too tied to the distribution trade and land ownership to be interested in manufacturing without state support. Commenting on the local capitalists he remarked: "They are specialists in

agriculture and commerce. They think in terms of import and export rather than of production. Some would even be hostile to domestic manufacture, which they see as a threat to their wholesale business." Cited in Widdicombe, *The Performance,* 85.

49. See Norman Girvan, *Foreign Capital and Economic Underdevelopment in Jamaica* (Kingston: Institute of Social and Economic Research, 1971).

50. See notes 47 and 49 above, and Paul Chen-Young, "A Study of Tax Incentives in Jamaica," *National Tax Journal* (Sept. 1967):292–308.

51. Arthur Lewis in 1964 remarked that this phase of development was unusual, accounting as it did for 42% of all investment in the 1956–61 period and averaging 7.3% of Gross Domestic Product. He concluded with the assessment that this rate of foreign investment "is most abnormal, and will not be repeated . . . It would be unwise even if it were possible." W. Arthur Lewis, "Finding the Money," *Daily Gleaner,* supplement on Jamaica's economic problems, Sept. 1964.

52. The share of local ownership of firms operating under the Import Incentive and the Pioneer Industries Laws in 1950–64 was 71.1% and 54.4%, respectively. See Chen-Young, "A Study," 296.

53. Part of the paradox of this pattern of industrial development in resource-limited countries is that import substitution strategies often rely heavily on imported raw materials.

54. For a recent documentation of the thesis that the postcolonial corporate economy is controlled by 21 families, see Stanley Reid, "An Introductory Approach to the Jamaican Corporate Economy and Notes on its Origins," in *Essays on Power and Change in Jamaica,* ed. Carl Stone and Aggrey Brown (Kingston: Jamaica Publishing House, 1977):15–44.

55. Matalon served in 1953–56 and again in 1960–64; *Daily Gleaner,* 4 Feb. 1966.

56. The Mona Heights, Harbour View, and Duhaney Park settlements in Kingston were part of the boom in the construction of new homes.

57. Carl Stone, "Political Aspects of Post-War Agricultural Policies in Jamaica (1945–1970)," *Social and Economic Studies* 23 (1974):145–75; Post, *Arise Ye Starvelings,* 87–88.

58. See Don Robotham, *Our Struggles* (Kingston: Workers Liberation League, 1975). See his complementary article, "Agrarian Relations in Jamaica," in *Power and Change,* ed. Carl Stone and Aggrey Brown, 45–57.

59. I use the term "dispossessed" here to refer to those farmers who were no longer engaged in cultivation, because they either had taken their land out of production or had "lost" it to bigger landowners. There are a number of puzzles here which my research has been unable to solve. One concerns the manner of liquidation of the small farmers' land. What was the mode of property transfer? Was their land sold to the big estates, as seems plausible? If so, for how much, and under what circumstances? What is not in dispute is that between 1958 and 1961 the big agricultural capitalists and the corporate estates together picked up 127,592 acres, and almost 50,000 small-to-medium farms ceased to exist.

60. For an analysis of this population movement, see O.C. Francis, *The People of Modern Jamaica* (Kingston: Jamaica, Dept. of Statistics, 1963), 2–3.

61. Jamaica, Committee for Relief of the Unemployed, *Interim Report* June 1950.

62. In the mid-forties, the colonial government already had recognized this problem. In its 1945 report, the Bentham Committee rejected local calls for import substitution and the protection of new industries, choosing instead to do nothing. At the same time, however, the committee was prescient in noting that foreign investment in the manufacturing sector would not solve the unemployment crisis. The committee noted that "manufacturing in Jamaica consists largely of processing local agricultural products and of producing goods, such as bread and ice. . . . All factories of every description together employ less than 20,000 workers . . . a few new factories may be set up but together they are unlikely to employ more than two or three thousand workers." Cited in Widdicombe, *Performance of Industrial Development Corporations*, 81.

63. Between 1950 and 1964, 130 firms were created under incentive legislation. Of these, 109 were operating in 1964. Chen-Young, "A Study," 295.

64. This much was confirmed in the case of returned veterans and farm workers who, having been placed in rural jobs, "settled in Kingston . . . owing to the greater social amenities available in the Corporate Area." See *Interim Report*, 1.

65. See W. Arthur Lewis, "Goals of Economic Development," *Daily Gleaner*, supplement on Jamaica's economic problems, Sept. 1964.

CHAPTER 3

1. For the details of the constitutional revisions between 1953 and 1959, which suggest the imminence of political independence, see Barnett, *Constitutional Law of Jamaica*, 18–21.

2. See "Report of the 2nd Annual Conference," PNP, Hart Collection, 4.

3. In contrast to the dominant interpretation within the postindependence Jamaican Left, my analysis of the middle class does not attribute to it any cultural class essence which doomed its members to a particular political orientation. Rather, I take their ideological orientation to be the product of a multiplicity of factors.

4. See, e.g., Leonard Barrett, *The Rastafarians: A Study in Messianic Cultism in Jamaica* (Puerto Rico: Institute of Caribbean Studies, 1969).

5. Several works treat the subject of religion, esp. its revivalist strain among the Jamaican peasantry. For two related texts, see: George E. Simpson, "Jamaican Revivalist Cults," *Social and Economic Studies* 5 (Dec. 1956):321–422; and Barry Chevannes, "Social Origins of the Rastafari Movement," typescript (Kingston: Institute of Social and Economic Research, 1979).

6. Of all the activities of the Rastafarians, perhaps none was so threatening to the British, and therefore so repeatedly repressed, as the militant promulgation of the notion that the authentic ruler of the black man was to be found in Africa and not in England. Carried out largely via itinerant preaching to mass audiences of peasants, this proselytizing, despite its being cloaked in a

religious garb, was recognized by the British for what it was—a form of popular mobilization against the British Crown.

7. These pioneers, Leonard Howell, Archibald Dunkley, and Joseph Hibbert, all were arrested and imprisoned for their activities. In Howell's case, he was indicted in 1935, according to a local newspaper report, for delivering "a seditious speech, in which he abused both the Governments of Great Britain and this Island, thereby intending to incite hatred and contempt for His Majesty the King and of those responsible for the government of this Island and to create dissatisfaction among the subjects of his majesty in this Island and to disturb the public peace and tranquility." Cited in Barrett, *The Rastafarians,* 73.

8. This group was called the "dreadlocks" because they wore their hair in long, matted locks. They were the harshest critics of the Anglophile middle class and the professional politicians. Reflecting on the period, Barrett noted: "It was a time of intense hatred for the established society. Rastafarians ran down the streets of Kingston, yelling fire, brimstone and Babylon, using the most profane language ever heard in public. To the community they seemed mad and several of them were apprehended . . . and sent to the asylum." Ibid., 76.

9. For example, in March 1958, one such convention was called by a notable Rastafarian, Prince Edward. The convention brought scores of Rastafarians to the West Kingston meeting with expectations that they would be departing for Africa. No such event transpired, and, the assemblage was forced to disperse in disappointment. For a discussion of these events, see the pioneering work of M.G. Smith, Roy Augier, and Rex Nettleford, *The Rastafarian Movement in Kingston* (Kingston: Institute of Social and Economic Research, 1960), 18–19.

10. It is not clear when Henry became a Rastafarian. However, at his trial for treason in Oct. 1960, he disclosed that as early as 1921, he was having visions and dreams; and he reported that he heard voices calling him to be a prophet. He recalled that the voices addressed him in the manner of Jeremiah 1:5: "Before I formed thee in the belly I knew thee; and before thou camest forth out of the womb I sanctified thee, and I ordained thee a prophet unto the nations." It was this conversion, with its implied charge to minister to the black poor and to predict the future, which set Henry on the road to Rastafarianism. He recalled being arrested by the colonial government in 1935 and charged first with preaching without a license and later with lunacy. This and all subsequent information on Henry is culled from the newspaper reportage on his trial. *Daily Gleaner,* 25 Oct. 1960.

11. Characteristically, the self-description was drawn from the Bible—in this instance, from Isaiah 58:12: "Thou shalt raise up the foundations of many generations; and thou shalt be called the Repairer of the Breach, the restorer of paths to dwell in."

12. Evidence given at the trial indicated that, in all, some 40,000 copies of different pamphlets were printed for Henry. *Daily Gleaner,* 11 Oct. 1960.

13. Ibid., 5.

14. Ibid.

15. See Alvin Gouldner, *The Dialectic of Ideology and Technology* (New York: Seabury, 1976).

16. Henry's willingness to give a specific date, Oct. 5, 1959, for the impending repatriation was only the latest in a series of failed predictions by self-appointed Jamaican prophets, from Alexander Bedward in the 1920s to Prince Edward in 1958. It appears that Henry blamed both the Manley regime and Queen Elizabeth II for his failure to repatriate his followers. Manley was accused of failing to live up to an alleged 1959 campaign promise to help in the repatriation effort, and the British monarch was blamed for withholding "money that was lodged in England for the slaves to go back to Africa." *Daily Gleaner* 11 Oct. 1960.

17. Recollections by prosecution witnesses at Henry's trial. *Daily Gleaner*, 7 Oct. 1960.

18. *Daily Gleaner*, 7 Apr. 1960.

19. The contents of this letter are instructive for what they indicate about the close attention Rastafarians paid to international affairs, particularly developments in Cuba. The letter read, in part:

> We wish to draw your attention to the conditions which confronts [*sic*] us today as poor, underpriviledged people which were brought here from Africa by the British slave traders over 400 years ago to serve as slaves. We now desire to return home in peace, to live under own vine and fig tree, otherwise a government like yours that give [*sic*] justice to the poor. All our efforts to have a peaceful repatriation has [*sic*] proven a total failure . . . therefore we want to assure your Sir, and your government that Jamaica and the rest of the British West Indies will be turned over to you and your government . . . we are getting ready for an invasion on the Jamaican Government therefore we need your help and personal service. [Letter cited in *Daily Gleaner*, 13 Oct. 1960.]

20. Consistent with the regime's efforts to prevent the entry of radical groups and ideas into the island, some 66 Afro-American black nationalists were barred from entering the country. All were members of an organization called the "First Africa Corps, Sons and Daughters of Africa." *Daily Gleaner*, 28 Oct. 1960.

21. These attacks on the Chinese involved criticisms and evaluations of their status in the country compared to blacks, rather than any damage to their property. One person making this comparison was Amy Jacques Garvey, widow of Marcus Garvey. She was reported to have spoken out on the issue and to have quoted her husband as having said: "As Blackmen and women you must stand up and claim your country, dedicate your lives to Jamaica, acquire the economic stability the 90 percent of the population should have in relation to the 30,000 Chinese here." Cited in *Daily Gleaner*, 19 Oct. 1960.

22. According to one estimate, the numbers of Chinese in clerical jobs in 1960 was "five times their proportion in the population." See Irving Kaplan et al., eds., *Area Handbook for Jamaica* (Washington: American Univ. Press, 1976), 102.

23. Ibid., 103; and H. Hoetink, "Race and Color in the Caribbean," in *Caribbean Contours*, ed. Sidney Mintz and Sally Price (Baltimore, Md.: Johns Hopkins Univ. Press, 1985), 71–73.

24. As an ideology which also served to cement the racial fault lines which had appeared in the country's social relations, Exceptionalism enjoyed wide support among civic and political leaders and was invoked repeatedly during postcolonial crises.

25. *Daily Gleaner,* 19 Oct. 1960. Bustamante's remarks were prompted by Mrs. Garvey's statement, cited in *Daily Gleaner,* 19 Oct. 1960 (see n. 21 above). It is clear, however, that his remarks were directed even more to groups connected with the current rise of black consciousness.

26. Ibid.

27. *Daily Gleaner,* 27 Oct. 1960.

28. For a valuable interpretation of the Gramscian approach to class hegemony, which sees hegemony as necessarily possessing a multiclass ideological appeal, see Chantal Mouffe, "Hegemony and Ideology in Gramsci," in Chantal Mouffe, ed., *Gramsci and Marxist Theory* (London: Routledge and Kegan Paul, 1979), 168–204.

29. Both Bustamante and the *Gleaner* appealed to Manley to speak out on this issue. See *Daily Gleaner,* 19 and 29 Oct. 1960.

30. Cited in *Daily Gleaner,* 31 Oct. 1960.

31. Manley's statement at the PNP's annual conference in Nov. 1960. Cited in *Daily Gleaner,* 22 Nov. 1960. Despite his claim that the resurfacing of racial protests was "the work of the devil," Manley nonetheless acknowledged the origins of these protests in the social relations of the society and reminded the party conference that the protests were occasioned partly by the uneven effects of economic growth.

32. Referring to the intractability of unemployment in the face of high economic growth, economist Arthur Lewis noted the irony of Jamaica's industrialization: "Between 1950 and 1960, production increased by somewhere between 80 and 100 percent. Also, about 11 percent of the labour force migrated. How does a country double its output, lose 11 percent of its labour force by migration, and still have 12 percent unemployment?" Lewis' answer was that foreign investment was "producing more goods without employing more people." See W. Arthur Lewis, "Goals of Economic Development," *Daily Gleaner,* supplement, Sept. 1964.

33. *Sunday Gleaner,* 10 Apr. 1960.

34. In Aug. 1960, Johnson reestablished in Kingston an organization he had founded in England in 1952 – the Afro–West Indian Cultural Center. See Gannon, "Origins and Development of Jamaica's Two-Party System," 262.

35. Ibid., 277.

36. Ibid.

37. In outlining its program for reform, the PPP seemed not to go beyond such generalities as "more uniform distribution of wealth to conform with the internationally recognized democratic principles of the greatest good for the greatest number." *Daily Gleaner* 14 Apr. 1961.

38. Despite similarities between Rastafarian and PPP race consciousness, there were sharp differences between the two nationalist tendencies. While the Rastafarians articulated the protest of the most destitute sectors of the urban

population, the PPP tended to speak for the independent artisans, manual laborers, small entrepreneurs, and workers on the lowest rungs of the service sector. Thus, the PPP's black nationalist appeals were directed less to the chronically unemployed or destitute poor, and more to those better-off elements at the bottom of the class structure who wanted to improve their lot in the urban economy. In this quest, the PPP, unlike the Rastafarians, was a model of political discretion. It pledged itself to peaceful boycotts and passive resistance if its "Jamaica for Jamaicans" demands were ignored, and generally conducted its opposition lawfully and with decorum.

39. M.G. Smith et al., *The Rastafarian Movement.*

40. See, e.g., M.G. Smith's reply to "Political Reporter," in the *Daily Gleaner,* 25 Aug. 1960.

41. *Daily Gleaner* 10 Apr. 1960.

42. Cited in *Daily Gleaner,* 22 Nov. 1960.

43. These were the 1961 referendum on Jamaica's continued participation in the West Indies Federation, and the final negotiations for an independence constitution. For a discussion of these events, see Trevor Munroe, *Politics of Decolonization,* chs. 4 and 5.

44. *Daily Gleaner,* 19 Apr. 1961.

45. For example, in April 1961, Bustamante lashed out at expatriates, apparently for their class snobbery. Addressing a mass meeting of party supporters at Half-Way-Tree Square in Kingston, he claimed, with characteristic bombast, that the real issue was one of class, not color: "It is not race or color, it's because once they have, they think themselves too damn good to associate with you. They feel they are better than you . . . Let me warn the 'haves' to change their ways or they will have to leave this country . . . I want to warn the 'haves' I am still alive." Cited in *Daily Gleaner,* 19 Apr. 1961.

46. In 1961 alone, these policies included a ban on socialist literature; the exclusion of Black Muslims, including Malcolm X, from the island; and prohibition of travel by a local communist, Ferdinand Smith, who was seeking medical help in Czechoslovakia. This latter ban was lifted after protests.

CHAPTER 4

1. Lloyd G. Barnett, "The Constitution: Ten Years After," *Jamaica Law Journal* 41 (1972):57.

2. In recounting the sorry story of the leaders' disinterest in protecting fundamental rights in the Independence Constitution, Barnett observed:

Public interest was displayed in the drafting of the Independence Constitution. By that time, too, Bills of Rights had become a feature of the Constitution of the newer Commonwealth Nations. *Yet, in Jamaica there was no discernable desire for such provisions among the political leaders.* The real impetus came from the claimant demands of the capitalist interests whose predominant advocacy was for the protection of property rights. The call for constitutional guarantees of human rights also received support from academic and middle class elements who probably apprehended future intrusion on the freedoms of conscience and expression. In the result, a chapter on Fundamental Rights and Freedoms was inserted in the Jamaican Constitution. [Ibid., 54; italics added.]

Barnett observed in his book, *The Constitutional Law of Jamaica*, that the reason given for the inclusion of Fundamental Rights was "to convince foreign investors that political freedom and constitutionalism would prevail in Jamaica," 377.

3. Of course, while full credit belongs to all the activists who struggled to keep this tradition alive in the bleak fifties—among them Arthur Henry, Ferdinand Smith, and Roland Simms—it was Hart's attention to cadre development that facilitated the regeneration of the Marxist tradition in the immediate postcolonial years.

4. Ben Monroe, interview with the author, summer 1979. Although other militants in the JFTU must have concurred with some of these charges, Monroe's allegations of "bureaucratism" were rejected as a "smokescreen" by the seasoned trade unionist and former JFTU activist, Chris Lawrence. In an interview, Lawrence made it clear that, while he shared Monroe's criticism of Hart's tactics and their consequences, the real issues which caused a split between Hart and Monroe concerned the latter's lack of personal integrity. Lawrence, interview with the author, summer 1979.

5. Ben Monroe, interview with the author, summer 1979.

6. In the wake of Monroe's damaging allegations, Hart apparently was unable to prevent a slide toward demoralization and indiscipline among the rank and file. Unwilling to confront the issue of how to deal with conflicts inside the party, Hart devoted less and less time to the PFM. Thus, instead of providing leadership on party discipline, Hart in effect drew back from a confrontation with Monroe. Increasingly, Hart turned his energies to his neglected law practice, while maintaining a correspondence with progressive forces worldwide.

7. Among the literature which the UWC disseminated were: Castro's "History will Absolve Me," and such pieces as "Cuba at Punte del Este," "Fidel and the Youth," and "Let the Philosophy of Plunder and War Disappear."

8. This group included the unemployed workers George Vassel and Raymond Ingram; the sign artist Headley Reynolds; the furniture maker Percival Graham, and the refrigeration mechanic George Meyers.

9. The grievous experience of decolonization apparently left Monroe with a marked distaste for all forms of political unionism, since he saw the latter as necessarily subordinating workers' interests to the needs of political parties. On this score, Monroe made no distinction between the PFM-JFTU and the other party-unions.

10. Although there were subsequent attempts to mobilize the urban poor, the UWC represented the only instance in which leadership came from the ranks of the unemployed.

11. The 1960 census, for example, put unemployment at 13%. That figure does not reflect the number of underemployed persons.

12. Post, *Arise Ye Starvelings*, 280.

13. As if in anticipation of precisely such an eruption, the *Gleaner*, early in 1962, called for increased emphasis on state security to deal with "the regular

habitual anti-social behaviour of those elements which follow crime or violence as their occasional or normal way of life." In the opinion of the editors, no means should be spared in dealing with the unruly poor:

> Every citizen has a responsibility to keep an eye on them, to keep a finger on them and if necessary to use violence against them in order that they may be made subordinate to good order. And in this duty the government as well as the civilian must have at his beck and call a specially trained, skillful, . . . and determined . . . security branch . . . [which] must actively undertake the continual patrolling of the ramparts of decency to the end that the criminal will be kept in proper check. [*Daily Gleaner,* 20 Mar. 1962.]

14. Invariably, these were civic leaders such as priests, schoolteachers, and newspaper editorial writers.

15. The link between the dramaturgy of the urban poor and their novel use of language needs to be investigated as a counter force challenging the rival dramaturgy and power of the bourgeois class.

16. Ben Monroe, interview with the author.

17. In his interview in summer 1979 Monroe located the origins of victimization in employment in the JLP's ten-year rule between 1945 and 1955. In his view, PNP supporters in that period were denied employment on government projects because the JLP made no distinction between PNP loyalists and socialists.

18. See Ernesto Laclau, *Politics and Ideology in Marxist Theory* (London: New Left Books, 1977), from which this critique comes.

19. Ben Monroe, interview with author, summer 1979.

20. This agitation at the refinery drew a sharp rebuke from the *Gleaner.* In an editorial entitled "Stop it," the paper condemned "those who regard the state of being unemployed as a license to terrorize the community" and endorsed the use of the police against the jobseekers. *Daily Gleaner,* 23 Mar. 1962.

21. The UWC apparently had some success here, as the Ministry of Labour agreed to recruit some 70 of these jobseekers, because many of them were fishermen and were willing to work long hours in the sea, where dredging was being carried out for construction of the refinery.

22. *Daily Gleaner,* 5 Jan. 1963.

23. In its coverage of the events, the *Gleaner* observed that "the project has been plagued by strikes ever since work began late last year." Ibid.

24. The *Gleaner* alluded to this with the following observation: "It is understood that the NWU supports the view that workers in the area are not given a fair share of employment on the project and this is one of the main reasons for the current stoppages." Ibid.

25. Ibid.

26. Ibid.

27. This settlement between the NWU and BITU did not bring peace to the project, however. Within a week of the demonstration, the BITU called its workers out to protest the registration list being used to poll the workers. *Daily Gleaner,* 16 Jan. 1963.

28. See the UWC pamphlet, "Why Tolerate Poverty and Oppression," 18 Aug. 1963, p. 5. Ben Monroe's personal files. Kingston, Jamaica. Complementing its activism to get jobs for the West Kingston poor, the council now identified itself with "workers, small and middle farmers, small business persons, students and professionals" and called on them to oppose the regime. However, given the lonely struggle of the UWC and the lowly origins of its leadership, it was unlikely that this rallying cry would be heeded.

29. It is probable that the now-entrenched clientelist practice of creating captive populations in the urban ghettos began with the construction of this Tivoli Gardens housing project.

30. The problem of urban squatting had reached a nodal point in the early sixties. According to a 1961 police estimate, there were some 20,000 squatters in Kingston alone, which in 1960 had a total population of just over 123,400 persons. This meant that at least 16% of the Kingston population lived under the horrific conditions of urban homelessness. To make matters worse, instead of finding temporary shelter for the squatters, the government pursued a callous slum-clearance policy which only exacerbated existing tensions.

31. The mobilizing role played by the UWC was alluded to by Minister of Housing D.C. Tavares, who referred to "agitators in this area [who] have been holding meetings and instigating squatters to be violent and to resist this operation . . . it is to these agitators that I attribute the behaviour of the people in this area today." *Daily Gleaner*, 5 Oct. 1963.

32. Ibid.

33. See, e.g., PNP criticism which tacked between support for the slum clearance and sympathy for the squatters. *Daily Gleaner*, 12 Oct. 1963.

34. *Daily Gleaner*, 14 Oct. 1963.

35. See the UWC pamphlet, "The Right to Work," 28 Nov. 1963. Ben Monroe's files, Kingston, Jamaica.

36. Ibid.

37. Ibid., 4.

38. UWC members attended the first congress of the league in Sept. 1963.

39. It should be noted, however, that this quiescence did not necessarily reflect labor's acceptance of racial inequalities.

40. *Daily Gleaner*, 7 Mar. 1963.

41. *Daily Gleaner*, 10 Mar. 1963.

42. In attempting to justify employers' playing ethnic favorites, the writer observed that "having . . . grown up in the business world it is just natural that we should have absorbed and gained practical experience in business which simply cannot be learned in a commercial school . . . we already have a basic knowledge of the running of a business and how to deal with the public, so from the very beginning we have the edge over our dark-skinned counterpart. Many employers recognize this and therefore feel safer in taking a bet on the Chinese when he has to choose between a Chinese and a coloured person." *Daily Gleaner*, 4 Oct. 1963.

43. Ibid.

44. *Daily Gleaner*, 8 Oct. 1963.

45. One such anti-Chinese smear was served up by an editorial writer for

the *Daily Chronicle* in 1914. After demanding that the colonial government limit "the number of celestials who are month after month being dumped onto the island," the writer delivered this demagogic assault:

> The Chinese question is one that concerns every businessman, and, in fact, every member of the community. It has been established beyond the shadow of a doubt that more Chinese are not wanted here . . . Honesty is no longer one of his chief characteristics . . . For him the brankruptcy court has no terrors. It matters not whether he is adjudged a fraudulent bankrupt and committed to jail, once he has achieved his object, viz., defrauding his creditors . . . Whether they come from Hong Kong or Canton, matters little. It is not to Jamaica's interests that they should continue to arrive in detachments, companies or battalions. To be perfectly frank, we prefer their room to their company. [*Daily Chronicle,* 7 July 1914.]

46. *Daily Gleaner,* 10 Oct. 1963.

47. UWC, "The Right to Work," 28 Nov. 1963.

CHAPTER 5

1. Among them were John Stephenson, secretary of Norman Manley's constituency. Others were: Gloria Davis, Paul Afflick, and Barry Moore – all members of the PNP's East Kingston Constituency Group. Apparently, none of them could have been over 35 years of age, since the organization they were to create only allowed those between 16 and 35 to join. See "Where Do We Go from Here," n.d., Papers of the Young Socialist League (hereafter referred to as YSL Papers), p. 1. These papers were held by former YSL activist Dennis Daley at the time this research was carried out.

2. "What Is the Young Socialist League?", n.d., YSL Papers.

3. Dennis Daley and Paul Afflick (former YSL members), interview with author, Kingston, Jamaica, summer 1979. The irony of Manley's offering his blessings to the YSL, despite the fact that he had helped to defeat a similar initiative 10 years earlier, did not escape UWC members who were in attendance. According to Ben Monroe of the UWC, he and others heckled and booed the party leader.

4. "Young Socialist League Annual Report," Sept. 1963, YSL Papers.

5. For example, it had difficulties establishing rural bases and witnessed the resignation of its president.

6. Draft statement by Daley, YSL Papers. This statement apparently was drafted in preparation for an appearance before the PNP disciplinary committee late in 1964.

7. "Draft Constitution," n.d., YSL Papers, p. 1.

8. "Socialism for Jamaica," n.d., YSL Papers, pp. 1–3.

9. Ibid., 6. This optimistic refrain seems especially puzzling, since the league's assessment of the political scene indicated that it believed the country had reached its political nadir.

10. The YSL paid scant attention to the ideological orthodoxies of the time.

The existing nuances and controversies in the world communist movement did not agitate the league. Instead, its members opted for an eclectic Marxism. Remarking on the absence of a dominant Marxist current in the league, Daley noted in an interview:

> The Marxists in the leadership of the YSL got their Marxism from varied sources. There was no one particular place where we got it. We all brought our own Marxism to the YSL with us. What we tried to impart was a hodge-podge of the variety of Marxisms. The division between Trotskyists and Leninists . . . meant nothing to us. We were pretty crude [in our approach].

11. The *Monthly Review* school of political economy appears to have been the only current of Marxism with a lasting effect on the YSL. Many articles on neocolonialism and underdevelopment from the journal were copied by the YSL and used as study aids. One noteworthy article which was seminal in influencing YSL thinking was "The Development of Underdevelopment" by the Latin American political economist Andre Gunder Frank. *Monthly Review*, 18, 4 (Sept. 1966):17–31.

12. "Report to the Second Annual Congress of the Young Socialist League," 23 Aug. 1964, YSL Papers, p. 2.

13. Munroe, along with K.D. Edwards, was given the responsibility for organizing a "regular bulletin" through which the league "could present to members and the public . . . a picture of the decadence and gross injustice of capitalist Jamaica." The result of their efforts was the publication of "Fact Sheets" which, the league noted, "have been a great success . . . [judging from] the frequency with which information from these sheets is quoted in all sections of the society." Ibid., 4.

14. Other members of the UWI Area Council were: K.D. Edwards, Hal Coore, and Hopeton Gordon.

15. "Minutes of Executive Meeting," 3 July 1964, YSL Papers, p. 1.

16. "Report to the Second Annual Congress," 1.

17. "Minutes of Meeting of the Executive of the YSL," 1 May 1964, YSL Papers, p. 2. Two leadership training courses were held in March, which the league termed "successful."

18. "Proposal for Work of Education and Training Subcommittes," 1964, YSL Papers, p. 2.

19. Ibid., 1. Expressing a sensitivity to the contradiction between the social origins of the organization's leadership and those of its potential support base, those preparing the pamphlets were encouraged to use "very simple language and homely analogies."

20. See "Minutes of the Meeting of the General Executive Committee," 3 May 1964, YSL Papers, p. 2.

21. See the untitled report on YSL organization drafted in 1964 by Dennis Daley, YSL Papers, pp. 1–10.

22. Ibid., 3.

23. "Minutes of the Meeting of the General Executive Committee," 3 May 1964, p. 1.

24. Ibid. The minutes did note that some of the JBC workers had shown some interest in the league after it held a public meeting on the strike.

25. "Report to the Second Annual Congress," 23 Aug. 1964, p. 5. Dr. Leroy Taylor, an economist at the university, represented the league.

26. Delegates representing rural areas came from: Savanna-la-Mar, Santa Cruz, Mandeville, Highgate, Porus, Annotto Bay, and Guy's Hill. *Daily Gleaner*, 25 Aug. 1964.

27. "Policy Statement," delivered to the Second Annual YSL Congress, Aug. 1964, YSL Papers, pp. 1–18.

28. Ibid., 10.

29. Ibid.

30. Ibid., 12.

31. See the article by "Special Correspondent," in *Public Opinion*, 12 June 1964, 3, and another by "a Young Socialist," in *Public Opinion*, 26 June 1964, 3.

32. "Minutes of the Meeting of the General Executive Council," 3 May 1964, YSL Papers, p. 3.

33. Arnett was PNP member of parliament (M.P.) for the Central Saint Andrew constituency, and mentor to the Young Socialists. Maxwell was editor of *Public Opinion* and an unabashed supporter of the league. He defended the YSL tactic of cooperating with the PNP, asserting that "in the present situation it is necessary, if you are to have any effective political voice, to join one of the two existing parties. You can of course, form a new party, or you can forsake the democratic method and take to the hills. Since I believe that it would be wasteful and destructive to form a new party and even more pointless . . . to take to the hills, I find myself along with a great host of others, compelled to work within the existing framework." *Public Opinion*, 3 July 1964, 4.

34. See O.T. Fairclough's dismissive reply to "special correspondent's" advocacy of workers' control in the trade unions. *Public Opinion*, 19 June 1964, 3.

35. Robert Hill, "An Open Letter to the Young Socialist League," 23 Aug. 1964, YSL Papers.

36. Ibid., 3.

37. Ibid.

38. Ibid., 7.

39. Ibid., 2.

40. Ibid., 6–7.

41. These included: the establishment of Workers' Councils, an alliance with the UWC, the circulation of a biweekly newsletter, and the development of a literacy project.

42. See the UWC's savage criticism of the YSL's tactic in "The Right to Work," 6 Nov. 1964.

43. *Daily Gleaner*, 25 Aug. 1964.

44. "Policy Statement," Aug. 1964, p. 2.

45. Hill, "An Open Letter," 3.

46. These included the notions that the right wing would definitely tolerate their maneuvers, and that bourgeois hegemony over the working class could be ended by capturing positions in these institution and taking them over.

47. *Daily Gleaner,* 12 Sept. 1964.
48. *Daily Gleaner,* 19 Sept. 1964.
49. Ibid.
50. Alluding to the deepening struggle within the party, the *Gleaner's* political reporter noted that "every person who has been a top-flight man in the PNP since 1938 is worried about the Young Socialists and their recent Annual Conference and the resolutions they passed at that Conference have not made them any easier for the old-timers to handle . . . although Mr. Manley argues and cajoles and more often than not gets the party to agree on a compromise, it is the group known as the Young Socialists which is now calling the tune within the People's National Party." *Sunday Gleaner,* 13 Sept. 1964.
51. UWC, "The Right to Work," 23 Oct. 1964.
52. Ibid., 5–6.
53. Ben Monroe, interview with author, summer 1979.
54. "The Right to Work," 30 Oct. 1964.
55. Small at this time was employed as a legal officer in the NWU. This precipitous action by the UWC was consistent with its politics of insurgency and surprise. Thus, within a week after making these disclosures, the council, though allied with the league and aware of its maneuvers to win positions on the PNP executive at the upcoming conference, published a scathing attack on the league. See *"The Right to Work,"* 6 Nov. 1964.
56. In part 2 of the published document, there is a remarkable rejection of the prior PNP strategy of externally-led industrialization. The document noted that "industrial development policy in Jamaica has so far been based on two doctrines. The first is that the development effort will come from private enterprise, the second is that development initiative and investment must come from abroad. These doctrines are unsound and their unsoundness has been amply established in the record of development. Private enterprise has no formal responsibility for the public good and is accountable to no authority but itself." *Daily Gleaner,* 9 Nov. 1964.
57. *Daily Gleaner,* 7 Nov. 1964.
58. Ibid.
59. Ibid.
60. Ibid.
61. Ibid. The inclusion of this proposal apparently was achieved only after a factional struggle. The *Gleaner* reported, for instance, that one faction wanted immediate nationalization of the Jamaica Public Service Co. (JPSCO), the Telephone Co., the Bybrook Milk Condensery, and the Cement Co. Another segment wanted to nationalize only the JPSCO, while a third faction wanted any nationalization to include wharves, the Jamaica Omnibus Service Co., and sugar factories. Only the proposal for nationalization of the JPSCO gained a majority vote in the PAC. *Daily Gleaner,* 7 Nov. 1964.
62. "Comments on the land policy," 1964, YSL Papers, p. 4.
63. Ibid.
64. Ibid., 3.
65. Ibid., 6.

66. "Manley's Statement to the PNP's National Executive Committee," YSL Papers, 2.

67. Ibid.

68. Cited in *Daily Gleaner*, 16 Nov. 1964.

69. For similar accounts of events at the conference, see Thomas Wright, "Candidly Yours," *Daily Gleaner*, 17 Nov. 1964, and "Vere Johns Says," *The Star*, 23 Nov. 1964.

70. For a discussion of this and other allegations made by the Young Socialists, see "Lessons from the November Conference," YSL Papers, 1-2.

71. *Sunday Gleaner*, 22 Nov., 1964. Throughout this period, *Gleaner* editorialists and columnists, their positions converging with those taken by the PNP opposition, did much to impugn the reforms. Perhaps the most militantly hostile of these columnists was "Jay Munroe," who denounced the reforms as "theoretical imbecilities" that were about "as relevant to Jamaica's *economic* needs as a pocomania ceremony."

72. Ibid.

73. For details of Small's removal from the NWU, see the exchange of letters between the latter and Thossy Kelly in *Daily Gleaner*, 26 Nov. 1964.

74. Monroe admitted in an interview that the tactics of the UWC were designed to undermine the PNP and embarrass the members of the YSL in it, because of the continuing rift over reforming the PNP.

75. Dennis Daley, interview with the author, summer 1979.

76. *Daily Gleaner*, 7 Dec. 1964.

77. *Daily Gleaner*, 8 Dec. 1964.

78. See Paul Afflick, YSL secretary, to the PNP, 4 Dec. 1964, YSL Papers.

79. Ibid., 2.

80. YSL pamphlet, n.d., YSL Papers, 1-2.

81. Dennis Daley, in an interview with the author, conceded that the league's defense of Norman Manley against the Right was not really a genuine reversal, but rather a ploy to gain rank-and-file support by "defending" Manley against his imagined enemies.

82. "The Desperate Men," YSL Papers, 2.

83. The *Gleaner*'s political reporter, who was following these developments closely, disclosed that Glasspole threatened to walk out of meetings of the executive, while Isaacs threatened to resign if the party's policy was not changed. *Daily Gleaner*, 17 Jan. 1965.

84. For the text of the revised program, see the *Daily Gleaner*, 23 Jan. 1965. Although *Gleaner* columnist Jay Munroe found the revised policy "an admirable statement without that hectoring . . . note of moral rectitude that marred the November manifesto," neither the paper's editorial writers nor the landowner-cum-columnist Morris Cargill was appeased. Both seemed to agree that the reforms were "unrealistic." See *Sunday Gleaner*, 31 Jan. 1965, and *Daily Gleaner*, 25 Feb. 1965.

85. *Daily Gleaner*, 7 Nov. 1964.

86. The one exception here was the case of the light and power company — perhaps the most embarrassing instance of a foreign-owned enterprise.

87. The proposal included the right to trade-union representation, equal pay for women, the right to reinstatement for wrongful dismissal, a literacy campaign, and a crash program for the chronically unemployed.

88. Isaacs and Glasspole were elected as first and second vice-presidents, respectively.

89. *Facing Reality* 1, no. 2 (Feb. 1965):3. YSL Papers.

90. Ibid.

91. Ibid.

92. Ibid. Italics mine.

93. Ibid., 6.

94. Ibid.

95. See ch. 5, no. 81 above.

96. This prompt response also was determined by the character of the dispute, which had a particular salience for the Young Socialists. A major concern of the league was the practice of political unionism and its tendency to subordinate the interests of the workers to the exigencies of party politics. Indeed, it was precisely Hugh Small's attempt to raise this issue with workers, as well as his call for an end to the misuse of union dues, which led to his dismissal from the NWU. See details of Small's letter to Thossy Kelly, in *Daily Gleaner*, 25 Nov. 1964; and *Daily Gleaner*, 2 Dec. 1964.

97. See Dennis Daley's 13 Feb. 1966 mimeographed draft statement to the PNP's National Executive Committee at the time of his expulsion, YSL Papers, 2.

98. This view was supported by Dennis Daley in an interview with me in 1979. Among other things, Daley noted that "there were misgivings about . . . whether we could undertake it. Whether we were sufficiently well organized. It presented . . . opportunities, but at the same time grave risks. We decided to take the risks. We felt we couldn't let down the workers who had been simply abandoned."

99. Daley estimated that about 1,000 of the approximately 5,000 sugar workers at Frome had resigned from both unions.

100. See "Transcript of a speech made by Mr. Hugh Small at a public meeting held at Frome on the night of 5th May, 1965" (hereafter referred to as "Small at Frome"), YSL Papers, 1–13.

101. Recounting this practice, Daley noted that both unions had agreed with the Sugar Manufacturers Association "to withhold 1^d in the 1/- of [the] 1964 bonus," to be paid in 1965 as a hedge against an expected fall in sugar prices. See D. Daley; "Draft Statement," n.d., YSL Papers.

102. "Small at Frome," 12.

103. The unions never could amass strike funds for the workers, because union organizers were part of the network of party organizers kept on retainer to be mobilized for party electoral campaigns. Dennis Daley, interview with the author, summer 1979.

104. It seems more likely that the unions were tardy in using the strike weapon, rather than unilaterally rejecting its use, as the league claimed. It must be said that the unions supported the strike belatedly, only after the workers had taken things into their own hands. Unilateral assurances against a strike could not

be given, because in Jamaica unionized workers repeatedly have struck employers with impunity and without approval from union leaders.

105. This was a disparaging reference to N.W. Manley and Alexander Bustamante, who were cousins as well as heads of their respective parties.

106. "Small at Frome," 3.

107. "Transcript of speech by Hugh Small at Grange Hill," 9 May 1965, YSL Papers.

108. Ibid., 4.

109. Ibid., 5.

110. Although workers at Inswood, New Yarmouth, Holland, and Richmond Estates were becoming restive because of the wage dispute, the actions of the Frome workers failed to trigger a revolt among those workers. The actions of the Frome workers were therefore the exception, with the obedient Monymusk workers representing the dominant trend.

111. Dennis Daley, interview with the author, summer 1979.

112. Ibid.

113. In the interim, the columnist Vere Johns expressed the alarm with which the incipient WLU was viewed in the media. After endorsing the refusal of the colonial state to recognize Ferdinand Smith's Sugar and Agricultural Workers Union in the fifties, Johns, in his 4 Aug. 1965 column in *The Star*, called for similar action against the WLU: "No government worth its salt would permit this WLU to operate, for it has nothing to offer the workers but certain ruin. Stamp it out good and hard and let Mr. Hugh Small go and seek a livelihood in the profession for which he was trained—law."

114. In an article on the commission's findings, the *Daily Gleaner* observed that "the report said the Commission was satisfied that Mr. Hugh Small, President of the Workers' Liberation Union, did great disservice to the workers' cause by arousing unwarranted discontent among them, but added his relevance was [that] the BITU and NWU should keep their members more informed . . . and imbued with a spirit of participation."

115. See *Facing Reality* 1, no. 2 (Feb. 1965), in YSL Papers; and a YSL letter in *Daily Gleaner*, 2 Feb. 1966.

116. See "Open Letter to A[ttorney] G[eneral], Prime Minister," 8 Sept. 1965, YSL Papers.

117. Dennis Daley, interview with the author, summer 1979.

118. In November, the commission upheld the workers' claim and recommended that WISCO pay them a bonus in 1965.

119. Hugh Small apparently was spared this trial since he claimed that he was not a member of the party.

120. See "Report of the Disciplinary Committee" [to investigate charges against Dennis Daley under Rule 16 of the party] (hereafter referred to as "Disciplinary Report"), 15 Nov. 1965, YSL Papers, pp. 1–8.

121. In addition to making the disclosure involving secret tape recordings of league meetings, the report showed that Daley regarded Small's use of the term "two-cousin" unions as inappropriate. As well, the report indicated that

Daley had repudiated the allegations of collusion with WISCO and of the NWU's abuse of union dues. "Disciplinary Report," 4–5.

122. Ibid., 7.

123. These included a January trip to the Tri-Continental Conference in Havana, letters in February protesting the numerous passport seizures which followed that trip, rallies in March decrying the British monarch's visit to Jamaica, and in July affirmations of solidarity with squatters whose shanties were to be razed.

124. It should be said, however, that the Young Socialists, having stumbled into the politics of the working class at the sugar estates, and subsequently having been reminded of the realities of state power and the limits of their practice, still gained a valuable apprenticeship at a time when many in the country — especially the middle class and the intellectuals — drew back from any activism against the state. The YSL's practice in the 1962–66 period therefore prepared the ground for a subsequent proliferation of movements opposed to the post-colonial state.

CHAPTER 6

1. In the midst of the growing debate on infringements of civil liberties, the *Gleaner* observed that, even though the debate was a legitimate one, "serious attention should also be paid to the conventions of good behaviour, to the need for self-restraint in all community matters and to the discouragement of the growth of an offensive [academic] elite." *Daily Gleaner*, 20 Aug. 1964.

2. *Daily Gleaner*, 19 Dec. 1964.

3. *Daily Gleaner*, 8 Dec. 1964.

4. *Daily Gleaner*, 29 Dec. 1964.

5. For example, in 1963, the regime introduced mandatory sentencing for major offenses against property and individuals. This law subjected prisoners to floggings and long prison terms at hard labor. See Lloyd G. Barnett, "The Constitution: Ten Years After," 57.

6. *Daily Gleaner*, 5 Aug. 1965.

7. Ibid. At uncomfortable moments like this, exponents of Exceptionalism could unsheathe the weapon of race. Witness Sangster's remark that "it is more than apparent to us that the new restrictions are based on colour and not on economic considerations."

8. The following PNP statement on the incident indicates that it was rebellious youths who were responsible: "The Police . . . have warned us that it is the young unemployed teenagers and persons in their early twenties who have never been employed in their lives who for the most part are involved in the present troubles." *Daily Gleaner*, 1 Sept. 1965.

9. For his part, the Chinese shopkeeper who was the target of the protesters noted that "this outbreak was not spontaneous. It's something that has been brewing and fermenting in the idle indigenous people around this area. When my father started business at this spot he was approached with threats and was propositioned on occasions to buy protection. He refused of course, and from

then on even after his death there exists a kind of resentment towards the family." Advertisement by Albert Lue in *Daily Gleaner* 3, Sept. 1965.

10. *Daily Gleaner,* 16 July 1966.

11. Mindful, perhaps, of the slum dwellers' penchant for attacks on government buildings, the JLP increased security at the prime minister's residence and the BITU offices during the evictions in July. *Daily Gleaner,* 13 July 1966.

12. It should be noted that the PNP also engaged in this practice. For a discussion of captive populations as "a group of people who are personally dependent upon, and excluded from independent political participation by, members of another class," see Goran Therborn, *What Does the Ruling Class Do When It Rules?* (London: New Left Books, 1978), 188.

13. For similar conclusions on the link between slum clearance and the JLP's consolidation of power, see Terry Lacey, *Violence and Politics in Jamaica, 1960–1970* (London: Manchester Univ. Press, 1977), 49.

14. Vernon Arnett, ally of the Young Socialists and PNP member of parliament (MP) for the Central St. Andrew constituency, was arrested for his actions. Furthermore, his criticism of a £58,000 government expenditure for an upcoming visit by the Queen not only exasperated the JLP MPs, but also earned him the censure of his PNP colleagues, who closed ranks against him in Parliament. In affirming that Arnett did not speak for the PNP, his nemesis, Wills Isaacs, observed: "Whatever I may have against the English people I shall abide by the Constitution . . . We shall take part in the welcome to her Majesty the Queen." *Daily Gleaner,* 17 Feb. 1966.

15. According to the *Gleaner*'s estimate, the shanty towns at both sites contained at least 800 shacks and sprawled over some 56 acres along Kingston's waterfront. *Daily Gleaner,* 14 July 1966.

16. Apart from UWC and YSL activists who championed the settlers' rights, the Jamaica Council of Churches (JCC) emerged as a major defender of the slum dwellers. It won delays for them and assisted in their relocation. It seems likely that the JCC also was instrumental in getting a reluctant JLP to contribute £10,000 to assist the squatters. *Daily Gleaner,* 20 July 1966.

17. *Daily Gleaner,* 16 Aug. 1966.

18. For the extraordinary measures taken by the JLP, see *Jamaica Gazette* 89, no. 141 (Oct. 1966).

19. This law was the Prevention of Crime (Special Provisions) Act No. 42, 1963.

20. This Dangerous Drugs Law, revised by Act 10 of 1964, imposed harsher sentences, ranging from a minimum of 5 years for a first conviction for cultivating, selling, or dealing in the drug, to a maximum of 10 years at hard labor for a second conviction for possession. See H. Aubrey Fraser, "The Law and Cannabis in the West Indies," *Jamaica Law Journal* (Apr. 1974): 26–36.

21. The cat-o-nine-tails refers to a whip made of nine thongs of 20-inch-long cotton rope, attached to a handle. For the grotesquerie involved in specifying the infliction of punishment on the prisoners, see *Jamaica Gazette* 88 (28 Jan. 1965).

22. Such policies, which were mild in comparison to the serious abuses of

human rights in other countries, did not prevent the government early in 1965 from becoming a member of the UN's Human Rights Commission.

23. During the communal violence, one of the JLP's top gunmen, Rudolph "Zackie" Lewis, was shot dead. His PNP counterpart, Douglas "Little Keith" Campbell, was killed by the police during the emergency.

24. Lacey, *Violence and Politics*, 87–88.

25. Of the record 98 work stoppages recorded for 1967, 48 (49%) of these were related to wage disputes. Jamaica, Central Planning Unit, *Economic Survey of Jamaica* (1968), 44.

26. For example, while Codrington College in Barbados did train school-teachers, it mainly prepared graduates for the clergy. In the early forties, the college had an average of only twenty students. On the other hand, the Imperial College of Tropical Agriculture in Trinidad trained British graduates destined for careers as agricultural specialists in the empire. For a discussion of colonial experiments in higher education in the West Indian colonies, see Hugh Springer, "The Historical Development, Hopes and Aims of the U.C.W.I.," *Journal of Negro Education*[31] (Winter 1962):9.

27. Ken Post, in discussing this issue, noted that in the 47 years between 1881 and 1928, only 17 people had chosen the external degree option. This paucity of enrollment for the external degree reflected the degree to which the more affluent classes sought higher education abroad. There seems to have been an underlying cultural reason for these low figures, for as the native opposition to the creation of a local university reveals, it regarded education in the colony as inferior to one acquired in the metropole. Post, *Arise Ye Starvelings*, 55.

28. This commission was chaired by the British High Court Judge, Sir Cyril Asquith.

29. The full committee included: Sir James Irvine, principal and vice-chancellor of the University of St. Andrews; W.D. Innis, from Trinidad; J.A. Lukkoo, member of the Executive and Legislative Councils in British Guiana; Margery Perham, expert on African colonial administration, Oxford University; R. E. Priestly, principal and vice-chancellor of the University of Birmingham; Philip M. Sherlock, secretary of the Institute of Jamaica; and Hugh Springer, member of the Barbados House of Assembly. Great Britain, Colonial Office, *Report of the West Indies Committee of the Commission on Higher Education in the Colonies* (hereafter referred to as "Irvine Committee"), CMD 6654, June 1945, p. 2.

30. As a keen student of these events later observed, opposition to the Asquith Commission by the Caribbean intelligentsia was futile, since they were too weak politically and economically to mount an effective challenge. See Trevor Munroe, "Developed Idealism and Early Materialism: 'Left' Caribbean Thought in Transition," photocopy (Kingston: Univ. of the West Indies, 1970), 31.

31. Irvine Committee, 61.

32. H. W. Springer, "University-Government Relationships in the West Indies," Extract from Collected Seminar Papers on Relations between Govern-

ments and Universities—The West Indies Case, offprint (U.W.I. Reference Collection, MONA, Jan.-May 1967):83–85.

33. I concur with Hugh Springer's reasoning when he argues that, had the university been "under conditions of political independence even under a federal regime, it is likely that it would have been allowed a good deal less freedom to manage its own affairs. It also would have been under much greater pressure to be a 'national' institution." H.W. Springer, "University-Government Relationships in the West Indies," 92.

34. The committee also proposed that the college be located in Jamaica, for a variety of reasons, including its "liberal and sympathetic attitude" and the "cooperative character of its racial structure." Irvine Committee, 19.

35. See Great Britain, Inter-University Council for Higher Education Overseas, *Report of Visitors* (1954), 41–44. This visiting team reported on the progress of the U.C.W.I.

36. Irvine Committee, 51. Emphasis mine.

37. Despite the initial projection of 500 students, only 33 students in the field of medicine were enrolled in 1948. Indeed, it was a decade before enrollment reached 622 students from 13 colonies in the region.

38. For a brief allusion to this oft-ignored link between the defeat of the federation and the revival of its basic tenets by the postcolonial intelligentsia, see Gordon Rohlehr's introduction to the *West Indian Social Science Index* [to the popular journals and newspapers, *Moko, New World Quarterly, Savacou,* and *Tapia,* for the years 1963–72], photocopy (Kingston: U.W.I. Reference Collection, 1974), iv.

39. University and Caribbean scholars also played an important role in the debate and preparations for federation. For example, the journal *Social and Economic Studies* in 1957 devoted an entire issue (vol. 6, no. 2) to the federation.

40. Within this contingent could be found disaffected PNP sympathizers such as the economist Leroy Taylor; the lecturer and student of Hegelian Marxism, Bertell Ollman; and Robert Hill and Trevor Munroe, both students whose radicalism veered toward militant laborism.

41. Quoted in an editorial, *Daily Gleaner,* 18 Aug. 1964.

42. Bustamante, letter to the press. Ibid.

43. This act—the Foreign Nationals and Commonwealth Citizens Employment Act—was passed in 1964, ostensibly to protect jobs for Jamaicans. However, as Norman Manley noted with dismay, "Nobody had then thought or dared to say in the House that the Bill might be used for security purposes—for the purpose of excluding from Jamaica people whose opinions they might not like." *Daily Gleaner,* 17 Mar. 1965.

44. Apart from a major outpost at the *Daily Gleaner,* the regime had few intellectuals who could elaborate its ideology.

45. It is important to maintain this distinction between what Alvin Gouldner calls "technical" and "humanistic" intelligentsia. In brief, the former are those intellectuals who are primarily engaged in puzzle solving and elaboration of technical problems; the latter are those concerned with social relations, ideology, and agency. At the University of the West Indies at Mona, there were several

members of the technical intelligentsia (e.g., statisticians, economic experts, etc.), who served the state as hired hands and regarded themselves as nonpartisan. Until the sixties, the self-understanding of some economists at the university placed them in this category, and the state had come to understand their function in this way. However, with the New World Group, this self-definition changed, as a new generation of economists rejected the role of technical expert to the state and took up positions critical of the state's economic policies. In this sense, they had explicitly thrown their lot with the humanistic wing of the intelligentsia. In part, it was this role-reversal, from technical experts to political critics, which antagonized Caribbean governments.

46. For a brief review of this development of the New World Group, see Mark Figueroa, "A Critical Essay on Caribbean Political Economy," photocopy (Kingston: Dept. of Economics, Univ. of the West Indies, Mona, Aug. 1977); 1–57.

47. Consistent with its regional focus, contributors to the *New World Quarterly* were drawn from Jamaica, Trinidad, and British Guiana.

48. Ibid. Emphasis mine.

49. In an important statement, Best lamented that "there has been no Press with the name, no professional societies organized to deal in opinion, no effective Guild of Graduates and not even much individual opinion willing to come out in public and defend reason against authority." Lloyd Best, "Whither New World?" *New World Quarterly* 4, no. 1 (1967):5.

50. For a discussion of modern nationalism and its links to "imagined communities," see Benedict Anderson, *Imagined Communities: Reflections on the Origin and Spread of Nationalism* (London: New Left Books, 1983).

51. For a collection of these writings, see Norman Girvan and Owen Jefferson, eds., *Readings in the Political Economy of the Caribbean* (Kingston: New World Group, 1971).

52. Trevor Munroe, "Developed Idealism and Early Materialism."

53. Best, "Whither New World?", 6.

54. Ibid.

55. *New World Quarterly* 2, no. 1, 2.

56. Ivar Oxaal, "The Dependency Economist as Grassroots Politician in the Caribbean," in *Beyond the Sociology of Development*, ed. Ivar Oxaal, Tony Barnett, and David Booth (London: Routledge & Kegan Paul, 1975), 34.

57. *Scope*, a UWI student publication, reported on 4 Oct. 1966 that Beckford's passport had been seized on 9 January as he was about to leave for the Windward Islands to conduct research financed by governments of the region. Since the historic Tri-Continental Conference was being held in Havana during that same week, it is not unlikely that the real reason for Beckford's interdiction was to prevent him from attending that conference.

58. Ollman's dismissal followed his forcible ejection from the university bookstore in December, for attempting to conduct his own investigation into its prices. What apparently sealed his fate was his ultimatum to the university administration [under Vice-Chancellor Philip Sherlock] that unless it formally

inquired into the matter, he would refuse to give exams or grade papers. See *Daily Gleaner*, 16 May 1966.

59. The Ollman incident ended a period of relative quiescence among the students and nudged them toward an increased critical awareness and activism. Led by Trevor Munroe, graduate student and YSL activist, the students, on 18 May, barricaded the vice-chancellor and other top administrators in the registry building for several hours, until they agreed to conduct an inquiry into the incident. This episode also had a dramatic effect on *Scope*, the student newspaper, which up until this time had contented itself with frivolous articles on student social activities. For a sense of this awakening, see "Back to the Ollman Affair," *Scope* 1, no. 21 (Aug. 1966).

60. This opposition came from the Bar, the teachers' unions, the churches, the university administration, and even sections of the bourgeoisie. Worthy of note here is that, running through some of these protests, there was not only a firm appeal that Dr. Beckford be given due process, but also assertions vouching for his "noncommunist" outlook. See, e.g., the vice-chancellor's statement, which noted in part that "he has assured me that he has no connection whatever with any group that is in anyway disloyal or subversive." *Daily Gleaner*, 14 May 1966.

61. Rebuffed in its attempts to get any explanation from the regime, the group protested by suspending its government-sponsored research in mid-September. *Scope* Oct. 1966.

62. Lloyd Best, "Independent Thought and Caribbean Freedom," in *Readings in the Political Economy of the Caribbean*, ed. Norman Girvan and Owen Jefferson, 7–28.

63. Ibid., 24.

64. Ibid., 23.

65. While his lively polemic called attention to such repressed topics in Marxism as the role of culture and the nature of Marxism's scientific status, Best allowed his critique to slide into a Cold-War caricature of Marxism, which he depicted as a religion with "Popes" in Moscow and Peking.

66. Best, "Independent Thought," 23.

67. Ibid., 22.

68. Ibid., 23.

69. Best, "Whither New World?", 1–6.

70. Ibid., 2.

71. Ibid., 3.

72. Referring to the distinct tasks of the activist and the intellectual, Best conceded that mobilization for political power was necessary. Consistent with his views, however, he noted that "these inputs of skill and leadership cannot be directly provided by New World as an organization. The individuals in the Group may, if they so wish, decide to work 'in the field.' But then their job in the intellectual system will only have to be done by others."

73. With the self-immolation of the Grenadian leadership in 1983, reflection on just these issues was imposed on the Caribbean Left.

74. Best argued, "The case for 'thought' rests on the need to erode the in-

tellectual foundations of the old order so as to guard against the mere substitution of one political elite for another." Best, "Whither New World?", 1.

75. See Norman Girvan, "Chairman's Report on the Jamaica New World Group, for the period August 1967 to September 1968," *New World Quarterly* 4, nos. 3, 4, (1968):1–6.

CHAPTER 7

1. Post, *Arise Ye Starvelings* 171.

2. Ibid., 160–61.

3. Early postcolonial political activism among the Rastafarians included participation in a 1961 mission to Africa to explore repatriation; running for political office in the 1962 general elections; attempting a putsch against the government; and forming various organizations to promote the welfare of Rastafarians. For a discussion of these activities, see Rex Nettleford, *Mirror, Mirror: Identity, Race and Protest in Jamaica* (Kingston: Williams Collins and Sangster, 1970), 75–76.

4. The others were: Lloyd Barnett, Dennis Sloly, Winston Spaulding, and Carl Rattray—all of whom had close links to the PNP.

5. In March, the New World Group convened a seminar on human rights; and, in Parliament, the PNP introduced a resolution calling for establishment of a Human Rights Commission. This was rejected by the JLP.

6. See the JCHR letter protesting these raids, *Daily Gleaner*, 15 July 1968.

7. Ibid.

8. See *Scope* (the undergraduate newspaper at the UWI), 10 May 1968.

9. *Sunday Gleaner*, 10 Apr. 1960.

10. Cited in "The Rhodesian Issue: Text of Petition to UK Government Signed by Over 600 Students (1965)," app. 2, in Trevor Munroe, "Our People's Struggle, The UWI-Marshall Administration and the Lewis Commission," n.d., Photocopy. Reference Collection, Univ. of the West Indies, Mona, pp. 1–21.

11. While Sherlock did not champion the independence of his institution forcefully, he did protest the seizure of Beckford's passport. Two years later, his attempt to balance respect for the institution's autonomy with sensitivity to the government's claims earned him the public rebuke of both the *Gleaner* and Edward Seaga, a JLP member of Parliament and state representative on the university's governing body.

12. *Scope* 1 No 11 24 (May 1966).

13. However, an article by one "Rick-Mel," three months later, characterized the students' demonstration on Ollman's behalf as a "dismal failure" and suggested that incorrect student tactics and the "basic spinelessness of the student body" allowed the administration to carry the day in the Ollman incident. *Scope* 1, no. 21 (Aug. 1966).

14. See, e.g. Walter Rodney, "African History and Culture," in his *The Groundings with my Brothers* (London: Bogle-L'Ouverture Publications, 1969), 35–50.

15. Rodney, "African History in the Service of Black Revolution," in Rodney, *Groundings*, 51.

16. Rodney's introduction to the urban poor was assisted by YSL activist Dennis Daley, who helped him make contact with cadres in the Kingston slums. Daley, interview with the author, summer 1979.

17. See Richard Small's introduction to Rodney, *Groundings*, 7.

18. No doubt due in part to increasing demands to end its isolation, the group, between Aug. 1967 and Sept. 1968, sponsored at least 10 public forums or teach-ins on such topics as the sugar industry, currency devaluation, the British invasion of Anguilla, unemployment, and the music of the rebellious youths. The group also disseminated four pamphlets on some of these topics. See Norman Girvan, "Report of Chairman" [Mona Group, 1967–68], *New World Quarterly* 4, no. 3 (1968): 4.

19. On 19 Mar. 1969, British paratroopers invaded the tiny Caribbean island of Anguilla, after Ronald Webster, the island's local leader, declared that country's independence from Britain and its secession from the Associated State of St. Kitts–Nevis–Anguilla. The invasion meant restoration of British colonial control, which lasted until Dec. 1980, when the island finally was granted its political independence.

20. Girvan, "Report of Chairman," 3.

21. On 2 Apr., the *Gleaner* published a report in which Prime Minister Hugh Shearer reacted to the outcry against the government's past seizures of academics' passports. In this report, Shearer indicated his awareness of activities which could only be associated with Rodney:

> I am an admirer of the university: I support the university; I welcome all the students of the university, and I want to see them making full use of the academic freedoms allowed.
>
> But I must say that I have cause to be very concerned about the abuse of this freedom by certain individuals up there, who are saying and doing things in Jamaica that they would not dare to say or do in their own country — individuals who are abusing sections of the population, deliberately stirring up strife, stirring up discontent among certain levels of the people of this country — something which they would not be allowed to do in the territories that they have come from. . . . I am hoping that those persons guilty of it will be persuaded to discontinue their anti-government campaign . . . under no circumstances will the government abdicate its responsibility to protect the interest of the nation as a whole. [*Daily Gleaner*, 2 Apr. 1968].

22. Rodney, "Black Power, A Basic Understanding," in Rodney, *Groundings*, 16–23.

23. Ibid., 22.

24. Ibid., 18.

25. Ibid., 19.

26. Rodney, "Black Power — Its Relevance to the West Indies," in Rodney, *Groundings*, 24–34.

27. Ibid., 28.

28. Ibid., 29.

29. Ibid.
30. Ibid., 28.
31. Ibid., 30.
32. When pressed, as they were in the late sixties, the middle and upper classes chose to define Black Power as black *political* incumbency in the aftermath of colonialism.
33. *Daily Gleaner*, 15 Nov. 1968. My emphasis.
34. *Scope*, 10 May 1968.
35. Ralph Gonsalves, "The Rodney Affair and its Aftermath," *Caribbean Quarterly* 25 no. 3 (Sept. 1979):3.
36. Ibid.
37. Ibid.
38. In addition to important figures from the U.S. Black Power movement such as Stokely Carmichael, the Montreal conference was attended by the West Indian activists Lloyd Best, Robert Hill, Richard Small, and C.L.R. James.
39. The exclusion also had larger consequences, including a major split in the New World Group, occasioned by Lloyd Best's slide into provincialism and anti-Black Power rhetoric; and the development of Black Power movements in several islands.
40. See the publication of this pamphlet in the *Daily Gleaner*, 27 Nov. 1968.
41. Cited in Gonsalves, "The Rodney Affair," 4.
42. Ibid., 6.
43. *Daily Gleaner*, 27 Nov. 1968.
44. For details on the students' march, I have relied on the document, "Diary of Events — October 16," issued by faculty and students the day after the demonstration and published in the Trinidad Black Power paper, *Moko*, 28 Oct. 1968.
45. Ibid.
46. Gonsalves, "The Rodney Affair," 8.
47. This serious charge never was substantiated with evidence other than what was widely known about Rodney's activities: that he was critical of the government and publicly expounded his views before different audiences. See Hugh Shearer, "Address to Parliament," 17 Oct. 1968, in *Jamaica Hansard*, Sessions 1968–69, vol. 1, no. 1, 392.
48. Roy McNeil, the minister of home affairs, also criticized the students for associating with "Rastafarian groups, known and dangerous criminals, political extremists and mal-contents," *Daily Gleaner,* 2 Nov. 1968.
49. Shearer, "Address," *Jamaica Hansard*, Sessions 1968–69, 392.
50. Ibid.
51. Edward Seaga took a slightly different approach. He expressed the government's dismay at the changing orientation of students who no longer saw the university simply "as a place to learn, as an institution for realizing occupational hopes, as a place where people are trained to add to the pool of skilled learning so as to enhance the development of the country." *Jamaica Hansard*, Sessions 1968–69, Vol. 1, no. 1, 406.
52. The charge that Jamaican students were being manipulated by their peers from other islands evidently was based on the fact that top positions in the

Guild of Undergraduates (president, first vice-president, and secretary) were held by non-Jamaicans. In their published statement, the students acknowledged this dominance but noted that a Jamaican was the guild's treasurer and that Jamaicans comprised 50% of the membership. *Sunday Gleaner*, 27 Nov. 1968.

53. *Daily Gleaner*, 17 Oct. 1968.

54. Ibid.

55. Editorial: "Communist Subversion, the University and Jamaica," *Sunday Gleaner*, 3 Nov. 1968.

56. Editorial: "Cave Mona," *Daily Gleaner*, 17 Oct. 1968.

57. Editorial: "Reconstruction," *Daily Gleaner*, 12 Nov. 1968.

58. Edward Seaga, comment in the House of Representatives, *Jamaica Hansard*, Sessions, 1968–69, vol., 1, no. 1.

59. In his farewell speech to the 1968 Party Conference, Norman Manley tartly observed "When the revolution comes to Jamaica and the Prime Minister of Jamaica says to the President of America, send us an army to save us in this part of the world, you think he would refuse? [Voices: No! No!]" Cited in *Daily Gleaner*, 11 Nov. 1968.

60. *Daily Gleaner*, 25 Nov. 1968.

61. *Daily Gleaner*, 6 Dec. 1968.

62. Unable to use the Immigration Restriction (Commonwealth Citizens) Law to bar Commonwealth lecturers, the JLP was forced to declare Rodney *persona non grata*. To ease future expulsions of dissidents, on 27 Dec. 1968 the JLP passed an amendment to the Commonwealth Citizens Law. This allowed the government to declare non-Jamaicans from other parts of the Caribbean to be undesirable aliens.

63. These included the *Gleaner*, the Farquharson Institute of Public Affairs, and the Incorporated Law Society. *Daily Gleaner*, 12 Dec. 1968.

64. See Jamaica, Dept. of Statistics, *A Survey of Housing Conditions in Trench Town*, Nov. 1968. This survey was conducted in Sept. and Oct. 1967.

CHAPTER 8

1. Indeed, as subsequent events in the region showed, student activism actually increased in the aftermath of October 1968.

2. According to Girvan, inspiration for *Moko* came from the distribution in Trinidad of copies of *Scope*, the student newspaper of the UWI at Mona, which was published at the height of the Rodney incident. See Norman Girvan, "Mona New World Report. Abeng, Moko and New World: A Review," *New World Quarterly*, 5, nos. 1 & 2 (1969):2.

3. *Moko*, 28 Oct. 1968.

4. Ibid.

5. *Sunday Gleaner*, 10 Nov. 1968.

6. Ibid.

7. Ibid.

8. *Trinidad Guardian*, 18 Nov. 1968.

9. This decision to create a communications medium, rather than a political organization, out of the coalition fashioned by Rodney seemed to be in part

a reflection of the fragmentation of political and organizational know-how within the intelligentsia, as well as the real gap that still existed between them and the Jamaican people.

10. Glenville Hinds, "The Theory and Practice of Abeng," photocopy (Kingston: Dept. of Government, Univ. of the West Indies, Mona, 1970), 2.

11. Editorial: "The Horn Reaches the People," *Abeng*, 8 Feb. 1969.

12. Hinds, "Theory and Practice," 21.

13. As Hinds would observe, the battle to get Garvey into the paper was "reminiscent of a PNP platform struggle on party policy," in which defenders of a Black Power focus for the newspaper "had to wage a determined struggle to have included a mere quotation from Marcus Garvey's first issue of *Black Man* in Easter of 1929." That quotation read: "We want our people to think for themselves. Just here we must begin." Ibid.

14. Ibid., 20.

15. In a novel incorporation of indigenous popular history in the newspaper, the founders recalled that the Abeng was an instrument, fashioned from a cow's horn and blown by the maroons when they wanted to summon each other using secret codes. They did this by varying the tonality of the horn. According to the editors, the newspaper would function in much the same fashion, as an ideological instrument to summon the people by sounding various messages. *Abeng*, 1 Feb. 1969.

16. In one statement, the editors noted that the newspaper wanted to appeal to all Jamaicans and would lead the effort to understand the ills of the society and how they might be remedied. Thus, in an injunction not unlike that of New World, the editors maintained that "the chief concern of this newspaper will be to ensure the widest possible participation of ideas coming from the people . . . a forum for the points of view of all groups, and an organ independent of existing political parties and commercial interests." *Abeng*, 1 Feb. 1969.

17. "What We Have to Do to Get Work," *Abeng*, 22 Feb. 1969.

18. After nearly eight weeks of publication, the paper reported that its vendors, drawn from the unemployed population, were "being intimidated by policemen." *Abeng*, 28 Mar. 1969.

19. As we observed earlier, the urgency of this issue led in Dec. 1967 to the formation of the watchdog group, the Jamaica Council for Human Rights—an exception and a minority trend in the legal profession at the time.

20. Observing that rude-boy music and dance parties were a means of communication, camaraderie, and cultural innovation, the Rastafarian poet Ras dizzy offered this poignant description of rude-boy culture: "The youths dance and as they creep up in numbers they like to greet and toast one another. The way they drink the beer and then how they dance to the beat of the blues show that they are sophisticated human beings searching for freedom and recreational facilities free from fear of force." Ras Dizzy, "Why Rudies Got to be Ruder," *Abeng*, 2 Aug. 1969.

21. *Abeng*, 28 Mar. 1969.

22. *Abeng*, 1 Mar. 1969.

23. By mid-February, censorship had been extended to include banning

from the airwaves such popular songs as Prince Buster's "Pharoah House Crash."

24. *Abeng*, 15 Feb. 1968.

25. Consistent with popular usage, *Abeng* substituted the singular noun for the plural "men," which is a Rastafarian epithet for sissies.

26. Jordan and Love were 19th-century reform leaders and newspaper publishers. Jordan, a colored Jamaican and antislavery activist, published several newspapers, the most notable being *Watchman*, a small Kingston newspaper which appeared in the 1830s. Love was a black medical doctor and anticolonial fighter who championed the cause of his race in his newspaper, *Jamaica Advocate*.

27. Editorial: "Overseer Day Done," *Abeng*, 1 Mar. 1969.

28. Commenting on the invasion, the paper berated Caribbean leaders for their "treachery" in abetting the invasion and asserted that the main conflict in the region was now between the Caribbean poor and "white imperialism." British troops remained on the island until September, but Anguilla eventually got its independence in Dec. 1980.

29. In this regard, the British invasion produced some salutary effects. On the one hand, it provided a negative lesson for political activists, by reminding them of the Caribbean's limited room for maneuver in a world in which the Great Powers jealously barred defections from their camps. Secondly, Anguilla's experience at last brought the *Abeng* around to a wider pan-Caribbean perspective, an orientation lacking at the start.

30. Without addressing the question of *political* alternatives, New World economists did draw up a nine-point agenda of economic reforms. Aside from the fanciful suggestion that the country "use nuclear power to produce electricity for aluminum production," the agenda included such longstanding New World proposals as a national employment program, land reform, and regional economic cooperation. *Abeng*, 22 Mar. 1969.

31. Editorial: "Abeng and Change," *Abeng*, 22 Mar. 1969.

32. Editorial: "The Way of Abeng," *Abeng*, 12 Apr. 1969.

33. *Abeng*, 1 Mar. 1969.

34. Sloly, who was also a founding member of the Jamaica Council for Human Rights, was killed in an automobile accident.

35. See eulogies by Abeng activists Rupert Lewis and Trevor Munroe, *Abeng*, 5 Apr. 1969.

36. *Abeng*, 5 Apr. 1969.

37. Sloly's loss was especially grievous. As Hinds reported, Sloly's example as an indefatigable worker, and his insistence that personnel be judged according to their productivity, was largely responsible for the efficient functioning of the *Abeng* committees. Hinds, "Theory and Practice of Abeng," 23.

38. "Statement from the Editors: Our Present Position," *Abeng*, 2 Aug. 1969.

39. In his criticism of the paper's politics, Trevor Munroe suggested this possibility: "One basis of some of the money and other troubles the paper is now experiencing may well lie in its alienation of die-hard bourgeois (who gave some support first because they wanted another paper) and its failure (partly

because more work has fallen on the rest) to bring in the sufferer to take their place." *Abeng*, 9 Aug. 1969.

40. In one chauvinist outburst aimed at Marxists on the *Abeng*, Garvey, Jr., proclaimed: "Garveys do not accept a class struggle. We only know a race struggle. Garveys are racists! I will never change. I cannot see the difference between one black man and another because one has more money . . . I'm not going to tear down a black man because he has made it good. No sir. There will be no class division in my movement. I believe in only one class the black class." Interview with Marcus Garvey, Jr., *Abeng*, 14 June 1969.

41. To remedy these absences, the paper substituted excerpts from the writings of Cuba's Fidel Castro and U.S. Black Power activists Bobby Seale and Stokely Carmichael. At the same time, the paper reserved space for popular grievances in a "Letters to the Editors" column.

42. Interview with Marcus Garvey, Jr., *Abeng*, 21 June 1969.

43. *Abeng*, 9 Apr. 1969.

44. As Munroe observed, the dilemma of the *Abeng* movement on this issue was partly self-created, since the very positions it adopted against the society were now turned against it. Ibid.

45. Ibid.

46. It's not clear how this suggestion would have worked, since Munroe also wanted the paper to "continue to accommodate all tendencies, racist, Marxist-Leninist, Maoist, Africanist, and Rasta[farian]." Ibid.

47. Ibid.

48. *Abeng*, 6 Sept. 1969.

49. *Abeng*, 13 Sept. 1969.

50. Marcus, "A Reply to Blackman," *Abeng*, 13 Sept. 1969.

51. Ibid.

CHAPTER 9

1. For example, in February 1969, Michael Manley, the new leader of the PNP, launched an attack on the government's policy that echoed all the concerns of the radical opposition. Three months later, the JLP introduced a "Reform Budget" which imposed new taxes on businesses. By July, the dominant parties had begun alluding to an as-yet-undefined effort to encourage "workers' participation." Finally, in September, both party leaders left for Africa on separate fact-finding trips.

2. *Economic Survey of Jamaica* (1970), 123.

3. *Economic Survey of Jamaica* (1968), 43.

4. In the late sixties, the employers' federation supported legislation, according to which an industrial court would impose sanctions and fines for strikes and other job actions. However, stiff opposition doomed this proposal. See Walter J. Gershenfeld, *Compulsory Arbitration in Jamaica: 1962–1969* (Kingston: Institute of Social and Economic Research, 1974), 64–65.

5. In 1951, Lawrence joined the TUC as an organizer and sat on its educational committee. Chris Lawrence, interview with the author, summer 1979.

6. The JCL represented workers in municipal departments, the shipping industry, and in laundry and dry-cleaning establishments. See ITAC booklet *The Independent Trade Unions* (Kingston: ITAC, 1970).

7. Ibid., 13.

8. Ibid., 15.

9. Ibid., 14–19.

10. For a standard reading for the Jamaican Left in this period, see Richard Hart, "The Origins and Development of the People of Jamaica," pamphlet (Kingston: Trade Union Congress, 1952).

11. Chris Lawrence, interview, summer 1979.

12. As late as 1972, Marxists within the ITAC were bemoaning the lack of "a proper understanding of the 'class struggle' and the need for strong working class discipline and consciousness . . . among the Officers of the Organizations and the rank and file." See "I.T.A.C.'s Programme and Projects to be Realized Within the Next Three Years: 1973–75," mimeo (Kingston, personal papers of Chris Lawrence, n.d.), 1.

13. In addition to moderating Communist ideology in the ITAC for fear of alienating the other leaders, Lawrence had another pragmatic reason: official hostility to communist unions which could make it next-to-impossible for such unions to operate. Chris Lawrence, interview, summer 1979.

14. Of roughly 2,000 workers eligible to cast ballots, only 803 actually voted. *Independent Trade Unions*, 17.

15. Ibid., 23.

16. It should be noted that the ITAC had its organic intellectuals. In addition to Chris Lawrence, there were at least two others: Winston Pusey and Irving Chong, both of whom were college-educated.

17. *Independent Trade Unions*, 26–27.

18. For an early example of agitational writing and political research produced by the UWI socialists, see *Independent Trade Unions*.

19. These resolutions included a protest against proposed increases in bus fares and gasoline prices, a demand that bus tickets be printed in the island, and a challenge to the government's practice of sending only the BITU and NWU to represent Jamaica at meetings of the International Labor Organization.

20. *Independent Trade Unions*, 25.

21. In February, it organized a teach-in to support West Indian students in Montreal, who were being charged with the destruction of computer facilities, and in March it backed the Mona students' occupation of the Creative Arts Center.

22. Gonsalves, "The Rodney Affair," 18–22.

23. In his account, Ralph Gonsalves noted that "JLP students" tried to oust him as guild president because they claimed he was disrespectful, first in not meeting with the prime minister and then, aggravating that refusal, in sending the prime minister an impertinent telegram which read: "Sorry cannot meet you tomorrow; probably some other time." Cited in Gonsalves, "The Rodney Affair," 22.

24. *Daily Gleaner*, 9 Nov. 1968.

25. The details of this Code of Conduct already had been under discussion in advance of Marshall's appointment. Nonetheless, its approval came during his administration.

26. Cited in the *Daily Gleaner*, 6 Sept. 1969.

27. Ibid.

28. Ibid.

29. Ibid.

30. In the period between mid- to late August, some six Commonwealth citizens were either deported or prevented from entering the island. Among them were Joey Jagan, the Guyanese student who participated in the February 1968 student demonstrations at the Sir George William University in Montreal, Canada; and Jacob Degia, a Barbadian teacher at Happy Grove School in Portland, who was deported for his Black Power sympathies. For details on the banning of other activists, see *Jamaica Gazette* 92 (1969):463.

31. In a contradictory statement which put the students on both sides of the issue, the Guild of Graduates maintained that the government should make a distinction between people who offered "objective opinions" and those who would "plot against the security of the state to the detriment of the majority of people in the country." *Daily Gleaner*, 6 Sept. 1969.

32. See letter to Marshall from the Guild of Undergraduates in *Daily Gleaner*, 24 Sept. 1969.

33. Dr. Kenneth McNeil, lecturer in the Dept. of Surgery and PNP member of Parliament, resigned in protest.

34. Statement by the PNP executive, *Daily Gleaner*, 4 Oct. 1969.

35. Ibid.

36. At the same time, he refused to back down on the Frater issue, calling instead on the University Council to endorse his decision in that matter. *Daily Gleaner* 19 Sept. 1969.

37. Cited in *Daily Gleaner*, 9 Oct. 1969.

38. For example, in defending the security minister's right to ban controversial lecturers, Marshall maintained that the minister's "responsibility is grave, particularly in developing countries such as ours, which having emerged from a long period of colonialism, remain vulnerable to many dangers." *Daily Gleaner*, 9 Oct. 1969.

39. Later, students would hem Marshall in his car, preventing his departure from the campus. *Daily Gleaner*, 14 Oct. 1969.

40. *Daily Gleaner*, 31 Oct. 1969.

41. *Scope* 13, no. 9 (11 Feb. 1971).

42. Divisions between the graduate and undergraduate student organizations were apparent, as the Guild of Graduates, without addressing the issue of the suspensions, called on the undergraduates to end their demonstration. See *Daily Gleaner*, 4 March 1970.

43. *Daily Gleaner*, 6 May 1970.

44. Kingston: House of Representatives, Ministry Paper no. 67, 6 Oct. 1970, 2.

45. At one of two dinners given in his honor in 1970 by a group of evidently prosperous young Jamaicans, the prime minister dismissed the plight of the vast

numbers of unemployed youths, with the claim that "what barriers there are, are self-generated and self-inculcated." See "The Prime Minister Speaks to Young Jamaica," Jamaica Information Service, 1970, p. 5.

46. *Daily Gleaner,* 16 Apr. 1971.

47. *Daily Gleaner,* 17 Apr. 1971.

48. For a time, WISCO retained ownership of the Frome and Monymusk estates. Kingston: House of Representatives, Ministry Paper no. 13, 15 June 1971, p. 2.

49. After stating its intention to sell back the land to "all classes of Jamaicans," the JLP acknowledged that the buyback would have political value, because "it is doubtful whether the present and forthcoming generations would accept a situation in which there is continuing foreign control of the majority of the best lands in the country." Ibid., 7.

50. As late as 1971, the regime still was excluding Caribbean academics from entering Jamaica.

51. *Daily Gleaner,* 28 Aug. 1969.

52. This protest was occasioned by a 1965 law establishing a national lottery.

53. See statement from the JLP executive, which noted in part that "after the October 16th incident . . . a number of citizens complained to the Prime Minister that . . . they had to listen to sermons by a few ministers . . . which were not merely critical of the Government, but which were abusive and apparently designed to increase the type of unrest on which subversion depends." *Daily Gleaner,* 10 Dec. 1968.

54. For example, see Havelock Brewster, "Sugar: Our life or Death?" in *Readings in the Political Economy of the Caribbean,* ed. Norman Girvan and Owen Jefferson, 37–54.

55. In 1966, the JLP appointed a Commission of Inquiry, which recommended, among other things, the gradual increase in the mechanization of the industry—a policy which inevitably would have created more unemployment among sugar workers. Following a further slide in production and a 1969 bid for increased government aid from cane farmers and sugar manufacturers, the government gave the industry additional assistance. By the 1970 crop year, additional mechanical harvesters were introduced. See Jamaica, Ministry of Rural Land Development, *First Report* (Jan. 1969 to Mar. 1970), 18.

56. Citing tax data for the years 1951–65, one report noted that there was little change in income distribution in this period, as some 8% of taxpayers received over a quarter of total national income. See Irving Kaplan et al., *Area Handbook for Jamaica,* 232.

57. Ibid.

58. Obviously annoyed at the criticism of young radicals who argued that political independence was a near-worthless achievement, Manley defended the aims of his generation:

Allow me to speak on some who I regard as mischief makers. I have said it before. I will say it again. The young new left-wing people of today cry down the work of the past and deny its value. They did not live when we were working for self-government. They know nothing of the dangers we faced. They know nothing of the fights we fought or how or when we overcame. They do not know the fight we had to win for them of this generation the tool of political power which they find in their hands. [*Daily Gleaner,* 11 Nov. 1968.]

59. *Daily Gleaner,* 10 Feb. 1969.

60. *Daily Gleaner* 27 Oct. 1969.

61. As the following statement by Michael Manley to the 1969 Annual Party Conference indicates, the PNP, despite the use of a livelier rhetoric, adopted essentially the same policy as the JLP. Thus, in defining what it meant by economic nationalism, the PNP asserted: "We mean an economy fundamentally under national control and an economy responsive to national needs. We mean an economy whose planning and directions are generated inside the country rather than from outside; and we mean an economy of maximum local participation. And most important of all, we mean a country whose basic assets are either locally owned or controlled and hence not at the mercy of the whims of an external ownership." *Daily Gleaner,* 27 Oct. 1969.

62. *Daily Gleaner,* 11 Oct. 1971.

63. In one typical invocation of the religious subjectivity of the Jamaican people, Manley solemnly observed, "We will face the election when it comes in the faith that the New Jerusalem is ours to build, and we will say with St. John in the Revelations, 'And I saw a new heaven and a new earth; for the first heaven and the first earth were passed away.'" Ibid.

64. As the Abeng Group noted in its postelection analysis, these slogans appealed to all classes. They could, the group argued, "appeal to the housewife and her gardener boy, [and] to the big capitalists, fearful that a third JLP term might embolden Edward Seaga in his bid to tax the rich." Abeng Group, "The Elections: Where from Here?" (Kingston, Jamaica: Abeng Group 1972), 2. Pamphlet.

65. The JLP's newspaper advertisements employed such bland slogans as "Change Without Chaos," and "One Good Term Deserves Another." From the standpoint of political appeal and media values, the JLP's unsophisticated newspaper advertisements during the campaign were an unmitigated disaster.

66. Abeng Group, "The Elections: Where from Here?", 2.

CHAPTER 11

1. Significant policies initiated by the PNP between 1972 and 1974 included the promotion of a New International Economic Order, a public housing program, lowering the voting age to 18, free secondary and university education, promotion of the Nonaligned movement, a national minimum wage, and imposition of a bauxite production levy which increased bauxite companies' royalties to the government.

2. For example, Mayer Matalon, a member of a prominent family of Jamaican businessmen with interests in real estate, manufacturing, and construction, was appointed to the National Bauxite Commission (NBC); his brother Eli was given the posts of minister of education and minister of security; and Pat Rousseau,

chairman of Life of Jamaica, a major insurance company, was appointed chair of the NBC.

3. In his retrospective on the period, Manley identified his intentions upon taking office:

> We began and ended with four basic commitments. . . . Firstly, we wanted to create an economy that would be more independent of foreign control and more responsive to the needs of the majority of the people at home. Secondly, we wanted to work for an egalitarian society both in terms of opportunity and also in the deeper sense of a society in which people felt that they were of equal worth and value. Thirdly, we wanted to develop a truly democratic society in which democracy was more than the attempt to manipulate votes every five years. Finally, we wanted to help, indeed accelerate, the process by which Jamaicans were retracing the steps of their history. We were convinced that it was only through the rediscovery of our heritage that we would evolve a culture that reflected the best in ourselves because it expressed pride in what we were and where we came from. [Michael Manley, *Jamaica Struggle in the Periphery* (London: Writers and Readers Publishing Cooperative Society, 1982), 39.]

4. Although the party's Nov. 1974 statement on democratic socialism was vague and not much different from the one articulated in 1964, this statement, presented in the context of the regime's other policies, increased the anxieties of businessmen and others who were concerned that the regime might be moving too far left.

5. These developments included: a sharp increase in the oil-import bill, brought on by the Organization of Petroleum Exporting Countries' 1973 decision to raise the price of oil; world inflation, which increased the price of imported goods; the imposition of austerity measures to contain the impact of world inflation on the domestic economy; and two consecutive years of negative growth in 1974 and 1975.

6. In addition to winning the post of general secretary, Duncan was credited with guiding the party to impressive victories in the 1974 parish council elections.

7. For the PNP's assessment of this period, see Manley, *Jamaica Struggle in the Periphery*, 223-37.

8. Michael Kaufman, *Jamaica Under Manley: Dilemmas of Socialism and Democracy* (Westport, Conn.: Lawrence Hill, 1985), 125-26.

9. This strategy entailed supporting the PNP's policies that helped workers and criticizing those that didn't.

10. In brief, the theory of the noncapitalist path argues that, because of the poorly-developed working class and bourgeoisie in the less-developed countries, the state is the leading force in economic development. This fact, advocates argue, necessitates an alliance of patriotic social classes if the transition is to succeed. See Evelyne Huber Stephens and John D. Stephens, *Democratic Socialism in Jamaica* (Princeton, N.J.: Princeton Univ. Press, 1986), 332.

11. The WPJ's prominence is explained by three factors: the attention given to WPJ positions by the *Gleaner*, in the hopes of stirring up fears of commu-

nism; announcement of WPJ positions by communist journalists working in the newsroom of the government-run Jamaica Broadcasting Corporation; and WPJ activism in the late seventies.

12. Cited in Kaufman, *Jamaica Under Manley*, 132.

13. Manley, *Jamaica: Struggle in the Periphery*, 153.

14. IMF agreements include quarterly performance tests which must be met in order to get further disbursement of funds. These tests determine whether the recipient country has met certain targets in its level of foreign reserves, extension of credit to the public and private sectors, and ratios in its net domestic assets. Failure to meet specific totals in any one of these areas usually leads to a suspension of the agreement. In December 1977, Jamaica failed the net-domestic-asset test by a small margin. See Kaufman, *Jamaica Under Manley*, 141.

15. For a discussion of the disastrous impact of the May 1978 IMF agreement, see Kaufman, *Jamaica Under Manley*, 146-49, and Stephens and Stephens, *Democratic Socialism in Jamaica*, 200.

16. Manley, *Jamaica Struggle in the Periphery*, 184.

17. Kaufman, *Jamaica Under Manley*, 184.

18. Small replaced Eric Bell, who resigned in protest against the decision to break with the IMF. Bell subsequently accepted a position with the IMF.

19. Carl Stone, "Running Out of Options in Jamaica," *Caribbean Review* 15 (Winter 1987):29.

20. See Jack W. Hopkins, ed., *Latin America and Caribbean Contemporary Record*, v. 1: 1981-82 (New York, Holmes and Meier, 1983), 589.

21. The IMF granted a new loan of US$625 million to be disbursed over three years; a World Bank–directed consortium of lenders contributed a loan of US$350 million; and the American government contributed aid in the amount of US$93 million, four times the 1980 contribution. See Carl Stone, "Jamaica: From Manley to Seaga," in *Revolution and Counterrevolution in Central America and the Caribbean*, ed. Donald E. Schulz and Douglas H. Graham (Boulder: Colo.: Westview, 1984), 404.

22. Prior to the conference, party chairman Dudley Thompson had made it clear that there was no room for communists in the party. See Jack W. Hopkins, ed., *Latin America and Caribbean Contemporary Record*, v. 2: 1982-83 (New York: Holmes and Meier, 1984), 713.

23. Ibid.

24. Ibid., 716.

25. Stephens and Stephens, *Democratic Socialism in Jamaica*, 263.

26. In the period, JLP support dropped from 59% to 55%, while the PNP's support grew from 41% to 45%. See Carl Stone, "Jamaica: From Manley to Seaga," 412.

27. In Duncan's case, it was alleged that his presence in the party made it impossible for the party to get sorely needed funds from the business community.

28. In boycotting the elections, the PNP argued that the JLP had broken an earlier agreement between the parties that no new elections would be held before an updating of the voters' list.

29. Jack W. Hopkins, ed., *Latin America and Caribbean Contemporary Record*, v. 4: 1984–85 (New York: Holmes and Meier, 1986), 749.

30. Abraham F. Lowenthal, ed., *Latin America and Caribbean Contemporary Record*, v. 6: 1986–87 (New York: 1989), Holmes and Meier, 527–28.

31. Lowenthal, ed., *Latin America and Caribbean Contemporary Record*, v. 5: 1985–86 (New York: Holmes and Meier, 1988), 574.

32. In the early eighties, the WPJ's popular support stood below 1%. Although the party increased its standing to 5% in a Dec. 1985 poll, by 1986 its support had fallen to the level of the early eighties. See Lowenthal, *Contemporary Record*, 5:573.

33. A resolution of the Fifth Plenary of the WPJ, Oct. 1986. Cited in Richard F. Starr, ed., *Yearbook on International Communist Affairs* 1988 (Stanford, Calif.: Hoover Institution Press, 1988), 93.

34. Preliminary results showed the PNP winning 57% of the vote and about 46 of 60 seats in the House of Representatives. A new ideological moderation was evident in the PNP's 1989 election campaign. The party, evidently chastened by its experience in the 1970s, stressed the need for good ties with Washington, emphasized that growth and production would be its priority, and indicated that Cuba would not assume a central place in Jamaica's foreign policy. At the same time, the PNP reiterated its commitment to improving the lives of the poorer classes.

35. As its dramatic slide in the polls continued, the JLP, under the pretext of carrying out an administrative overhaul of local government, postponed local government elections in 1984 and 1985. See Hopkins, *Contemporary Record*, 4:744–45.

Selected Bibliography

I . BOOKS
Ake, Claude. *Revolutionary Pressures in Africa*. London: Zed Press, 1978.
Althusser, Louis, *Lenin and Philosophy*. New York: Monthly Review Press, 1971.
Anderson, Benedict. *Imagined Communities: Reflections on the Origin and Spread of Nationalism*. London: New Left Books, 1983.
Barnett, Lloyd. *The Constitutional Law of Jamaica*. London: Oxford University Press, 1977.
Barrett, Leonard. *The Rastafarians: A Study in Messianic Cultism in Jamaica*. Puerto Rico: Institute of Caribbean Studies, 1969.
Carnegie, James. *Some Aspects of Jamaica's Politics: 1918-1938*. Kingston: Institute of Jamaica, 1973.
Eaton, George. *Alexander Bustamante and Modern Jamaica*. Kingston: Kingston Publishers, 1975.
Francis, O. C. *The People of Modern Jamaica*. Kingston: Department of Statistics, 1963.
Gershenfeld, Walter J. *Compulsory Arbitration in Jamaica: 1962-1969*. Kingston: Institute of Social and Economic Research, 1974.
Girvan, Norman. *Foreign Capital and Economic Underdevelopment in Jamaica*. Kingston: Institute of Social and Economic Research, 1971.
Girvan, Norman, and Owen Jefferson, eds. *Readings in the Political Economy of the Caribbean*, Kingston: New World Group, 1971.
Gouldner, Alvin. *The Dialectic of Ideology and Technology*. New York: Seabury Press, 1976.
————. *The Future of Intellectuals and the Rise of the New Class*. New York: Seabury Press, 1979.
Hall, Douglas, *Free Jamaica*. New Haven, Conn.: Yale University Press, 1959.
Hopkins, Jack W., ed. *Latin America and Caribbean Contemporary Record*. Vol. 1:1981-82. New York: Holmes and Meier, 1983.
Hyden, Goran. *No Shortcuts to Progress*. Berkeley: University of California Press, 1983.
Jefferson, Owen. *The Post-War Economic Development of Jamaica*. Kingston: Institute of Social and Economic Research, 1972.
Kaufman, Michael. *Jamaica Under Manley: Dilemmas of Socialism and Democracy*. Westport, Conn.: Lawrence Hill, 1985.

Kaplan, Irving, et al., eds. *Area Handbook for Jamaica.* Washington, D.C.: American University Press, 1976.

Lacey, Terry. *Violence and Politics in Jamaica: 1960-1970.* London: Manchester University Press, 1972.

Lewis, Gordon K. *The Growth of the Modern West Indies.* New York: Monthly Review Press, 1968.

Lowenthal, Abraham F., ed. *Latin America and Caribbean Contemporary Record.* Vol. 6: 1986-87. New York: Holmes and Meier, 1989.

Manley, Michael. *Jamaica Struggle in the Periphery.* London: Writers and Readers Publishing Cooperative Society, 1982.

Mintz, Sidney, and Sally Price, eds. *Caribbean Contours.* Baltimore, Md.: Johns Hopkins University Press, 1985.

Mouffe, Chantal, ed. *Gramsci and Marxist Theory.* London: Routledge and Kegan Paul, 1979.

Munroe, Trevor. *The Politics of Constitutional Decolonization.* Kingston: Institute of Social and Economic Research, 1972.

Nettleford, Rex. *Mirror, Mirror: Identity, Race and Protest in Jamaica.* Kingston: William Collins and Sangster, 1970.

Oxaal, Ivar; Tony Barnett; and David Booth, eds. *Beyond the Sociology of Development.* London: Routledge and Kegan Paul, 1975.

Post, Ken. *Arise Ye Starvelings: The Jamaica Labour Rebellion of 1938 and Its Aftermath.* The Hague: Martinus Nijoff, 1978.

Robotham, Don. *Our Struggles.* Kingston: Workers' Liberation League, 1975.

Rodney, Walter. *The Groundings With My Brothers.* London: Bogle-L'Ouverture Publications, 1969.

Sandbrook, Richard. *The Politics of Africa's Economic Stagnation.* New York: Cambridge University Press, 1985.

Smith, M.G.; Roy Augier; and Rex Nettleford. *The Rastafarian Movement in Kingston, Jamaica.* Kingston: Institute of Social and Economic Research, 1960.

Starr, Richard F., ed. *Yearbook on International Communist Affairs* 1988. Stanford, Calif.: Hoover Institution Press, 1988.

Stephens, Evelyne Huber, and John D. Stephens. *Democratic Socialism in Jamaica.* Princeton, N.J.: Princeton University Press, 1986.

Stone, Carl. *Class, Race and Political Behaviour in Urban Jamaica.* Kingston: Institute of Social and Economic Research, 1973.

———. *Democracy and Clientelism in Jamaica.* New Brunswick, N.J.: Transaction, 1980.

Stone, Carl, and Aggrey Brown, eds. *Essays on Power and Change in Jamaica.* Kingston: Jamaica Publishing House, 1977.

The Independent Trade Unions. Kingston: ITAC, 1970. In YSL Papers.

Therborn, Goran. *What Does the Ruling Class Do When It Rules?* London: New Left Books, 1978.

Widdicombe, Stacey. *The Performance of Industrial Development Corporations: The Case of Jamaica.* New York: Praeger, 1972.

2. ARTICLES

Barnett, Lloyd. "The Constitution: Twenty Years After." *Jamaica Law Journal* 41 (1972):49–58.

Bradley, C. Paul. "Mass Parties in Jamaica: Structure and Organization." *Social and Economic Studies* 9 (Dec. 1960):375–416.

Chen-Young, Paul. "A Study of Tax Incentives in Jamaica." *National Tax Journal* (Sept. 1967):292–308.

Fraser, H. Aubrey. "The Law and Cannabis in the West Indies." *Jamaica Law Journal* (Apr. 1974):26–36.

Girvan, Norman. "October Counter-revolution in Jamaica." *New World Quarterly* 4 (1968):59–68.

Huntington, Samuel P. "Will More Countries Become Democratic?" *Political Science Quarterly* 99 (1984):193–218.

Kirkpatrick, Jeanne. "Dictatorships and Double Standards." *Commentary* 68 (Nov. 1979):34–45.

Lipset, Seymour Martin. "Some Social Requisites of Democracy: Economic Development and Political Legitimacy." *American Political Science Review* 53 (Mar. 1959):69–105.

Munroe, Trevor. "The Bustamante Letters: 1935." *Jamaica Journal* 8 (Mar. 1974):2–15.

O'Donnell, Guillermo. "Tensions in the Bureaucratic-Authoritarian State and the Question of Democracy." In *The New Authoritarianism in Latin America*, edited by David Collier, 285–318. Princeton: Princeton University Press, 1979.

Owens, J.V. "Literature on the Rastafari: 1955–1974. A Review." *Savacou* 11 & 12 (Sept. 1975):86–105.

Phelps, O.W. "The Rise of the Labour Movement in Jamaica." *Social and Economic Studies* 9 (Dec. 1960):417–68.

Simpson, George E. "Jamaican Revivalist Cults." *Social and Economic Studies* 5 (Dec. 1956):321–422.

Springer, Hugh. "The Historical Development, Hopes and Aims of the U.C.W.I." *Journal of Negro Education* 31 (Winter 1962):8–15.

Stone, Carl. "Political Aspects of Post-War Agricultural Policies in Jamaica (1945–1970)." *Social and Economic Studies* 23 (1974):145–75.

———. "Running Out of Options in Jamaica." *Caribbean Review* 15 (Winter 1987):10–12, 29–32.

———. "Jamaica: From Manley to Seaga." In *Revolution and Counterrevolution in Central America and the Caribbean* edited by Donald E. Schulz and Douglas H. Graham, 385–419. Boulder: Westview Press, 1984.

Therborn, Goran. "The Rule of Capital and the Rise of Democracy." *New Left Review* 103 (May–June 1977):3–41.

———. "The Travail of Latin American Democracy." *New Left Review* 113–14 (Jan.–Apr. 1979):71–109.

3. THESES AND DISSERTATIONS

Albuquerque, Klaus de. "Millenarian Movements and the Politics of Liberation: The Rastafarians of Jamaica." Ph.D. dissertation Virginia Polytechnic
Institute and State University, 1977.

Benn, Dennis M. "The Growth and Development of Political Ideas in the Caribbean." Ph.D. dissertation, University of Manchester, England, 1973.

————. "Historical and Contemporary Expressions of Black Consciousness in
the Caribbean." M.Sc. thesis. University of the West Indies, 1972.

Brown, Headley A. "The Import Substitution Process as a Model of Development: A Case Study of the Jamaican Economy, 1957–1966." Ph.D. dissertation, University of the West Indies, 1969.

Gannon, John C. "The Origins and Development of Jamaica's Two-Party System,
1930–1975." Ph.D. dissertation, Washington University, 1976.

Munroe, Trevor. "The People's National Party, 1939–1944. A View of the Early
Nationalist Movement in Jamaica." M.Sc. thesis, University of the West Indies, 1966.

4. UNPUBLISHED ARTICLES AND MANUSCRIPTS

Chevannes, Barry. "Social Origins of the Rastafari Movement." Typescript.
Kingston: Institute of Social and Economic Research, 1979. ISER Library,
Kingston.

Figueroa, Mark. "A Critical Essay on Caribbean Political Economy." Photocopy. Kingston: Dept. of Economics, University of the West Indies, Mona
Campus, (Aug. 1977), ISER Library, Kingston.

Gonsalves, Ralph. "The Trade Union Movement in the West Indies." Photocopy. Kingston: University of the West Indies, 1974. ISER Library, Kingston.

Hinds, Glenville. "The Theory and Practice of Abeng." Photocopy. Kingston:
Department of Government, University of the West Indies, (Mona,) 1970.
ISER Library, Kingston.

Levy, Jacqueline. "The Economic Role of the Chinese in Jamaica: The Grocery
Retail Trade." Photocopy. Kingston: University of the West Indies, 1967. ISER
Library, Kingston.

Lindsay, Louis. "The Myth of Independence: Middle Class Politics and Non-
Mobilization in Jamaica." Working Paper no. 6. Kingston: Institute of So-
cial and Economic Research, University of the West Indies, 1975. ISER
Library, Kingston.

Munroe, Trevor. "Developed Idealism and Early Materialism: 'Left' Caribbean
Thought in Transition." Photocopy. Kingston: Department of Government,
University of the West Indies, 1970. ISER Library, Kingston.

————. "The Marxist 'Left' in Jamaica: 1940–50." Working Paper no. 15
Kingston: Institute of Social and Economic Research, University of the West
Indies, 1977. ISER Library, Kingston.

5. GOVERNMENT DOCUMENTS AND REPORTS

Great Britain. Inter-University Council for Higher Education Overseas. *Report
of Visitors.* 1954.

Great Britain. Colonial Office. *Report of the West Indies Committee of the Com-mission on Higher Education in the Colonies.* June 1945. CMD 6654.

Jamaica. Jamaica Committee for Relief of the Unemployed. *Interim Report.* June 1950.

Jamaica. Department of Statistics. *A Survey of Housing Conditions in Trench Town.* November 1968. The Latin American Collection, University of Florida, Gainesville.

Jamaica. Jamaica Industrial Development Corporation. Office of Economic Research. *A Review of Industrial Development in Jamaica, W.I.* March 1962.

Jamaica. Central Bureau of Statistics. *Trade Unionism in Jamaica 1918–1946.* 1946.

Jamaica. Ministry of Rural Land Development. *First Report.* Jan. 1969 to Mar. 1970.

6. NEWSPAPERS AND JOURNALS

Abeng (Jamaica). 1969.

Daily Gleaner (Jamaica). 1960–72.

Moko (Trinidad). 1968.

New World Quarterly. 1963–71.

Public Opinion (Jamaica). 1964.

Scope (Jamaica). 1967–71.

7. INTERVIEWS WITH AUTHOR

Afflick, Paul. Kingston, Jamaica. Summer 1979. Tape recording.

Daley, Dennis, Kingston, Jamaica. Summer 1979. Tape recording.

Lawrence, Chris. Kingston, Jamaica. Summer 1979. Tape recording.

Lewis, Rupert. Kingston, Jamaica. Summer 1979. Tape recording.

Monroe, Ben. Kingston, Jamaica. Summer 1979. Tape recording.

Index

Abeng, definition of, 263n
Abeng Group, 188-89, 204, 218, 269n
Abeng newspaper movement: criticisms
of, 181-82, 264-65n; ending of, 183;
financial crisis and incidents of
political intimidation, 176-77, 263n;
founding of, 171, 208; ideology of,
171-75, 177-81, 210, 211, 212, 263n,
265n; intelligentsia and, 169-70,
186-87, 188
Afflick, Paul, 246n
Africa: *Abeng* newspaper and, 177;
blacks' identification with, 22, 48,
49, 60, 145, 147, 152-53, 211, 214,
238n, 239n; blacks' repatriation to,
48, 49, 211, 239n; blacks' repatriation to, 48, 49, 211, 239n, 240n,
259n; fact-finding trips to, 265n; national liberation movement in, 132;
neo-Marxist analysis of, 5; personal
rule in, 4; socialism in, 89
African Reformed Church, 49, 51
Afro-West Indian Cultural Center, 241n
agricultural workers, 19-20, 27, 29, 36,
67, 109-14, 251n, 252n, 253n; *see
also* peasants
agriculture: crisis in 1970s, 199; estate
workers and, 19-20; landowners and,
19, 41, 42, 43, 237n; multinational
firms and, 19, 41; number and size
of farms, 42, 43, 237n; strikes and,
27, 36
Ake, Claude, 5
American Black Power movement,
149-51, 153-54, 194-95, 209, 261n,
265n
American Civil Rights movement, 12,
209

Anguilla, 153, 174, 177, 260n, 264n
Arnett, Vernon, 60, 95, 103, 113, 120,
248n, 254n
artisans, 59, 70-71, 243n
Ashenheim, Neville, 197
Asquith Commission, 125, 255n
authoritarian democracy, in Jamaica,
6-11, 33-35, 63-66, 123

banana cultivation, 29, 41
Bar Association, 198
Bar Council, 164
Barbados, 124, 194, 255n
Barnett, Lloyd, 64, 259n
Beckford, George, 137, 170, 173, 257n,
259n
Bedward, Alexander, 240n
Bentham Committee, 236n, 238n
Bertram, Arnold, 221
Best, Lloyd, 136, 137, 138-42, 167-69,
257n, 258-59n, 261n
Bishop, Maurice, 225, 227, 228
BITU. *See* Bustamante Industrial Trade
Union (BITU)
Black Muslims, 63, 179, 242n
black nationalism: attacks on, 56-57,
61, 66, 82-86, 241n; conflict with
Exceptionalism, 56-57, 61, 63, 82-86,
115, 146-47; intelligentsia and,
147-48; Jamaica Labour Party's opposition to, 63, 150, 195, 198, 210;
of peasants, 20-21; political parties
and, 60; of Rastafarians, 63, 77, 78,
84, 143, 208, 210; unemployed and,
14; Unemployed Workers' Council
and, 85-86; in urban areas, 63, 85,
115, 212; *see also* Rastafarian
movement

democratization: authoritarian democracy in Jamaica, 6–11, 33–35,
63–66, 123; electoralist approach to
definition of, 7–8, 234n; factors
affecting, 2–4, 233n
dissident movements. *See* social
movements
Domingo, W.A., 25
"dreadlocks," 239n
Duncan, D.K., 217, 218, 220–23, 226,
227, 270n, 271n
Dunkley, Archibald, 239n

Eaton, George, 29, 33
Edward, Prince, 239n, 240n
Edwards, K.D., 247n
Elizabeth II, Queen, 240n
Emergency Powers Law, 28, 121
employment. *See* agricultural workers;
unemployed; workers
Engels, Friedrich, 68
Esso Oil Company, 79, 119
estate workers. *See* agricultural workers
Ethiopianism, 20
Exceptionalism, 54–56, 61, 63, 82–86,
87, 112, 115, 129, 195, 24n, 253n
Export Incentives Encouragement Law,
38
export-import trade. *See* import-export
trade

Fairclough, O.T., 25, 26, 30
Farquharson Institute of Public Affairs,
262n
"February Revolution," 194, 195
Federation of Citizens' Association, 23
Flogging Regulation Law, 122
foreign investment in the economy,
36–42, 45, 57, 99, 173, 196–97, 227,
236n, 237n, 241n, 249n, 250n, 268n
Foreign Nationals and Commonwealth
Citizens Employment Act, 256n
Frater, Eric, 191–92, 267n
Frome sugar estate, 27, 109, 110, 112,
113, 251n, 252n, 268n

gangs, 75, 116, 118, 120–21, 122, 220
ganja law, 122
Garvey, Amy Jacques, 240n, 241n
Garvey, Marcus, 16, 25, 145, 170, 172,
196, 240n, 263n

Garvey, Marcus, Jr., 172, 176, 178, 265n
Garveyites, 51, 63, 145, 147, 178
Girvan, Norman, 170, 262n
Glasspole, Florizel, 104, 105, 106, 107,
250n
Gleaner, 160, 161, 162, 164, 166, 190,
195, 220, 223, 243n, 244n, 249n,
250n, 252n, 253n, 259n, 262n, 270n
Gonsalves, Ralph, 266n
Gouldner, Alvin, 256n
Graham, Percival, 243n
Graham, Russell, 117
Grant, Victor, 156
Grenada, 225, 227, 258n

Hart, Richard, 35, 36, 47, 67, 243n
Henry, Arthur, 35, 243n
Henry, Claudius, 49–51, 149, 161, 181,
239–40n
Henry, Ronald, 51
Hibbert, Joseph, 239n
Higher education. *See* University of the
West Indies (UWI); and names of
other universities
Hill, Frank, 25, 26, 35
Hill, Ken, 26, 35
Hill, Robert, 95–97, 98, 99, 107, 170,
256n, 261n
Hinds, Glenville, 170, 263n, 264n
housing projects, 119, 120, 245n, 269n
Howard University, 125
Howell, Leonard, 239n
human rights, 149, 164, 209, 254–55n,
259n; *see also* civil and political
liberties
Huntington, Samuel, 3, 233n, 234n

I.C.D. Group, 40
IMF. *See* International Monetary Fund
(IMF)
Immigration Restriction (Commonwealth
Citizens) Law, 262n
Imperial College of Tropical Agriculture,
255n
Import Incentive Law, 38, 237n
import-export trade, 16, 17, 38, 40,
237n, 238n
Incentive Laws, 37
Incorporated Law Society, 262n
Independent Trade Union Advisory
Council (ITAC), 184–89, 212, 266n

SNCC. *See* Student Nonviolent Coordinating Committee (SNCC)
social classes: class arrogance and, 115–16; Gramscian approach to class hegemony, 241n; incompatible rival models of "Jamaican-ness," 13; public perception of class inequality, 199; *see also* middle class; poor; unemployed; upper class; workers
social movements: deficiencies of, 210–12; importance in Jamaica, 11–13, 213–15; internal growth and maturation of, 214–15; internal growth and maturation of, 214–15; leverage of, 208–209; means for effective opposition, 206–10; during 1970s and 1980s, 229–31; persistence and expansion of, 208; *see also* Rastafarian movement; rebellious youth movement; and names of specific organizations
Spaulding, Anthony, 226, 227
Spaulding, Winston, 259n
Springer, Hugh, 125, 256n
squatters, 80–82, 119–21, 245n, 254n
SSAU. *See* Service Stations Attendants Union (SSAU)
Standard Oil Company, 79
Stephenson, John, 246n
Stone, Carl, 8–9
street vendors, 70, 71–72
strikes: of agricultural workers, 20, 27, 36, 67, 109–14; during decolonization, 31; government sanctions and fines on, 265n; labor rebellion of 1938, 12, 14, 25, 27–30, 69, 177; during 1960s, 79–80, 93, 122, 184, 244n; unemployed as scabs, 77; unions' tardiness in use of, 251–52n
Strong, William, 84–85
student activism, 122, 138, 151, 158–60, 161–62, 166, 169, 189–95, 196, 213, 257–59n, 261–62n, 266n, 267n
Student Nonviolent Coordinating Committee (SNCC), 151
subordinate classes. *See* agricultural workers; peasants; poor; unemployed; workers
Sugar and Agricultural Workers' Union (SAWU), 36, 252n

sugar industry, 27, 41, 67, 109–14, 197–98, 199, 249n, 251n, 253n, 260n, 268n
Sugar Manufacturers Association, 251n
Syrians, 53, 155

Tate and Lyle, 27, 41, 111, 197, 199
Tavares, D.C., 245n
Taylor, Leroy, 91, 256n
Therborn, Goran, 7
Third World: democratization and, 2–4; demonstration elections in, 8; Jamaica as advocate for, 221, 225; narrow definition of democracy and, 7–8; national liberation movement in, 132; neo-Marxist analysis of, 4–6; noncapitalist path of, 221, 270n; political modernization theory and, 2–4, 6–7
Thomas, Clive, 191, 192
Thompson, Dudley, 271n
Tivoli housing project, 119, 120, 245n
trade unions. *See* unions
Trades Union Advisory Council (TUAC), 31
Trades Union Congress (TUC), 35–36, 184, 265n
Trades Union Council (TUC), 31
Trinidad, 58, 124, 166–67, 169, 193, 194, 255n
TUAC. *See* Trades Union Advisory Council (TUAC)
TUC. *See* Trades Union Council (TUC)

UAWU. *See* University and Allied Workers' Union (UAWA)
unemployed: alliance with students and intelligentsia, 156, 160; black nationalism of, 14; foreign investment and, 37, 38, 45, 57, 241n; government dismissal of problems of, 267–68n; impact on People's National Party, 129; importance of export of labor to ease unemployment, 118; indictment of *Abeng* newspaper movement, 181–82; in Kingston during 1960s, 70–73; militancy of, 72–73, 116–23, 254n; in 1950s, 57–58, 62, 236n; in 1960s, 199, 243n; in opposition to workers, 77–78; peasants' exodus to urban areas and,

Printed in the United States
91187LV00003B/104/A